John Adams _In volumes neatly bound_

Rufus King — do

Ph. Schuyler — do

Ralph Izard — do

Benjamin Hawkins — do

Pierce Butler — do

G. Frisbie — do

John Langdon — do

Oliv. Ellsworth — do

Richard Bassett — do

Theodore Foster — do

Ch. Carroll of Carrollton
in volumes neatly bound — do

Tristram Dalton — do

Caleb Strong — do

Rob. Morris — do

Jno. Henry — do

Jas. Monroe — do

Richard Henry Lee — do

Joseph Stanton Jr — do

P. Butler _in vol. neatly bound_

James Gunn — do

Paine Wingate

Samuel Livermore

George Thatcher _in volms. neatly bound_

Fred. Muhlenberg — do

John Laurance _in volumes to be neatly bound_

Elias Boudinot — do

Egbt. Benson — do do

Theodore Sedgwick do do

Samuel Griffin do do

Jona. Trumbull — do do

Wm. B. Giles Jr — do do

George Gale — do do

Lambt. Cadwalader — do

Tho. Hartley — do do

Jere. Wadsworth One in volumes
one in numbers

John Vining

John Beckley _one in volumes_

Hen. Tho. Tucker

J. Parker

A. Moore

Alex White

M. J. Stone _in volumes bound_

J. B. Ashe

J. Smith S.C.

Wm. Floyd

P. Muhlenberg

Jos. Van Rensselaer

R. Sherman _in volumes bound_

Ab. Baldwin _bound_

P. Sylvester _in Vols. neatly bound_
B. Bourn _in Boards_
Ad. Burke
Tho. Scott, _in Vols. neatly bound_
Richd. Bland — do do
Wm. Duer — do do
Th. Jefferson _in volumes neatly bound_
Edm. Randolph _in volumes neatly bound_
Lynch Coxe _in Numbers_
Jeremiah Smith _in Vol_

Ben. Contee, _in Boards._
John Hathorn, _bound._
N. Gilman _in Vols. neatly bound._
Henry Wynkoop, _in Vols. neatly bound_
Andrew G. Fraunces
Daniel Hiester
Natha. Niles

THE
FIRST FEDERAL
CONGRESS
1789–1791

BY MARGARET C. S. CHRISTMAN

PUBLISHED BY THE
SMITHSONIAN INSTITUTION PRESS
FOR THE NATIONAL PORTRAIT GALLERY AND
THE UNITED STATES CONGRESS
WASHINGTON CITY
1989

An exhibition at the National Portrait Gallery

March 2 to July 23, 1989

ALAN FERN
Director

BEVERLY J. COX
Curator of Exhibitions

SUZANNE C. JENKINS
Registrar

NELLO MARCONI
Chief, Design and Production

FRANCES KELLOGG STEVENSON
Publications Officer

This exhibition has been made possible, in part, by the Commission on the Bicentennial of The United States Constitution.

Library of Congress Cataloging-in-Publication Data
Christman, Margaret C. S.
The first federal congress, 1789–1791
"An exhibition at the National Portrait Gallery, March 2 to July 23, 1989" —
T.p. verso.
Bibliography: p.
Includes index.
1. Legislators — United States — Portraits — Exhibitions. 2. United States.
Congress (1st: 1789–1791) — Biography — Portraits — Exhibitions. 3. United
States — Politics and government — 1789–1797 — Exhibitions. I. National
Portrait Gallery (Smithsonian Institution) II. United States. Congress. III.
Title.
E302.5.C5 1989   328.73′092′2 [B]   88-43524
ISBN 0-87474-313-3

Half-title page: Signatures of members of the First Congress attached to Ebenezer Hazard's proposal for the printing of "A Collection of State Papers." The Historical Society of Pennsylvania, Philadelphia

Cover illustration: Frederick Augustus Conrad Muhlenberg (1750–1801) by Joseph Wright (1756–1793); oil on canvas, 1790. National Portrait Gallery, Smithsonian Institution, Washington, D.C.

CONTENTS

FOREWORD

The observance of the bicentennial of the Constitution of the United States provides an opportunity for reflection upon the lessons that remarkable document can teach. If we take the trouble to read the Constitution carefully, we find that it sets forth in exceptionally clear language the functions and responsibilities of the several parts of our government. Certain rights are guaranteed to the citizens of our nation, and these were to be secured by the actions of their elected representatives: the First Federal Congress, celebrated in this book and in the exhibition mounted at the National Portrait Gallery as one of its contributions to the bicentennial.

How that First Congress was to function once it was elected, what issues the first Senators and Representatives would face once they had assembled, and how they were selected in the first place are the issues dealt with here. Of the first Senators and Congressmen, some were notable for their intellectual power, their vision, or their good sense. Others had narrower views, concerned with more petty matters, or were stubborn in their adherence to a single issue. It cannot have been easy for such a diverse group to function, especially in the absence of any precedents, but function they did — and today we celebrate the two-hundredth anniversary of the institution they established so solidly.

It is particularly appropriate that the book before you should have been prepared at the National Portrait Gallery. The Gallery was established by Act of Congress in 1962 to collect and to display the portraits of the men and women who have contributed notably to the United States of America. It is unlikely that the First Federal Congress would ever have imagined that its implied powers from the Constitution would later encompass the creation of a National Portrait Gallery.

In thinking about the people who should be celebrated on our walls, those of us on the staff of the Gallery have concentrated on the lives and achievements of many individuals. Our collections have inspired those who work here to a special interest in biography, and they tend to explore past events in the context of the lives and attitudes of those who participated in them. Curiously, we have paid scant attention to the Congress until now, except for dealing with it as part of a larger story. The executive branch of government is a constant presence in our Hall of Presidents, but only selected Senators and Representatives are present in our permanent collection. Yet no American political entity is more enduring or more influential than the Congress, and it is high time we recognize its special significance.

Here for the first time we concentrate on the United States Senate and House, and Margaret Christman has used the biographical approach with great effectiveness in her account. She has made the political issues of the day as vivid as those in the election just past, and has brought to life a group of people unknown to many of us until now.

This is the first time that the National Portrait Gallery has undertaken a project jointly with the Senate and the House of Representatives, and we are proud that the opening of our exhibition on the First Federal Congress will also mark the opening of the congressional celebration of its own bicentennial. We are grateful to the leadership of both houses of Congress, and to their staffs, for their collegial support. Nor has the significance of the occasion been lost on the many institutional and private collectors who have made available many portraits and associative objects never before loaned for exhibition or for reproduction in a book of this kind. The Gallery and the Congress are deeply grateful to these generous lenders, and to all who have assisted in this pioneering effort.

ALAN FERN
Director
National Portrait Gallery

ON BEHALF
OF THE
UNITED STATES CONGRESS

This exhibition celebrates the lives of those remarkable individuals who met in New York's Federal Hall two hundred years ago to give life to a new form of government. Elected from a population of four million, they held positions as diverse as the constituencies they represented. These were Harvard-educated ministers and wealthy financiers, Indian fighters and land speculators, Irish-born jurists, members of state assemblies, and future Presidents of the United States. Now, our distinguished predecessors have assembled once again, through the medium of this landmark exhibition.

What better way to understand those who influenced so profoundly the course of our federal legislature than through a careful examination of their portraits? These likenesses, rendered by some of the leading painters and sculptors of the period, allow us to tap a rich vein of graphic memoirs. Here, you will find Joseph Wright's elegant study of the first Speaker of the House of Representatives, Frederick Augustus Conrad Muhlenberg. The rotund Pennsylvanian, with quill firmly in hand and bills ready for signing, is shown seated in the Speaker's chair in Federal Hall's House chamber. Wright's work is probably the only contemporary depiction of the interior of this historic meeting-place. Here, too, is John Singleton Copley's celebrated portrait of John Adams: the "Father of American Independence" and first President of the United States Senate, captured on canvas by the most eminent portrait painter of the colonial period.

For Thomas Carlyle, ". . . a Portrait is superior in real instruction to half-a-dozen written 'Biographies.'" Readers who consider the prodigious research which is reflected in this scholarly volume might argue with Carlyle, but all will agree that the wealth of visual documentation provided by the exhibition is without equal. On behalf of our colleagues in the 101st Congress, we are honored to join with the National Portrait Gallery in presenting "The First Federal Congress, 1789–1791."

LINDY (MRS. HALE) BOGGS
Chairman
Commission on the United States House of Representatives Bicentenary

ROBERT C. BYRD
Chairman
Commission on the Bicentennial of the United States Senate

ACKNOWLEDGMENTS

Preeminent among those to whom I have cause to be grateful is James Roe Ketchum, Curator of the United States Senate, who proposed that the National Portrait Gallery join with the Senate and House of Representatives in a tribute to the First Federal Congress. I am very glad that he did.

To say that I am thankful for the existence of the *Documentary History of the First Federal Congress*, sponsored since 1966 by the National Historical Publications and Records Commission and George Washington University, is an understatement. Charlene Bangs Bickford, Editor of the projected twenty-volume series, allowed me free access to a virtual treasure trove of official documents, newspaper accounts, and private correspondence collected from depositories throughout the country. Associate Editor Kenneth R. Bowling has shared with me his long study, his shrewd insights, his favorite anecdotes, and has valiantly tried — I fear without complete success — to keep me from error.

My portrait search was made immeasurably easier by the accumulated research of the National Portrait Gallery's Catalog of American Portraits, a national reference center that has recorded more than eighty thousand likenesses of the famous, the near-famous, the forgotten famous, and indeed some who were never famous at all.

I am indebted to Robert G. Stewart, Chief Curator of the National Portrait Gallery, who provided art-historical advice, and to Photographer Rolland White, who never flinched as I requested picture after picture, many of them seemingly impossible to capture. At the National Museum of American History, Lynn W. Vosloh of the National Numismatic Collection took pains to help me find concrete illustrations for the abstractions of funding and assumption, and Kathryn Henderson in Political History also went out of her way to assist me.

Particularly am I under obligation to Claire Kelly, assistant to the Curator of Exhibitions, who shouldered a myriad of details and remained cheerful throughout. Indispensable has been Beverly Jones Cox, Curator of Exhibitions, whose judgment and persistence I value more than words can convey.

I have long been fortunate in having a superb editor, Publications Officer Frances Stevenson, but upon this occasion I have been doubly blessed. Not only did I have the benefit of Frances's exquisite sense, but also the diligent attention of Assistant Editor Dru Dowdy. To Dru, who has had the chief burden of saving me from a world of embarrassment, and who has shared with me her enthusiasm for the people and events of post-revolutionary America, I must render special thanks.

No one who touches upon the First Federal Congress comes away without a profound obligation to Senator William Maclay of Pennsylvania. His acerbic diary, published in a new edition as volume nine of the *Documentary History of the First Federal Congress,* is the stuff of history as it was lived. To my unceasing regret — despite the efforts of numerous Maclay descendants — his miniature portrait has not been located, but his words are the spice and flavor of this effort.

Finally, a note of appreciation to my long-suffering spouse, whose willingness to ferry me up and down the Eastern Seaboard made an important part of my research feasible.

MARGARET C. S. CHRISTMAN
Washington City, November 1988

LENDERS TO THE EXHIBITION

Charles F. Adams

American Antiquarian Society, Worcester, Massachusetts

The Baltimore Museum of Art, Maryland

Cynthia (Beverley Tucker Kimbrough) Barlowe

Mary Thurber Clark

The Connecticut Historical Society, Hartford

The Currier Gallery of Art, Manchester, New Hampshire

H. Richard Dietrich, Jr.

Donaldson, Lufkin & Jenrette, New York, New York

Duke University Library, Durham, North Carolina

Fogg Art Museum, Harvard University, Cambridge, Massachusetts

Henry Ford Museum & Greenfield Village, Dearborn, Michigan

Fraunces Tavern Museum, New York, New York

The Gibbes Art Gallery, Carolina Art Association, Charleston, South Carolina

Harvard University, Cambridge, Massachusetts

The Hibernian Society of Charleston, South Carolina

Historical Society of Berks County, Reading, Pennsylvania

Historical Society of Delaware, Wilmington

The Historical Society of Pennsylvania, Philadelphia

Historic Deerfield, Inc., Deerfield, Massachusetts

Louisa Catharine Adams Clement Hull

Independence National Historical Park, Philadelphia, Pennsylvania

The Library Company of Philadelphia, Pennsylvania

Library of Congress, Washington, D.C.

The Manney Collection

Private collections

Theodore Sedgwick

Society for the Preservation of New England Antiquities, Boston, Massachusetts

Stockbridge Library Association, Massachusetts

The Supreme Court of the United States, Washington, D.C.

S. Robert Teitelman

Telfair Academy of Arts and Sciences, Savannah, Georgia

Tennessee State Library and Archives, Nashville

Tennessee State Museum, Nashville

United States Senate Collection, Washington, D.C.

Virginia Museum of Fine Arts, Richmond

Wadsworth Atheneum, Hartford, Connecticut

Mr. and Mrs. Christopher W. Wood

Yale University Art Gallery, New Haven, Connecticut

THE MEMBERS
OF THE
FIRST FEDERAL CONGRESS

John Adams, President of the Senate
Frederick Muhlenberg, Speaker of the House

CONNECTICUT

Oliver Ellsworth, Senator
William Samuel Johnson, Senator
*Benjamin Huntington, Representative
Roger Sherman, Representative
*Jonathan Sturges, Representative
Jonathan Trumbull, Representative
Jeremiah Wadsworth, Representative

DELAWARE

Richard Bassett, Senator
George Read, Senator
*John Vining, Representative

GEORGIA

William Few, Senator
*James Gunn, Senator
Abraham Baldwin, Representative
James Jackson, Representative
*George Mathews, Representative

MARYLAND

Charles Carroll of Carrollton, Senator
*John Henry, Senator
Daniel Carroll, Representative
*Benjamin Contee, Representative
*George Gale, Representative
*Joshua Seney, Representative
William Smith, Representative
*Michael Jenifer Stone, Representative

MASSACHUSETTS

Tristram Dalton, Senator
Caleb Strong, Senator
Fisher Ames, Representative
Elbridge Gerry, Representative
Benjamin Goodhue, Representative
*Jonathan Grout, Representative
*George Leonard, Representative
George Partridge, Representative
Theodore Sedgwick, Representative
*George Thatcher, Representative

NEW HAMPSHIRE

John Langdon, Senator
*Paine Wingate, Senator
*Abiel Foster, Representative
Nicholas Gilman, Representative
Samuel Livermore, Representative

NEW JERSEY

*Jonathan Elmer, Senator
William Paterson, Senator (resigned November 13, 1790)
*Philemon Dickinson, Senator
Elias Boudinot, Representative
Lambert Cadwalader, Representative
*James Schureman, Representative
*Thomas Sinnickson, Representative

NEW YORK

Rufus King, Senator
Philip John Schuyler, Senator
Egbert Benson, Representative
*William Floyd, Representative
*John Hathorn, Representative
John Laurance, Representative
*Peter Silvester, Representative
*Jeremiah Van Rensselaer, Representative

NORTH CAROLINA

*Benjamin Hawkins, Senator
*Samuel Johnston, Senator
*John Baptista Ashe, Representative
*Timothy Bloodworth, Representative
John Sevier, Representative
John Steele, Representative
Hugh Williamson, Representative

PENNSYLVANIA

*William Maclay, Senator
Robert Morris, Senator
George Clymer, Representative
*Thomas Fitzsimons, Representative
Thomas Hartley, Representative
*Daniel Hiester, Representative
Frederick A.C. Muhlenberg, Speaker of the House
*John Peter G. Muhlenberg, Representative
*Thomas Scott, Representative
Henry Wynkoop, Representative

RHODE ISLAND

*Theodore Foster, Senator
*Joseph Stanton, Jr., Senator
Benjamin Bourn, Representative

SOUTH CAROLINA

*Pierce Butler, Senator
Ralph Izard, Senator
Aedanus Burke, Representative
*Daniel Huger, Representative
William Loughton Smith, Representative
Thomas Sumter, Representative
Thomas Tudor Tucker, Representative

16

VIRGINIA

*William Grayson, Senator (died in office, March 12, 1790)

Richard Henry Lee, Senator

James Monroe, Senator (filled William Grayson's seat)

*John Walker, Senator (temporarily filled William Grayson's seat)

*Theodorick Bland, Representative (died in office, June 1, 1790)

John Brown, Representative

*Isaac Coles, Representative

*William Branch Giles, Representative (filled Theodorick Bland's seat)

Samuel Griffin, Representative

Richard Bland Lee, Representative

James Madison, Representative

*Andrew Moore, Representative

John Page, Representative

Josiah Parker, Representative

*Alexander White, Representative

*indicates that the members are not in exhibition

Overleaf: Federal Hall and the upper end of Broad Street in New York City by George Holland; watercolor, 1797. The I.N. Phelps Stokes Collection, The Miriam and Ira B. Wallach Division of Art, Prints and Photographs, The New York Public Library, New York City; Astor, Lenox and Tilden Foundations

The ELECTION

Zealous Patriots heading rabbles,
Orators promoting squabbles;
Free Electors always swilling,
Candidates not worth a shilling!
Butchers, Farmers, and Carmen,
Half-pay Officers, and Chairmen;
Many Zealots, not worth nothing,
Many perjured Persons voting;
Candidates, with Tradesmen pissing,
Cleavers, Bagpipes, Clapping, Hissing;
Warmest Friends in Opposition,
Hottest Foes in Coalition!
Open Houses, paid to tempt the
Rotten Votes, with Bellies empty;
Boxing, Drinking Rhyming Swearing,
Some Fools laughing, some despairing;
Fevers, Fractures, Inflammations,
Bonfires, Squibs, Illuminations;
Murd'rers, daring all detection,
Pray, Gentlemen, how do you like the Election,

R.

Trenton *Federal Post*, November 18, 1788

PART ONE

THE

CONGRESS

IS

CHOSEN

THE STAGE IS SET

In the wake of the Declaration of Independence, a committee of the Continental Congress set about drawing up a constitution for the new nation. The resulting Articles of Confederation, which loosely bound the thirteen sovereign states together, was agreed to by the Congress in 1777 and sent to the states for unanimous ratification. Not until 1781, however, when the holdout Maryland legislature bestowed its consent, did the Articles become official, and the Continental Congress was thereby transformed into the Confederation Congress.

From the first, however, the inefficacy of this system of government—administered by a single-chamber legislature in which each state delegation had an equal vote — was manifest. "The fundamental defect," Alexander Hamilton clearly saw, "is a want of power in Congress." Dependent for revenue on requisitions levied on the individual states, the Congress had no means of enforcing compliance. It had no authority to regulate commerce between the states or to negotiate treaties with foreign nations. Nothing of significance could be undertaken without the vote of at least nine states, and amendments to the Articles required consent from all thirteen. "There is no measure, however wise or necessary," Hugh Williamson of North Carolina exclaimed in frustration, "that may not be defeated by any Single State, however small or wrong-headed."

Robert Morris, named superintendent of finance by the Congress in 1781, was charged with the formidable task of introducing order into the chaotic finances of a virtually bankrupt government. In vain he pleaded with the states for funds to pay the army and fulfill obligations to foreign and domestic creditors. "I know there is a Delicacy which influences some minds to treat the States with Tenderness and even adulation," he complained to Congress in February 1782, "while they are in the habitual Inattention to the Calls of national Interest and Honor. I know that Delicacy and I disclaim it." In his November 1784 "Statement of Accounts and Farewell to the Inhabitants of the United States," Morris warned, "If there be not one government, which can draw forth and direct the efforts, the combined efforts of United America, our independence is but a name, our freedom a shadow, and our dignity a dream."

Two major attempts had been made to give the Congress an independent source of revenue. In 1781 a tax on imports was proposed, to be levied with the proceeds used to discharge the principal and interest on the national debt. Rhode Island refused its consent, and the measure died. The

Confederation Congress tried again in 1783, but as Connecticut Congressman William Samuel Johnson reported on March 26, 1785, "the Senate of NY by a Majority of two rejected the Impost Bill and Dashed all our fond Hopes of a speedy establishment of our Regulation for Justice Interest and Honor. What shall we do next?"

What in fact did happen was that the initiative toward strengthening the central government was taken outside of Congress. In September 1786, a dozen deputies from five states gathered at Annapolis "To take into consideration the trade of the United States." Without waiting for a quorum to assemble, they adjourned with a resolution — drafted by Alexander Hamilton — for a meeting that would have the broader agenda of devising "such further Provisions as shall appear to them necessary to render the Constitution of the Federal Government adequate to the exigencies of the Union."

Eighteenth-century walnut ballot box from the Delaware Valley. Independence National Historical Park Collection, Philadelphia, Pennsylvania

Governor Edmund Randolph of Virginia responded in November by sending out a call for all the states to meet. While the Confederation Congress, in residence at New York since 1785, was pondering just what action it might take, five states joined Virginia in authorizing delegates. On February 21, 1787, Congress reacted. Naming the same time and place as the Annapolis resolution, it called for a Grand Convention at Philadelphia in May "for the sole and express purpose of revising the Articles of Confederation."

The Constitution that was unveiled to the public on September 18, 1787, abolished the confederacy and in its place created a national government that would act directly on the people instead of on the states. "Who authorized them," asked a horrified Patrick Henry when he read what the framers had wrought, "to speak the language of 'We, the People' instead of 'We, the States'?"

At the Philadelphia Grand Convention the framers had determined that the Constitution should not be submitted to the Confederation Congress for approval, but should merely be transmitted to the states. Ratification would be sought, not from the state legislatures, but from special conventions elected by the people. Approval by nine states would be sufficient to bring the new government into operation for those states.

Men for and against ratification divided into two main camps — Federalists and Antifederalists. *Those who were called antifederalists at the time complained that they had injustice done them by the title, because they were in favor of a federal government, and the others in favor of a national one; the federalists were for ratifying the constitution as it stood, and the others not until amendments were made,* explained Elbridge Gerry, one of the three framers who had refused to sign the Constitution. "Their names then ought not have been distinguished by federalists and antifederalists, but rats and antirats."

The objections of the Antifederalists were various, but in general they feared centralized power, were jealous of state interests, and were suspicious of "aristocratical" influences. Many declared that the ratio of one Representative for thirty thousand people was inadequate, that presidential and senatorial terms were too long, and that all elected officials should be subject to limited terms in office, as they were under the Articles of Confederation. Some protested that they would be taxed to support "expensive courts of judicature" and "a princely president." Some warned that the prohibition of religious tests would open public office to "pagans, deists, and Mahometans," and that the proposed seat of government, under the exclusive jurisdiction of Congress, "would be the asylum of the base, idle, avaricious and ambitious." Most tellingly, the Antifederalists cried out that the Constitution included no bill of rights, and refused to be silenced by the Federalist contention that the people retained everything they did not expressly give up. Wrote Antifederalist Richard Henry Lee in derision, *They have reserved from their Legislature a power to prevent the importation of Slaves for 20 years, and also from*

Creating Titles. But they have no reservation in favor of the Press, Rights of Conscience, Trial by Jury in Civil Cases, or Common Law securities. As if these were of less importance to the happiness of Mankind than the making of Lords, or the importation of Slaves!

By July of 1788, all the states except North Carolina and Rhode Island had approved the Constitution. Ratification, however, had been a very near thing in the key states of Massachusetts, Virginia, and New York, and in these three as well as in South Carolina and New Hampshire, the states' conventions recommended a great number of amendments for the consideration of the First Federal Congress.

The Constitution had directed that the House of Representatives "shall be composed of Members chosen every second Year by the People of the several States." The people were defined as those qualified to vote for the most numerous branch of the state legislatures, which in effect meant white males who possessed some degree of property. "The Senate of the United States," it was specified in the Constitution, "shall be composed of two Senators from each State chosen by the Legislature thereof." Although Congress retained power to "alter such regulations" in the selection of House members, to the states themselves was left the time and manner of choosing their Senators and Representatives.

On the last day of September in 1788, the business of selecting the members of the First Federal Congress began with Pennsylvania's designation of William Maclay and Robert Morris as its two Senators. Not until December 17, 1790 — when Benjamin Bourn, the Representative from straggling Rhode Island, took his seat — was the full component of twenty-six Senators and sixty-five Representatives in place.

In the First Federal elections, amendments to the Constitution were the great national issue. The differences between Federalists and Antifederalists were brought to the fore by opposing slates in Pennsylvania and Maryland and by individual candidates in Massachusetts, South Carolina, New Hampshire, Virginia, and New York. No declared Antifederalists, however, came forth in Delaware, New Jersey, Connecticut, or Georgia to disturb the general satisfaction with the Constitution as it stood.

Irreconcilable Antifederalists, particularly Patrick Henry, wanted nothing so much as to call a second Constitutional Convention, but as the elections proceeded, the more moderate among the Antifederalists advocated alteration, not destruction, of the innovative system. Antifederalist Samuel Osgood, who had told Samuel Adams that it had cost him "many a sleepless night to find out the most obnoxious Part of the proposed Plan," was among those who came to the conclusion that the new government should be given a fair trial. "I consider the first Congress," said Osgood, in expressing a sentiment held by a great many critics of the Constitution, "as a second Convention."

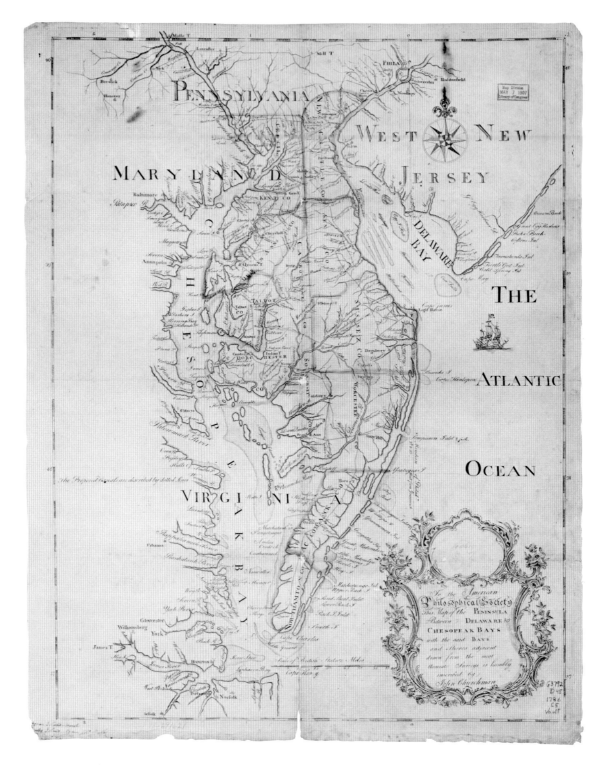

Map of the Peninsula Between Delaware & Chesopeak Bays; published by John Churchman, 1787. Geography and Map Division, Library of Congress, Washington, D.C.

DELAWARE

Perspective View of the Country between Wilmington and the Delaware; engraved for the *Columbian Magazine*, April 1787. Robert G. Stewart

Delaware, the first state to ratify the Constitution, chose its Senators on October 25, 1788. The state Assembly elected Richard Bassett (q.v.) and George Read (q.v.) — both of whom had been framers of the Constitution — overriding the nomination of Gunning Bedford, Jr., who had also signed the document. Some had hoped that framer John Dickinson, the celebrated penman of the Revolution, might agree to serve, but he pleaded that "the Weakness of my Health will not permit Me to go through the fatigues of a close Attention to such momentous Business."

As the least populous state, Delaware was entitled to but a single Representative. Several candidates offered, but the contest came down to Gunning Bedford, Jr., and John Vining. In the election, held on January 9, 1789, Bedford won his home county of New Castle, but Vining, prevailing in Sussex and Kent, was the victor.

Thirty-one-year-old Vining was a protégé of George Read, with whom he had studied law. He had been in the Confederation Congress and was then a member of the Delaware House of Assembly. Famous for his wit and conviviality, Vining is referred to in the state annals as "the pet of Delaware."

Federalists all were the men from Delaware.

PENNSYLVANIA

All politics is local," Speaker of the House Thomas P. "Tip" O'Neill was wont to proclaim. Never was this more true than in eighteenth-century Pennsylvania, where all elections revolved around the divisions in state politics. The Constitutionalists, those who were sworn to protect the radical state constitution of 1776, were now called Antifederalists. Their adversaries, the Republicans, intent on a more conservative system, were nationally known as Federalists.

As soon as the Confederation Congress adopted an election ordinance on September 13, 1788, the Republican-controlled Pennsylvania legislature made haste to determine upon their United States Senators, lest their majority be lost in the upcoming October elections. Among the names mentioned in Republican circles were John Armstrong, Jr., William Irvine, and William Bingham —all of them then in the Confederation Congress. An obvious candidate was Robert Morris (q.v.), signer of the Constitution and pivotal figure in local and national politics. Unknown nationally was William Maclay, a surveyor and lawyer who had represented Northumberland County in the Assembly and was currently on the Supreme Executive Council. Maclay, married to the daughter of Harrisburg founder John Harris, had the rare distinction of being a Republican from inland Pennsylvania.

John Armstrong, author of the 1783 Newburg addresses demanding back pay from the Congress on behalf of the Continental army officers, was just barely old enough to qualify as a Senator. He had many friends among the Federalists, however, and if geographic balance was to be a consideration, he had the advantage of coming from inland: Carlisle.

Also from Carlisle was General William Irvine, an Irish-born doctor who had been a brigadier general during the Revolution. Although Irvine was a Republican, he had alienated many Federalists when he charged that Robert Morris had mishandled public money during his tenure as superintendent of finance.

Robert Morris and William Bingham, both wealthy merchants from Philadelphia and closely allied in business and in Republican politics, appealed to the same constituency. In the interest of diversity, Bingham, the younger and less experienced of the two, was ultimately dropped from consideration. Bingham's turn would come in 1795 when he became Robert Morris's successor.

After much maneuvering behind the scenes, the Assembly on September 30, 1788, elected the first two Senators to the United States Congress. The

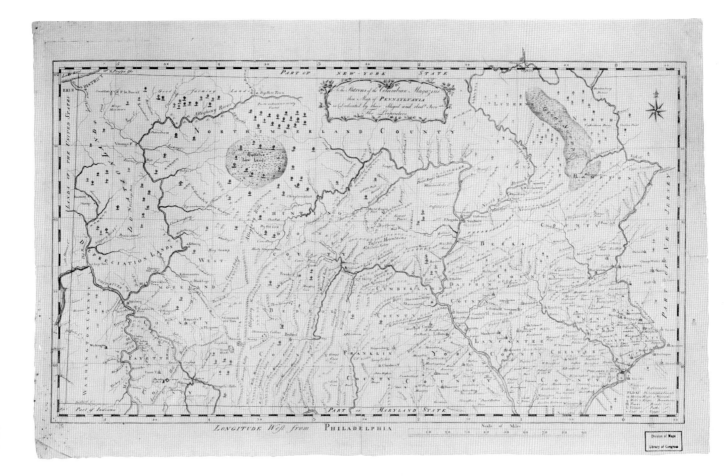

Map of Pennsylvania, 1787; published in the *Columbian Magazine*, 1788. Geography and Map Division, Library of Congress, Washington, D.C.

final vote stood at 66 for William Maclay, 37 for Robert Morris, and 31 for William Irvine. Except for one country Federalist, the choice of Maclay was unanimous.

Dr. Benjamin Rush, the Federalist confidant, explained, "Young General Armstrong was opposed to Mr. Maclay as a Senator, but at a meeting previous to the day of the election he had only 7 out of 33 votes. Maclay's age and steadiness of character were urged against his youth and inexperience in public business."

George Thatcher, Massachusetts delegate to the dying Congress at New York, heard that "the city party strove hard to command the election and held up Morris and our *loquacious* Armstrong. The country party was willing the trading interest should have one choice; but they thought the country was entitled to the other." William Maclay, Thatcher detailed, "was originally, a lawyer. He lives now on a large farm upon the River Susquehanna, about one hundred and ten or twenty miles from Philadelphia. He is a member of the

Council in that state and highly respected by the *landed interest*, as *Morris is by the mercantile.*"

Tench Coxe told James Madison, *You will have great satisfaction in hearing that Mr. Maclay, our agricultural Senator is a decided Federalist, of a neat clean landed property, with law education, a very straight head, of much more reading than the country gentlemen in the Middle States usually are, a man of fair character and great assiduity in business.* Rush testified that Maclay "is alike independent in fortune and spirit. In his manners he is a perfect republican."

When it came to choosing Pennsylvania's eight delegates to the House of Representatives, the Constitutionalists were thwarted in their attempt to divide the state into electoral districts. "By obliging the whole state to vote in

Credentials of William Maclay and Robert Morris, Senators from Pennsylvania. National Archives, Washington, D.C.

one ticket," Benjamin Rush acknowledged, "it is expected the Federalists will prevail by a majority of two to one in the choice of Representatives for the lower house of Congress."

The Antifederalists, meeting at Harrisburg in early September, drafted proposals for amendments to the Constitution, and on November 5 a "Harrisburg" or "Amendments" ticket was published. Five of the nominees for the House of Representatives — Robert Whitehill, William Findley, Charles Pettit, William Montgomery, and Blair McClenachan — were Constitutionalists. Rounding out the ticket were two Republicans, chosen because of their German ancestry — Peter Muhlenberg and Daniel Hiester. Muhlenberg, the son of the founder of the Lutheran Church in America, had left the ministry in 1776 to command a Virginia regiment and by the end of the war was a major general in the Continental army; Hiester was a farmer and tanner from Montgomery County. A third Republican was added in the person of defeated senatorial candidate William Irvine.

The Republican members of the Assembly countered with a ticket chosen at a Lancaster meeting on November 3, 1788. Their eight nominees were Thomas Hartley (q.v.), George Clymer (q.v.), Henry Wynkoop (q.v.), Thomas Scott, Stephen Chambers, Thomas Fitzsimons, John Allison, and Frederick Muhlenberg (q.v.). All were Republicans.

A correspondent to the *Pennsylvania Packet,* lauding the Lancaster ticket on November 10, pointed out that "no part of the state has escaped the notice of the conferees. From the banks of Delaware they have travelled to the further bank of the Ohio, with wisdom and justice." From Philadelphia came George Clymer, merchant and stalwart conservative, who had been a signer of the Constitution. The second city Representative was Thomas Fitzsimons, Irish and Catholic, a business associate of Robert Morris and also a framer of the Constitution. To give a voice to western Pennsylvania, Thomas Scott, lawyer and justice of the peace and pleas from Washington County, was selected. And a nominee from the newly established county of Franklin was chosen in the person of John Allison, who had represented his area at the state ratifying convention. The newspaper correspondent went on, "Two of the gentlemen are of the law, but both reside near the Susquehanna." The reference here was to Thomas Hartley of York County and Stephen Chambers of Lancaster County. "The German gentleman," added the writer, alluding to Frederick Muhlenberg, "has been honored with the chair of speaker of the legislature, and was president of the state Convention." The eighth candidate was Henry Wynkoop, a large Bucks County landholder who was justice of the court of common pleas and orphan's court. Concluded the author, "It is impossible for a ticket more completely to embrace the various interests of Pennsylvania."

One Federalist grumbled privately to Tench Coxe, an active Philadelphia Federalist who had been kept off the ticket since the country delegates had been unwilling to accept a third nominee from the city, "We have need, upon

Engraved by J. Wiggin.

D.ᴿ BENJAMIN RUSH.

Dr. Benjamin Rush (1745–1813), signer of the Declaration of Independence and longtime influential figure in Pennsylvania politics, played a guiding role, not only in the federal elections, but afterward, when various members of Congress corresponded with him on a regular basis.

By James Akin (circa 1773–1846), after Jeremiah Paul, Jr.; engraving, 1800. National Portrait Gallery, Smithsonian Institution, Washington, D.C.

this great occasion, of more important characters, men of science and of large minds. Our ticket may indeed be called a *good one*." But he fretted, "Our sister states will probably send some of their first and ablest characters. I hope their brilliancy may not diminish our splendor, nor their importance decrease our weight in the national scale."

On November 13 there appeared a broadside written in German and soon translated into English for the *Pennsylvania Packet*, pointing out that the Germans, who comprised at least a third of the population of Pennsylvania, were not adequately represented on either the Lancaster or Harrisburg tickets. Its author, or at least its instigator, Dr. Benjamin Rush, called upon the Germans to "muster all your strength in the ensuing election, and neither receive nor give a ticket which has not at least three Germans on it." It was proposed that Peter Muhlenberg and Daniel Hiester be substituted in the place of Stephen Chambers and John Allison on the Lancaster ticket, and that the Harrisburg ticket be altered to include Frederick A. Muhlenberg's name instead of Robert Whitehill.

In the elections, held on November 26, the German Lancaster ticket swept the field with Frederick Muhlenberg, who was also on the German Harrisburg list, receiving more votes than any other candidate.

After the election was over, Benjamin Rush wrote to Tench Coxe, "There is great wrath, I hear, against me in York and Lancaster for favoring the German alterations in the Federal ticket. They do me great honor, for it has saved the state." Had not the Federalists adopted Peter Muhlenberg and Daniel Hiester, Rush declared, the Germans would either have voted for the German Harrisburg ticket or remained away from the polls altogether, which "would have thrown the six Antifederalists into Congress by a majority of several hundred votes."

It was with relief that Coxe reported to Massachusetts Federalist Timothy Pickering that the election had resulted in "eight safe members for Pennsylvania, none of whom will injure and some of whom can essentially serve the Constitution." Speaking of George Clymer and Thomas Fitzsimons, Coxe added, *We have great satisfaction in knowing that of the merchants we have the two ablest — of the Germans the two ablest and three of the most respectable — that among the other landed Representatives Wynkoop and Scott are equal to anybody we could send, and in Hartley we have an upright lawyer, beloved by his country.* The gentlemen elected "are pretty good judges [of] what the people of Pennsylvania can do and what they can be brought to undertake." Coxe concluded, "Some of them are men of experience and resource. I am upon the whole much more than satisfied with the ticket, for five are as good as we could send, the rest are very well, none bad."

NEW JERSEY

On November 15, 1788, the New Jersey legislature, with the geographic cleavage of the state distinctly in mind, met to choose United States Senators. Agreed upon were William Paterson (q.v.) from East Jersey — the northern urban area, economically tied to New York, and Jonathan Elmer from West Jersey — the southern rural part of the state, which was oriented toward Philadelphia. Paterson received 45 out of a possible 50 votes and Elmer, 29. Abraham Clark, the radical leader from East Jersey, was given 19 votes, and Elias Boudinot, a former president of the Confederation Congress, also from East Jersey, garnered 7 ballots.

Paterson, who had led the revolt of the small states at the Constitutional Convention, was now solidly in the Federalist camp. Dr. Elmer had been a regimental surgeon during the Revolution, and afterward, giving up medicine for politics, he had been elected to the legislative council and the Confederation Congress. Like most others in New Jersey, Elmer had favored the swift ratification of the Constitution.

For purposes of choosing delegates to the House of Representatives, each voter was permitted to submit four names from any part of the state. "Thirty or forty are said to be in nomination," it was reported, "and near half that number are very busy in making interest either in person or by their friends." Some of those named, however, hastened to advertise in the press that they declined to be considered — among them Philemon Dickinson of Trenton, in West Jersey, who would later fill out William Paterson's term in the first Senate.

To the conservatives, the election came down to anybody other than Abraham Clark of Essex County, a man who had espoused paper money and sought to reform the legal system to the disadvantage of lawyers. In a move to keep out Clark, a number of conservative assemblymen, most of them from West Jersey, organized a ticket in support of Elias Boudinot (q.v.) and James Schureman from East Jersey, together with Thomas Sinnickson and Lambert Cadwalader (q.v.) from West Jersey. Schureman was a merchant who had fought in the Revolution and had been in the old Congress. Sinnickson, who was descended from one of New Jersey's old Swedish families, had also served in the war. Both Schureman and Sinnickson were currently members of the state Assembly. Cadwalader, a member of a prominent Quaker family, had nonetheless been a colonel of the Fourth Pennsylvania Line and had represented New Jersey at the old Congress from 1784 to 1787.

"I apprehend the house of Representatives will afford a greater field for

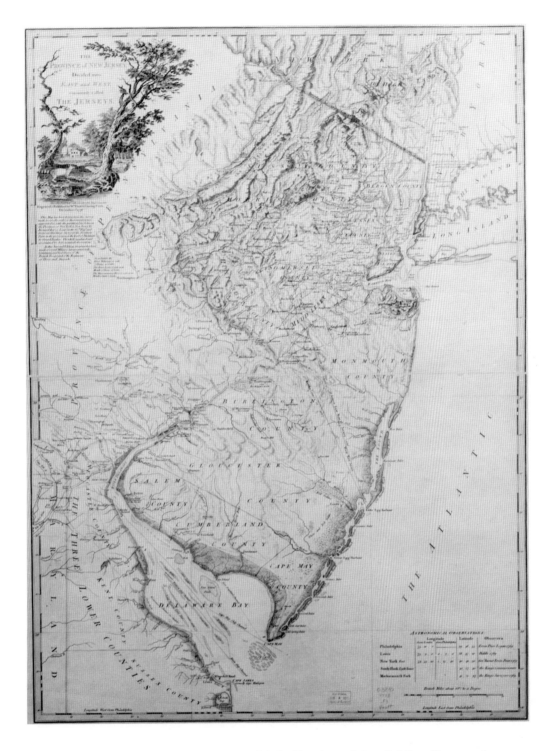

Map of the province of New Jersey, with indication of the dividing line run in 1743 between East New Jersey and West New Jersey.

Engraved and published by William Faden, 1778. Geography and Map Division, Library of Congress, Washington, D.C.

James Schureman (1757–1815), the leading vote-getter in New Jersey's first federal elections, was not returned to the Second Congress. His portrait shows him in later life and reveals the loss of his eye because of smallpox.

From a portrait illustrated in Clarence Winthrop Bowen's *The History of the Centennial Celebration of the Inauguration of George Washington* (New York, 1892)

talents, & usefulness than the Senate," Elias Boudinot was advised by his son-in-law, William Bradford, Jr. "That assembly will undoubtedly be in a great degree a popular one in which eloquence & abilities will have a greater chance for success than in the select body of Senators."

The opposition to the West Jersey, or Junto, ticket was dispersed and unorganized. Fifty-four candidates were nominated by the East Jersey forces, chiefly Abraham Clark and Jonathan Dayton. Dayton had been the youngest delegate at the Federal Convention, and as a faithful member of the Continental army from 1776 to 1783, he expected that his brethren in the Society of the Cincinnati would "use their utmost endeavors" in his favor.

Since Clark had failed to embrace the new Constitution — which was universally seen as advantageous to New Jersey — with unreserved enthusiasm, his enemies readily painted him as an Antifederalist. "At present I am attacked not openly in the public prints that I have heard of," Clark protested in a letter to the *New Jersey Journal*, "but in a secret manner by letters, certificates, etc. sent privately into every part of the state, containing gross misrepresentations, and the most palpable falsehood, in order to prejudice the minds of the citizens against me at the coming election." He went on to protest that the epithet of Antifederalism "is frequently given to all those who dare venture to suspect the least defect in the Constitution, in which is included by far the greatest part of the inhabitants of the United States."

Advocates of the Junto ticket, Jonathan Dayton was apprised by one of his supporters, went among the Quakers of West Jersey saying, "Dayton & Clarke are bloody men — are men for War — they want another War that they may make their fortunes." On the other hand, "The Gentlemen in our West-Jersey-Ticket, are good peaceable Men, — they will oppose all War-measures." Elias Boudinot, the voters were reminded, had pleaded with the Pennsylvania government to spare the life of Quaker Abraham Carlisle, convicted of treason in 1778; and after he was hanged, Lambert Cadwalader's brother had protested the deed in print. James Schureman was touted as the person "who last Fall got the law passed to free the Poor Negroes," and "as to Sinnicksen the last name in this printed ticket, You know He lives in Salem & all his Family-connections are Friends." The Quakers were exhorted, "These are honest, good men you ought to Vote for — But if you want War and to be persecuted by the Presbyterians, — Stay at home, & see who will pity You when Your goods are distrained and Your Meeting-Houses are made barracks."

On February 11, 1789, the voting began, and since the law had set no specific time for the closing of the polls, the balloting continued for weeks. "New Jersey have been in Strife between Eastern & Western Counties," Benjamin Huntington of Connecticut reported on March 11. "The Object of the Western Counties is to gain strength to remove Congress to Philadelphia & for that purpose to keep open the Poll until a Day or two since in order to bring every body in to Vote and by that Means carry the Choice."

The polls were declared closed on March 18 and Governor William Livingston proclaimed Boudinot, Cadwalader, Sinnickson, and Schureman duly elected. Even so, voters continued to cast their ballots in Essex County until April 27, and supporters of Clark and Dayton, charging election irregularities, appealed the election to the recently convened House of Representatives.

The committee of the House appointed to look into the matter sought to take evidence in New Jersey, but the full House denied them authority to do so, and their investigation was confined to oral testimony taken in New York. In their report, the committee summarized the evidence but made no recommendations. On September 2 the House of Representatives ruled that the disputed members, who had been seated before the challenge, "were duly elected, and returned."

Credentials of William Few, Senator from Georgia. National Archives, Washington, D.C.

GEORGIA

Geography was very much on the minds of the Georgia legislature as it chose United States Senators and drafted the ordinance for the elections to the House of Representatives.

On January 17, 1789, William Few (q.v.) from up-country Georgia and James Gunn from the low country were named by the legislature to the Senate of the United States. Few had put his name to the Constitution and was a member of the dying Congress. The Virginia-born Gunn was a member of the House of Assembly from Chatham County.

Gunn was unknown outside of Georgia, and Catharine Greene, the widow of General Nathanael Greene, characterized him contemptuously to Jeremiah Wadsworth, Representative from Connecticut, as *"Captain Gun* of the Lighthorse the Most ignorant and infamous fellow in the whole army — he was disgraced — ran away to Georgia. Married a pretty fortune here found means to purchase the votes of the common people (which the assembly is composed of) and which have made him Senator." It might be pointed out that Gunn, a quarrelsome man of violent temper, had challenged Mrs. Greene's husband to a duel in 1785.

Another of Gunn's detractors was General Anthony Wayne, under whom Gunn had served in the campaign around Savannah, and who himself aspired to represent Georgia in the Senate. Although Wayne had voted for the Constitution as a member of the Pennsylvania ratifying convention, he claimed Georgia residence, since his wartime services had won him citizenship and a plantation twelve miles northwest of Savannah.

Abraham Baldwin (q.v.), who had been Georgia's most faithful and active delegate at the Grand Convention, had also hoped to be chosen for the Senate. But he was absent from the state during the winter of 1788–1789 because of his assignment to the commission appointed to settle the tangled financial accounts between the national government and the several states. Baldwin was greatly annoyed to find that false rumors of his having accepted federal appointment had precluded his name from senatorial consideration.

Georgia's potential for growth had so impressed the framers of the Constitution that, pending the conduct of the 1790 census, the sparsely settled state had been awarded three seats in the House of Representatives. For the purpose of electing Representatives, the legislature divided the state into three districts, but all voters could vote for three Representatives. Candidates must be residents of the district that they aspired to serve for three years standing — a stringent requirement for a raw state of emerging

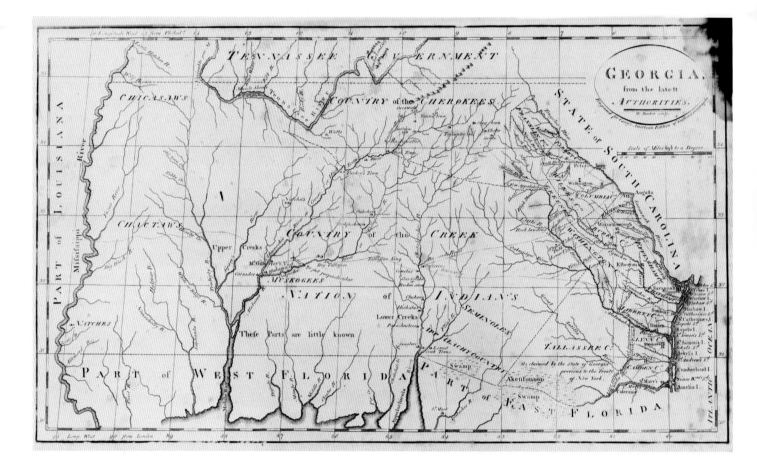

Georgia, from the Latest Authorities by William Barker; engraved for William Guthrie's *A New System of Modern Geography.* Geography and Map Division, Library of Congress, Washington, D.C.

population. The candidates in Georgia, James Madison was assured, "are well affected to the Constitution."

The first, lower, or eastern district — with a population of only 16,250 — was the smallest congressional district in the nation. Four candidates presented themselves, and James Jackson (q.v.), a young Revolutionary War hero currently serving Chatham County in the Assembly, won by a margin of 196 votes out of a total of 616, only 216 of which were from his home district. In 1788 Jackson had declined election as governor of Georgia on the grounds of youth and inexperience. According to James Madison, Jackson's main competition came from Henry Osborne, a former member of the Congress and chief justice of Georgia. Another opponent was framer William Houstoun, a member of one of the first families of Georgia. Houstoun, who had left the Federal Convention to return to New York on business and to court the lady he married in 1788, had been in Georgia only spasmodically since that time. In February 1790, however, he was reported to be "electioneering in the Upper Counties."

In the second, middle, or center district, there was no opposition to Abraham Baldwin.

Candidates for the third, upper, or western district were Isaac Briggs and George Mathews. Briggs, a civil engineer and surveyor who had migrated to Georgia after his graduation from the College of Philadelphia to engage in a project to develop steamboating on the Savannah River, received only 42 votes. Mathews, who amassed a count of 1,054, proved to be the leading vote-getter in the state.

George Mathews, a product of the western Virginia frontier, had been elected governor of Georgia only two years after he had settled there, partly on the basis of his wartime reputation as a general of militia in Greene's southern army. Gifted with an extraordinary memory, Mathews could allegedly recite the names of the owners of almost every lot of land in the state. He was, at the time of his election to the House, an assemblyman from Wilkes County. All but illiterate, he was described as "a Ruff brave Soldier," whose strong talents were not much polished. Contemporaries later recalled that Mathews acknowledged but two superiors, George Washington and the Lord Almighty, and with the passing of time he had some doubts about the former.

After the congressional elections had been decided, Mrs. Greene commented to Wadsworth, "I think however that the representatives are a little better than the Senators. Col Jackson is a Lawyer of tolerable repute and an honest Man but has a very hot head — Mathews they Say is tolerable Sensible which is all the information I can give you."

CONNECTICUT

On October 15 and 16, 1788, the Connecticut General Assembly chose Oliver Ellsworth (q.v.) and William Samuel Johnson (q.v.) to represent the state in the first Senate of the United States. Both men had played significant roles in the drafting of the Constitution.

Each freeman in Connecticut was at liberty to stand up at his town meeting and nominate twelve candidates for the House of Representatives. Some 399 names were suggested. The twelve who received the most votes were listed on a broadside, and from these each voter might select five.

Personalities, not issues, governed the Connecticut elections. Most people were well satisfied with the Constitution as it stood; there had been no agitation for amendments at the state ratifying convention. "I learn that the Constitution is very agreeable to Connecticutt," Gouverneur Morris jested to Jeremiah Wadsworth, who had been commissary general for the Continental army, "Excepting always that certain People called Cincinnatti do not think it sufficiently energetic and that a certain person called Jeremiah Wadsworth declares it to be highly objectionable on that Score but is willing to take it for the present in Hopes of Something better by and bye."

There appears to have been no public campaigning in Connecticut, but the voters had the opportunity to select from an extraordinarily well-qualified group — most of them college educated and politically seasoned.

In order of result, those elected on December 22 were Jonathan Sturges, Roger Sherman (q.v.), Benjamin Huntington, Jonathan Trumbull, Jr. (q.v.), and Jeremiah Wadsworth (q.v.).

Sturges was a Yale-educated lawyer from Fairfield, who had served in the state Assembly and was a judge of the probate court.

Huntington, likewise a graduate of Yale, had for twenty years past been in public office — as mayor of Norwich, member of the state legislature, and representative to the old Congress.

Trumbull, a Harvard man, had been Washington's aide and later commissary general. Elected to the Assembly from Lebanon, he was speaker of the state House of Representatives.

Sherman, signer of the Declaration of Independence, the Articles of Confederation, and the Constitution, was Hartford's mayor. He gave up the judgeship that he had held for twenty-three years in order to take his seat in the House of Representatives. Last among the victors was Jeremiah Wadsworth, a master in the world of commerce but a comparative political neophyte. He was inclined at first to refuse the seat, but as he explained to

Connecticut and Parts adjacent compiled by Bernard Romans; published by Covens & Mortier, Amsterdam, 1777. Geography and Map Division, Library of Congress, Washington, D.C.

Alexander Hamilton, "My friends would hear nothing of my being withdrawn from ye representation in Congress as there was great pains taken to oppose me by ye antis," among whom was his "Antifederal relation," James Wadsworth, who "has acquired much influence in our lower House, and is opposed to every thing of National concern." Jeremiah Wadsworth concluded to Hamilton, "Tho I may be less usefull in ye assembly than in some other place I flatter my self some of my friends will be placed where you wish me & in that case I shall be perfectly satisfied."

Connecticut would have the distinction of being the only state to have its entire delegation present on the day appointed for the Congress to assemble.

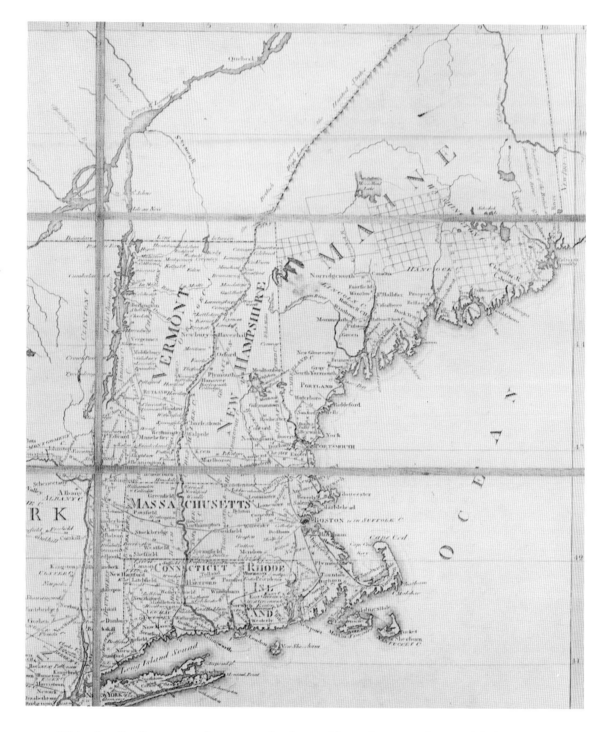

This detail of a map of post roads shows Massachusetts along with its Maine section.

Map of the United States, Exhibiting Post Roads; published by Abraham Bradley, Jr., Philadelphia, 1796. Geography and Map Division, Library of Congress, Washington, D.C.

MASSACHUSETTS

O ur legislature have not yet been able to agree upon a mode of electing Senators," the Boston *Herald of Freedom* reported on November 20, 1788. "Each branch is extremely tenacious of its authority."

The Massachusetts Senate insisted that each house vote separately, but Theodore Sedgwick (q.v.), speaker of the House of Representatives, pushed for a joint ballot in the expectation that his colleagues in the more numerous branch would favor his candidacy. At length the House proposed a compromise, suggesting that two nominees be submitted to the Senate, and if they were rejected, new names would be submitted. After an initial refusal, the Senate accepted the plan.

From the first there seems to have been a general agreement that one Senator should represent the western agricultural part of the state, and the other the eastern mercantile interests. Caleb Strong (q.v.), a lawyer from Northampton, and Dr. Charles Jarvis, a legislative representative from Boston, were the first choices of the House. Strong, who had been a delegate at the Philadelphia convention, was an outspoken advocate of the Constitution, whereas Jarvis was politically attached to Governor John Hancock, whose last-minute support for the Constitution had come about only by Federalist connivance.

The Senate readily agreed to Strong — thus blasting the hopes of Theodore Sedgwick, who was also from the western part of the state — but twice proposed other names in place of Jarvis. In rejecting Jarvis for the third time, the Senate put forward Tristram Dalton (q.v.) of Newburyport, a merchant and a Senator from Essex County. By a vote of 78 to 70, the House refused Dalton. The stalemate was finally broken when Jarvis withdrew, and on November 24 the House voted for Dalton and the Senate concurred. "Our Senators are Federal indeed," General Benjamin Lincoln assured George Washington.

If Massachusetts had difficulties enough in settling on her Senators, they were as nothing compared to the protracted process of electing her eight Representatives to Congress.

The General Court, as the Massachusetts legislature was called, divided the state into eight electoral districts, which were drawn to favor the eastern Federalists and disadvantage the western counties of Hampshire and Berkshire, as well as the Maine district — the areas that had inundated the ratifying convention with Antifederalist delegates. No candidate could be

45

elected until he received the majority of the votes cast.

On December 18, 1788, the balloting began, and the *Massachusetts Centinel* reported, "The elections in the country have, in general, been very thinly attended—owing in some measure to the late fall of snow, making the passing bad." Decisions were made in four districts — Suffolk (which included Boston); Plymouth-Barnstable; Bristol-Dukes-Nantucket; and York-Cumberland-Lincoln (Maine). Further elections were scheduled to decide the remaining four districts.

Suffolk District

In the Suffolk district, the leading Federalist candidate was Fisher Ames (q.v.), a thirty-one-year-old lawyer from Dedham who had won accolades for his eloquent defense of the Constitution at the Massachusetts ratifying convention. The old revolutionary, Samuel Adams, who had reluctantly voted to ratify what he considered a document much in need of amendment, was the candidate of the *Boston Gazette* and also the *Independent Chronicle*. A third candidate, Samuel Allyne Otis, a member of the Confederation Congress, was neatly disposed of by the *Chronicle* when they asked if a bankrupt person should be elected to Congress. Otis would later serve as the able secretary to the Senate.

All sides utilized the press to carry on a spirited letter-writing campaign. A communication from an Adams supporter acknowledged that Ames was "a man of agreeable, amiable manners; is possessed of abilities and information; and in time we doubt not will make a good legislator." Then the writer went on in defense of Adams, "It has been said he is old and Antifederal. My fellow citizens, be not deceived; his age and experience are the very qualifications you want." The Adams partisan proclaimed, *"His influence caused the Constitution to be adopted in this state,* and if he fails to give it his support for a fair trial, remember it will be the first time he ever failed you. In forty years he has never deceived you."

"There were great exertions made for Mr. Samuel Adams," Benjamin Lincoln told George Washington. "He would probably have carried the vote, could the people have been persuaded that he was in heart a Federalist." As it turned out, Fisher Ames (q.v.) easily won the outlying areas and even overcame Adams in Boston.

Plymouth-Barnstable District

The Antifederalists in the Plymouth-Barnstable district were hard put to find a candidate to run against George Partridge (q.v.), sheriff of Plymouth County and former delegate to the Continental and Confederation congresses. The *Herald of Freedom* had it that the "Anties" talked of running a man

Caleb Strong (1745–1819), described as an educated lawyer who looked and talked like a farmer, was the easy choice of the Massachusetts legislature for one of the places in the United States Senate.

By John Christian Rauschner (born 1760); wax, 1800–1810. Massachusetts Historical Society, Boston

with a large family of children, "lately accused of copulation — with a young girl of about 17 years old, who is now pregnant." Partridge received 501 out of the 554 votes cast.

Bristol-Dukes-Nantucket District

Two Federalists, George Leonard and Dr. David Cobb, as well as Antifederalist Phaneul Bishop, contested for the congressional seat in the Bristol-Dukes-Nantucket district on lower Cape Cod. The victor was George Leonard of Norton, a graduate of Harvard and currently justice of the court of common pleas of Bristol County. His family had long been active in the political affairs of the area. Leonard's "ample landed possession," said one supporter in the press, "will render him watchful of the interests of the *farmer* and *mechanic*." Privately, Leonard was assessed as "a gentleman of good disposition, but an inefficient politician." When he ran unsuccessfully for reelection in 1790, it was complained "that he has not taken so active a part in the debates of Congress as was proper."

It was not so much that Leonard won the election, but that Cobb lost it. Dr. Cobb, who had fought in the Revolution, was in high repute among the Federalists for his role in dispersing the mob that had threatened to close the court at Taunton in 1786. Cobb would have been elected by a large majority, one of his friends grumbled, had he not hesitated so long about becoming a candidate. When he at first declined, those who might have supported him turned to Leonard.

Phaneul Bishop had been the leader of the rebels put down by Cobb. At the state convention he had been decidedly against the Constitution.

York-Cumberland-Lincoln District (Maine)

The three counties comprising the Maine part of Massachusetts had a population of 90,000, but only 948 freemen cast votes in the congressional election. George Thatcher was the winner with a count of 588. His two chief opponents, Josiah Thacher and Nathaniel Wells, justices of the court of common pleas in Cumberland and York counties, respectively, together received 255 votes. Ten other candidates divided the remaining 105 ballots.

George Thatcher, a Massachusetts native, had set up a law practice in Biddleford in 1782, and in 1787 was elected to the Confederation Congress. Thomas B. Wait, publisher of the Portland *Cumberland Gazette* and a strong Thatcher supporter, apprised his friend that some discontents would not "say a syllable in your favor. You are said to be a man of no religion," and what was more, *unprincipled, light, frothy and even boyish in your conduct and conversation, in private and public life — at home, among your friends and acquaintance, and while at New York, and to such a degree, that it was feared the credit of the state which you*

George Leonard's (1729–1819) appearance has been recorded in a lithograph that appeared in George F. Clark's *History of Norton*, but the original portrait is unlocated.

    National Portrait Gallery, Smithsonian Institution, Washington, D.C.

GEO. THACHER.
Member of the Continental Congress.

George Thatcher

George Thatcher (1754–1824), a man famous for his irony and satire, was described as the antipode, in character as well as in politics, of Elbridge Gerry. Thatcher was "eccentric, witty, downright and sarcastic; and seemed to take pleasure in worrying his more sensitive colleague." Charges of impiety and irreligion were raised against Thatcher at every election. "When 'tis objected against me that I am not a man of Religion," Thatcher declared, "I would not wish my friends even to deny the charge; because the people might thereby be led to imagine me religious after their own ideas of religion—which is not the fact."

By Leopold Grozelier (1830–1865), after Henry Williams; lithograph, not dated. National Portrait Gallery, Smithsonian Institution, Washington, D.C.

represented would suffer, and your constituents disgraced.

Thatcher survived allegations of irreligion and impiety and remained in Congress until 1801, when he retired to take an appointment as associate judge of the Supreme Judicial Court of Massachusetts.

Essex District

Four candidates figured in the first Essex election on December 18, 1788, and no one of them was able to claim a majority. Benjamin Goodhue (q.v.), a Salem merchant and Essex County Senator, received the most votes. Goodhue was a dependable Federalist. Next placed Jonathan Jackson, a quixotic Federalist of Newburyport who had riled the waters with a pamphlet in which he declared the people incapable of electing political officials. A distant third was Nathan Dane of Beverly, a former member of the state legislature and presently a delegate to the Congress. He had opposed ratification of the Constitution. Last was Samuel Holten of Danvers, a doctor-turned-politician who had served in the state legislature and in the Congress. He had also voted against the Constitution.

Dane and Holten withdrew, and the runoff election on January 29, 1789, pitted the two Federalist candidates, Goodhue and Jackson, against each other. The great issue became which town — Goodhue's Salem or Jackson's Newburyport — should have the representation. Since Tristram Dalton of Newburyport had been selected for the Senate, Goodhue's supporters claimed that, in fairness and justice, Salem should have the seat in the House of Representatives. Goodhue prevailed with 569 votes to Jackson's 390.

Middlesex District

The first election in the Middlesex district — the area northwest of Boston — brought out 1,473 voters but no winning candidate. Nathaniel Gorham, who had signed the Constitution, received 536 votes; Elbridge Gerry (q.v.) who had refused to do so, was next with 384; Joseph Varnum, a farmer who was a member of the Massachusetts Senate, garnered 254 votes. An Antifederalist at the ratifying convention, Varnum was among those persuaded to change his vote after it was agreed that amendments should be recommended. John Brooks, a Continental army doctor who as a major general of the Middlesex militia had helped to suppress the debtor insurrection led by Daniel Shays, received 106 votes. The remaining 193 votes were scattered among eleven other candidates.

As the second election approached, it was reported in Federalist circles that Nathaniel Gorham "gave out publicly and in the most positive manner before he set out for New York that he would not accept if chosen." General John Brooks "positively declines going." The correspondent added on

January 11, 1789, that Joseph Varnum would not be chosen, "as he is disliked by both parties." Elbridge Gerry refused to say flat out that he would accept if chosen, although most Federalists feared that he certainly had no intention of withdrawing from the stage.

Gerry, whose public rantings against the Constitution had won him the everlasting enmity of former friends, was pilloried in the Boston press. An anti-Gerry piece appearing in the *Massachusetts Centinel* on January 7 sneered, "Where Mr. Gerry is best known, it is said, he has the smallest number of votes. Now I do not aver this to be the truth, but this I can say, that although a resident, he had but three votes out of seventy-one in the town of Cambridge." One who signed himself "An Elector" asked in the *Massachusetts Centinel* on January 10, "What sort of amendments would Mr. Gerry aim at? Where would they terminate? I answer that he would probably pursue amendments until nothing of the original was left."

The Antifederalists shot back with reminders of Gerry's spirited advocacy of independence — the time when John Adams wrote from the Congress at Philadelphia, "If every Man here was a Gerry, the Liberties of America would be safe against the Gates of Earth and Hell." Gerry, his supporters maintained, had no wish to annihilate the new Constitution, but only to amend it. When the election was held in January, he was elected with a count of 1,140, more than three times the number given to his nearest competitor, Joseph B. Varnum.

Worcester District

In 1786 the Worcester district had been caught up in the insurrection led by Daniel Shays. At the December 1788 election, state Senator Jonathan Grout, who had been sympathetic to the disaffected farmers and who had voted against the Constitution, led the field of candidates, although he failed to secure a majority. Trailing in second and third places were Grout's senate colleague, Timothy Paine, and Artemas Ward, an old soldier who had done much to bring Massachusetts into rebellion against the British and who had commanded the patriotic forces around Boston until he was forced to relinquish his position to George Washington. Sixteen other candidates shared 376 votes.

"Worcester are very much divided," Benjamin Lincoln, the commander who had repulsed Shays's attack on the federal arsenal at Springfield, apprised George Washington after the first election. "The struggle there finally will be, I think, between Mr. Paine who was one of the mandamus councillors [under the British crown], a gentleman of abilities and a good Federalist, and a Colonel Grout of a different character."

A letter printed in the Boston Antifederalist *Independent Chronicle* declared, "the parties run very high, but rather from affection to their leaders, than from any essential difference of opinion, for in order to have any votes, a man must be known to be in favor of the amendments."

The results of the second election showed that Paine had superseded Grout as the high vote-getter, with 1,040 to Grout's 956, but was short of a majority. Ward had received only 258 votes.

A letter published in the Worcester *Massachusetts Spy*, declaring that it was almost certain that the victor would either be Timothy Paine or Jonathan Grout, compared the two candidates. Paine, a graduate of Harvard, the writer acknowledged, "early received a liberal education, and has always been esteemed a man of real substantial abilities, though not of the most splendid kind. Yet he is possessed of the kind of knowledge, which really will always render him extremely useful in public assemblies." The writer did not fail to point out that Paine was "a man of large landed property" in Massachusetts, primarily in the Worcester district; "consequently he is a proper person to represent the yeomanry . . . added to this, his easy circumstances, and leisure, will admit his constant attendance at the federal court." Then the writer turned to Grout. *Grout's advantages, in the early part of life, were by no means equal to Mr. Paine's. No one will deny that Mr. Grout is a man of good natural capacity; but to say that he is a man of real science would be doubted as would also, by many, his having abilities every way adequate to represent the great and important District of Worcester.* Moreover, the author pointed out that all of Grout's "real estate, except a small farm at Petersham is supposed to lie in Vermont and New Hampshire." He continued that "every man who knows him, knows that he is extremely attached to the management of his estates in Vermont and New Hampshire, and is constantly in one or the other of those governments, excepting the short time he is in the legislature of Massachusetts."

Another writer in the *Massachusetts Spy* came to Grout's defense. "From the first infringement of American liberty by the hand of British tyrants, Mr. Grout has boldly advocated the independence of America." Whereas "Mr. Paine, it is well known, has been extremely attached to the British administration, and has therefore been opposed to the independence of America." As to experience, Grout "has been a member of the legislature almost every year since our rights were first invaded by foreign and domestic foes; and, he has therefore had a greater opportunity of being acquainted with our laws and government." Paine's *acquaintance with mankind is by no means adequate to Mr. Grout's. Mr. Grout has had occasion to attend the general assemblies in almost every state east of Pennsylvania, to transact business for himself, and others, by which means he has had an opportunity to form a more particular acquaintance with political characters, than the other candidate.* In a final thrust, the suspicious Antifederalist author declared that Paine's friends were perhaps acting from "sinister motives, viz.: they may vote for him because they wish to have laws made that shall abolish equality, and raise *them* and *their sons*, to *honors*, *titles*, and *dignities*, in conformity to the British government."

In the third election, held on March 2, 1789, Jonathan Grout, with a total of 1,968, achieved a majority over Timothy Paine's 1,241 votes and Artemas Ward's 256.

"I would fondly hope," jested presidential elector Dr. Samuel P. Savage of Barnstable, that Grout "has honesty, sense, and patriotism, for if he has not something excellent within to balance the inharmoniousness of his name, I cannot conceive any person who is blessed with ears would ever vote for him."

Hampshire-Berkshire District

It took five elections before any candidate was able to achieve a majority in the sprawling Hampshire-Berkshire district in western Massachusetts.

In the first election, 2,251 freemen cast ballots for twenty-two candidates. Although the district had been a hotbed of rebellion in the days of Shays and had sent a large Antifederalist contingent to the Massachusetts convention, five of those who finished among the top six were Federalists. Heading the list with 801 votes, 325 votes short of a majority, was Theodore Sedgwick of Berkshire County who, when confronted a mob of insurgents in 1786, had simply stared them down and told them to go home. Sedgwick was reputed to have been "as sore as a man can be" when he was not elected to the first United States Senate.

Another candidate was John Worthington of Springfield, once a scorned Tory but now lauded for his knowledge "of the landed interests of his fellow citizens, his literary talents, and republican character." Worthington's daughter was on the verge of marriage with Boston's new Congressman Fisher Ames.

In the second go-round the field was reduced to ten, and Sedgwick's vote was diminished to 716, allowing Samuel Lyman, a Hampshire County lawyer who served in the Massachusetts House, to supersede him by a single vote.

The campaign was carried on in the newspapers, by private letters, and was fueled by rumors and innuendos. "Never at any time hath the rancor of party been more virulent," complained Sedgwick to Benjamin Lincoln on February 6, 1789. *With regard to myself there is no character which is odious and detestable that has not been given me, excepting that it has not been said that I am a whoremaster. Mean, servile, and fawning to great men (pray have you observed it?); proud, haughty, and imperious to those in lower stations; a public peculator and a private usurer; and above all things opposed to any amendments.*

Rumors that Sedgwick was a Deist —started by the Reverend John Taylor, minister at Deerfield in Hampshire County — circulated throughout the district. "The Reverend Zealot! has made a journey through this town," Sedgwick was told, "to Westfield and the towns around exhorting people not to build up Anti-Christ, not to vote for a Deist, etc. etc. etc."

Supporters of Theodore Sedgwick made plans to take advantage of the feeling among Berkshiremen that since Senator Caleb Strong came from Hampshire County, the seat in the House of Representatives rightfully belonged to them. "County pride would easily kindle," one of Sedgwick's friends suggested, "if a few prudent persons would gently fan the latent sparks, and feed the spreading flame with the oil of friendship." On the other side, Sedgwick's opponents spread rumors that his supporters were about to leave him in favor of another candidate, and they also put about false reports that he was a defaulter who owed the public fifteen hundred dollars.

Sedgwick's rather arrogant personality was inserted into the campaign. "Mr. Lyman is a man who is possessed of a soft, easy manner of behavior, which wins the good will of the company he is in," a writer to the *Hampshire Gazette* pointedly observed. "He has no such thing as haughtiness and pride about him, but he will be familiar with anybody." Aiming another shaft at Sedgwick, the Lyman partisan went on, "I never saw his countenance change in my life, but tis always exactly the same, equally smooth, good-natured, and smiling — not ruffled by passion and anger, as other people's are I could mention." Then the writer got directly to Sedgwick. "He is a gentleman of some abilities and some experience, but surely not worth all this fuss that is made about it. Is there a man in this county equal to Mr. Sedgwick, and must we go to the county of Berkshire for a Representative?" The correspondent concluded, *I have heard a great deal about Mr. Sedgwick being a grand speaker, and what a figure he makes; but for my part I own I never could see anything very extraordinary in him besides a great fat belly, and a great loud voice; or as we say, "all talk and no cider."*

Most damaging to Sedgwick were the doubts entertained on his willingness to support amendments to the Constitution. As the fifth election approached, Sedgwick's allies pressed on him the necessity of presenting a public statement in favor of the recommendations made by the Massachusetts ratifying convention. Although Sedgwick had at the time seen no need for amendments, he announced in the press on May 6, "My friends and acquaintance know, and all with whom I have had the pleasure of conversing on the subject, know, that I have been, and now am, a zealous advocate for many amendments."

The fifth election, held on May 27, 1789 — nearly three months after the First Federal Congress had been scheduled to commence — finally concluded the business. Theodore Sedgwick, with a count of 2,056, was elected with eight votes to spare.

One of Maryland's United States Senators, the General Assembly decided, should be a resident of the Eastern Shore; and the other should come from the western shore. Nominated for the eastern seat were John Henry and George Gale; for the western place, Charles Carroll of Carrollton (q.v.) and Uriah Forrest.

Dr. Henry, who represented Dorchester County in the Maryland Senate,

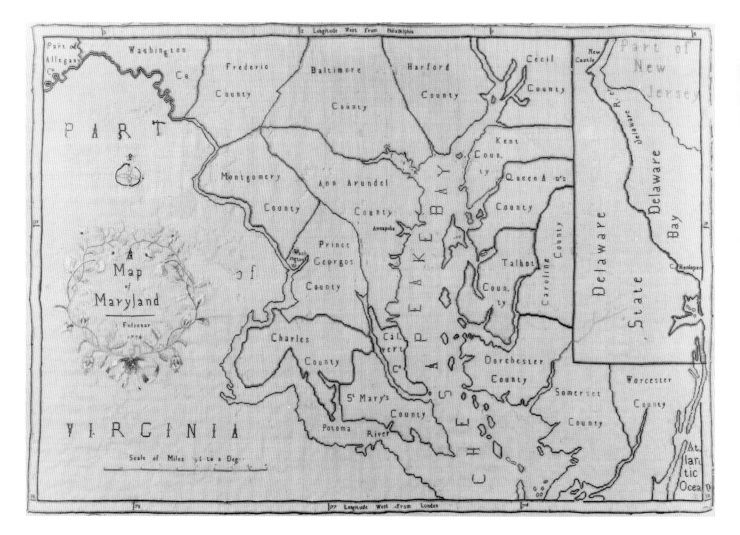

Map of Maryland; cross-stitch on linen, circa 1798. Maryland Historical Society, Baltimore

was a graduate of the College of New Jersey and had studied law at the Middle Temple in London.

George Gale from Somerset County had been in the House of Delegates before his appointment to fill a vacancy in the state Senate, where he allied himself with the Potomac interest. As a delegate to the Maryland convention, he voted to ratify the Constitution.

Charles Carroll of Carrollton, a manor of some 10,000 acres in Frederick County, had been active in the political life of Maryland even before the strictures against Catholics holding public office had been removed. A signer of the Declaration of Independence, Carroll would have been a framer of the Constitution had he not feared to leave Maryland at a time when Samuel Chase was stirring up the populace in favor of a paper-money issue.

Uriah Forrest, a delegate to the Confederation Congress in 1787, represented Montgomery County in the House of Delegates.

On December 9, 1788, the legislature chose John Henry by joint ballot and the day following elected Charles Carroll. Henry had been drawn reluctantly into the "Tumult and vexations of public life," he explained to a friend, "by a strange and unaccountable combination of circumstances." Accusations that he was unfriendly to the new government made it "necessary for me in justification of the principles which I really hold, to stand for the appointment which I at present fill."

"I am glad, that Mr. *Henry* is chosen," proclaimed an anonymous writer in the *Maryland Gazette*, "because he has been *twelve* years in our service, five of them in congress, and therefore experienced in continental affairs." Mr. Gale, on the other hand, "has only been *four* years in the senate of our state, and never in congress at all, consequently cannot be equal to his competitor in continental knowledge, although his character for abilities, integrity, and close application to public business, stands remarkably high." Thereupon the author expressed the wish of seeing Gale as "one of our six representatives, if he will consent to serve."

Secure in their control of the General Assembly, the Federalists drew up an election ordinance that would insure a Federalist sweep of Maryland's six seats in the House of Representatives. Although the state was divided into districts, the candidates for each of them—as was the case in Georgia—would be voted upon by the entire electorate. This arrangement effectively diluted the Antifederalist strength, which was concentrated in Anne Arundel, Baltimore, and Harford counties. The campaign time was exceedingly brief —the election law was passed on December 22 with voting scheduled for January 7–10.

Federal and Antifederal tickets were quickly organized, although the most prominent of the Antifederalists—Samuel Chase, William Paca, and Luther Martin—did not offer their names.

In the first district (Calvert, Charles, and St. Marys counties), Federalist

Michael Jenifer Stone, who had represented Charles County in the House of Delegates from 1781 to 1783, was opposed by George Dent, his successor in the state legislature.

Joshua Seney, in the second district (Cecil, Kent, Queen Annes, and Talbot counties), was the only candidate to be endorsed by both tickets. Educated at the College of Philadelphia, Seney had been a member of the House of Delegates from 1785 until he was chosen for the Confederation Congress in 1788.

The third district (City of Annapolis and Anne Arundel and Prince Georges counties) pitted Benjamin Contee, a lawyer and merchant, against John Francis Mercer, who had left the Constitutional Convention in high outrage and who had been denouncing the Constitution ever since.

William Smith (q.v.), a leading Baltimore merchant, carried the Federal banner in the fourth district (Town of Baltimore and Baltimore and Harford counties). His opponent was Samuel Sterett, likewise a merchant, and Baltimore's representative in the House of Delegates. "I am for Mr. *William Smith*," declared one who signed himself "A Marylander," because "we ought to have *one commercial character* in the house of representatives; he served in congress with reputation, and was a very useful member in the commercial and marine committees, and at the treasury board, besides which his character and foederalism are irreproachable." Smith's adversary, Sterett, the same correspondent declared, although "a man of abilities and merit, and having been secretary to two presidents of congress, must be well acquainted with continental affairs," had not boldly come forth to say *"where he would stop with his amendments."*

The unsuccessful senatorial candidate George Gale was the Federalist choice in the fifth district on the lower Eastern Shore (Caroline, Dorchester, Somerset, and Worcester counties). William Vans Murray of Dorchester County, who had recently returned to Maryland after legal studies at the Middle Temple in London and was a member of the House of Delegates, competed for the seat.

Framer Daniel Carroll (q.v.) stood in the sixth district (Frederick, Montgomery, and Washington counties) against Abraham Faw. Faw had been in the House of Delegates from 1785 and, despite his presence on the Antifederalist ticket, had in fact voted to ratify the Constitution. He kept a tavern in Montgomery County and served as an agent for Amelung glassworks in Frederick County. "A Marylander" pronounced that Carroll should be the choice here "because of his integrity, acquaintance with continental business and the fidelity, with which he has served us in council, congress, and the senate for more than ten years."

The Federalist ticket was triumphant. But if the electors had been confined to voting for members of their own district, a writer to the *Maryland Journal* complained, the results would have been quite different. Joshua Seney, who

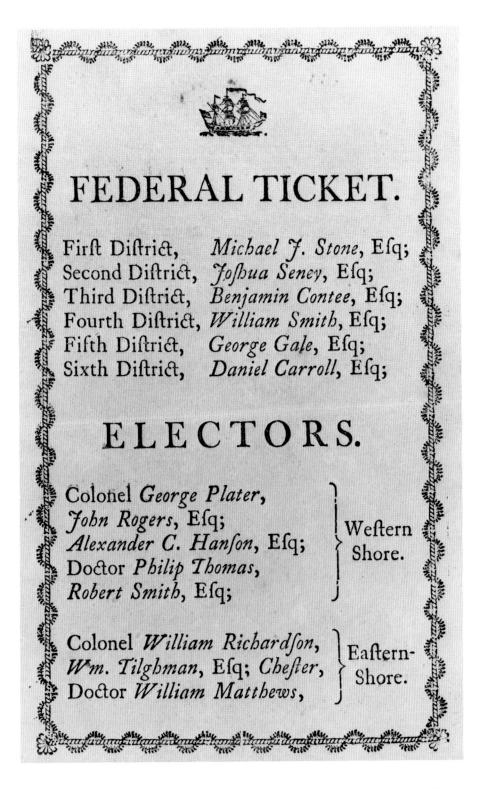

FEDERAL TICKET.

First District,   *Michael J. Stone*, Esq;
Second District,   *Joshua Seney*, Esq;
Third District,   *Benjamin Contee*, Esq;
Fourth District,   *William Smith*, Esq;
Fifth District,   *George Gale*, Esq;
Sixth District,   *Daniel Carroll*, Esq;

ELECTORS.

Colonel *George Plater*,
John Rogers, Esq;
Alexander C. Hanson, Esq;   } Western Shore.
Doctor *Philip Thomas*,
Robert Smith, Esq;

Colonel *William Richardson*,
Wm. Tilghman, Esq; *Chester*,   } Eastern-Shore.
Doctor *William Matthews*,

Broadside of Maryland federal electoral ticket, 1789. Maryland Historical Society, Baltimore

was on both tickets, and Daniel Carroll — who had received 2,308 votes against only 6 for his rival — would have prevailed, but otherwise the Antifederalists Samuel Sterett, John Francis Mercer, George Dent, and George Gale would have carried the vote. Asked the irate correspondent, *Is it just or wise to compel the People to vote for Persons they do not know? Is it proper that Washington and Frederick Counties should elect for the People of Baltimore and Harford Counties, and thereby prevent them from having the Man of their Choice, and impose on them the Man they very generally reject?*

A letter from a German farmer carried in the *Maryland Journal* on January 16, 1789, gave an account of the proceedings in Washington County. "We thought it right to call the Friends of the New Government to give in their Votes at the Court-House, so we made out so many as 1167 for the Federal Ticket, and no Man said against it." Of the two or three thousand people assembled, the writer declared that there was "not one Anti." He went on, "An Ox roasted whole, Hoof and Horn, was divided into Morsels, and every one would taste a Bit. . . . They were as happy to get a Piece of *Federal Ox* as ever superstitious Christians, or *Anti*-Christians were to get Relicts from Jerusalem."

Federalist jubilation could not be contained. Baltimore, always a Federal town, held a public celebration at Fells Point as soon as the polls had closed, bringing forth the little ship that had been featured in the grand parade held in honor of ratification, as well as "other Emblems descriptive of the Occasion," including "a Figure representing the Goddess of Federalism, and an excellent Painting of General Washington."

The federal ship *Union,* which was the highlight of all the state processions in celebration of ratification of the Constitution, was used once more at Baltimore to acclaim the Federalist victory in the first federal elections.

Published in Francis Hopkinson, "An Account of the Grand Federal Procession," *American Museum,* 1788

SOUTH CAROLINA

South Carolina was the only state — except for stalemated New York — to choose her Representatives before fixing upon her Senators. Elections for the House of Representatives were set for November 24–25, 1788, the earliest in the nation. The state was divided into five districts, but the legislature decreed that the candidate need not be a resident of the area he aimed to represent. Save for the Charleston district, there is scant information about the contests — not even the vote tallies are extant.

Low-country planter Daniel Huger was the choice in the combined Geeorgetown-Cheraw district. Huger, brother of three prominent patriots, had taken an oath of loyalty to the British after the fall of Charles Town but nonetheless escaped property confiscation. At the time of his election, he was serving in the old Congress. There is no information as to whether Huger — who was believed to be a supporter of the Constitution — had opposition.

Aedanus Burke (q.v.), the victor in the combined Beaufort-Orangeburg district, was challenged by Robert Barnwell, who had voted in support of the Constitution at the state ratifying convention. Barnwell, a planter, carried only his native St. Helena's Parish. The Irish-born Burke, a circuit judge in the backcountry, resided at Charleston and had in 1783 created a considerable stir by the publication of two pamphlets, one attacking the Society of the Cincinnati and the other calling for amnesty for South Carolina's Loyalists. Burke was a decided Antifederalist.

The backcountry Camden district elected Thomas Sumter (q.v.), the feisty leader of the celebrated guerrilla force that had bedeviled British Colonel Banastre Tarleton during the Revolution. Sumter had been in the state legislature since 1782. He was outspoken in his opposition to the Constitution and had voted against its ratification. Who, if anyone, opposed Sumter is not known.

Ninety-Six, the frontier district that bordered on Georgia and the Cherokee Indian lands, selected Dr. Thomas Tudor Tucker (q.v.) of Charleston. Tucker, a University of Edinburgh-educated physician, was Bermuda born. He had served as a surgeon in the Continental army and was then a member of the Confederation Congress. Interestingly, Charles Pinckney the framer, writing on January 26, 1789, identified all of the South Carolina delegates by political label except for Tucker, "whose sentiments I am unacquainted with." There soon would be no doubt that Dr. Tucker was thoroughly Antifederalist.

The seat in the Charleston district was contested by three candidates —

Commodore Alexander Gillon, Dr. David Ramsay, and William Smith (q.v.). Smith, who some years later would add Loughton as a middle name to distinguish himself from another South Carolina Smith, will thus be referred to at the First Federal Congress in order to differentiate him from William Smith of Maryland.

Gillon, born in Amsterdam and trained as a merchant in London, had been in South Carolina since 1766. Appointed commodore in the South Carolina navy during the war, he had been a successful privateer until his ship was captured in 1782. Leader of the agitation against returning Loyalist merchants, Gillon was popular with the artisans of Charleston. "My friends have applied to me to go to Congress for Charleston District," Gillon wrote, "as they wish a commercial character to be in Congress."

A native of Pennsylvania, Ramsay had been educated at the College of New Jersey and received his medical degree from the College of Philadelphia. He moved to Charleston in 1773, was soon elected to the state legislature, and from 1782 to 1785 served in the Congress. At the state ratifying convention Ramsay had been a stout advocate of the Constitution.

Smith, also a Federalist, the candidate favored by the Charleston establishment and the Goose Creek planters, was a wealthy lawyer who had been sent to Europe for his education in his twelfth year. He had studied law at the Middle Temple in London and traveled extensively before his return to South Carolina in 1783. A little more than a year later, he was elected to the state legislature.

Just days before the election, a heated exchange between Ramsay and Smith was carried by local newspapers and in broadsides distributed throughout the city. Dr. Ramsay charged that Smith, because of his long residence in Europe, did not meet the seven-year citizenship requirement set by the Constitution. Smith retorted that Ramsay's own vote for his election to the privy council in 1785 was an acknowledgment of his citizenship. In a countercharge, the Smith forces accused Ramsay of distributing antislavery pamphlets. Ramsay avowed that he was opposed to the emancipation of slaves, but Smith shot back, "It is very well known, that *he is principled against slavery,* and it is idle for him to contradict *what is universally known.*"

After the votes were counted, Ramsay declared that he had "lost my election on two grounds. One was that I was a Northward man and the other that I was represented as favoring the abolition of slavery. Such is the temper of our people here that it is unpopular to be unfriendly to the further importation of slaves."

The final tally showed that Smith had received more votes than his two opponents combined — 600 to Gillon's 386 and Ramsay's 191. There had been, detailed the local newspaper, "an uncommon number of voters at this election."

John F. Grimké, an active South Carolina Federalist, noting that Aedanus

Burke, Thomas Sumter, and Dr. Tudor Tucker were clearly Antifederal and that Daniel Huger was inclined to be "doubtful," wrote, "What a black list. We must endeavor to mend it by our election of Senators."

In January 1789 the legislature got down to the business of deciding on the state's two Senators. Charles Pinckney declared to his friends that he certainly would have been elected had not his obligations to his mother, wife, and new son prevented him from offering his services. Rawlins Lowndes, the

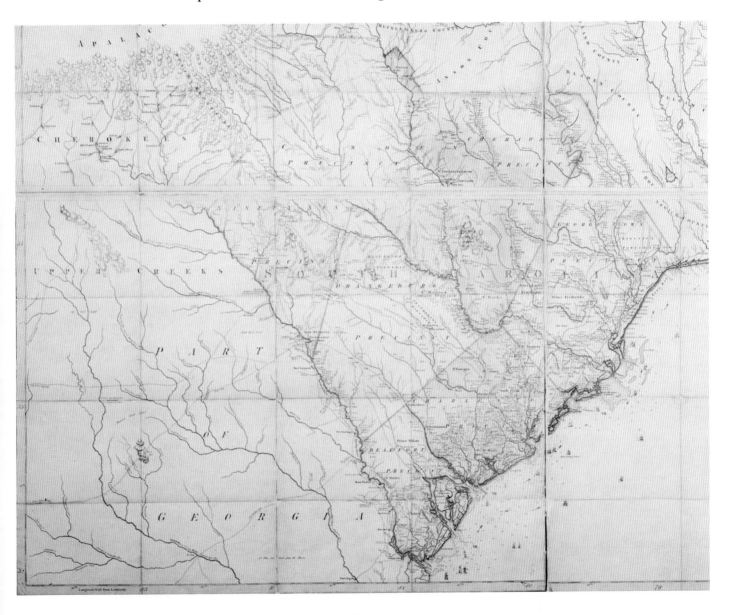

An Accurate Map of North and South Carolina (detail of South Carolina) from Henry Mouzon *et al.*; published by Robert Sayer and John Bennett, London, 1775. Geography and Map Division, Library of Congress, Washington, D.C.

A DOSE for the DOCTOR.

ECCE *iterum Crispinus!* or in plain English, the Dr. has again intruded himself on the patience of the public. Finding that arguments have failed him, he is obliged to have recourse to misquotations, quibbles, distinctions without a difference, and to laws made to answer temporary purposes, which by no means apply to the present question. What have we, for example, to do with *virtual citizenship,* when I am in possession of, and never have been deprived of *actual citizenship?* May not the Dr. with propriety be compared to a certain cunning animal, who when hard run, and all his windings, artifices and tricks have availed him nothing, steeps his tail in an unsavoury liquor, and endeavours to whisk it into the eyes of his pursuers.

The Dr. asserts that by the generosity of this country I had the advantage of aliens so far, that at any time on application I might be admitted to citizenship. Here then is a new class of men never known in society before!—not aliens—not citizens—but an intermediate set of beings, who neither aliens nor citizens, partake of the nature of both, and may be compared to what is very well understood by the Dr. under the name of a *tertium quid.*

I think it unnecessary to follow the Dr. through all his subterfuges, but shall attach myself to the main point, to which I flatter myself I shall give a satisfactory answer by condemning him out of his own mouth. The Dr. has declared, that *I was,* at the time of my election, *qualified to be a privy counsellor.* Let us examine then the qualification of a privy counsellor—the following are the words of the constitution : ——— " The members of the privy council shall have been *residents in this state five years preceding their election.*" I arrived here from Europe in *November* 1783—I qualified as a privy counsellor in *August* 1785, the short *space* of 21 *months.* The Dr. however *admits* that *I had a qualification*—what then was my qualification ? If my residence here, during my minority, and previous to my going to Europe, was not considered as part of the residence of five years required by the constitution, how could I have possibly been qualified, or what does the Dr. conceive could have been my qualification ? Had I arrived here in Nov. 1783, *an alien,* a *British subject,* could I have been elected a privy counsellor and qualified in August 1785 ? *Will the Dr. say I could ?* The Dr. we know is fond of *paradoxes* : a stronger proof than the following cannot be adduced. In *his Calm Reply,* he says I was, in Nov. 1783, *a British subject* : in his *Short Reply,* he says I was in August 1785 eligible to the office of privy counsellor, and in October 1785, I actually had *his vote* for that office. Let him reconcile this monstrous absurdity ! Should the Dr. favor us with another reply, whether it be *calm* or *short,* I hope he will be able to extricate himself from this difficulty. I shall conclude with a word of advice to the Dr. He frequently speaks of his *candor* and *his regard for the good of the state* : these expressions have been so hackneyed, that every person who has had any transactions in public life, must now be sickened with them : they have been often made use of as a *step-ladder,* to mount into popularity, or a *mask* to conceal the most ambitious designs.

The Doctor says *he had a regard for me* : the public will not be imposed upon his words, but will judge from his actions. I am conscious of never having injured him in the course of my life ; and yet when he found that I was likely to obtain the suffrages of my fellow citizens, his regard vanished : malevolence, and detraction were substituted in the room of it, and one single object seemed to engross his attention, namely, the gratification of his ambition.—He has confessed that if at the declaration of Independence I was a party to it, either personally *or representatively, he gives up the argument.* That I was so, must be now apparent, even to the most prejudiced of his friends, and therefore I hope he will adhere to his word.

He must, I believe, not only give up the argument, but likewise the good opinion which has hitherto been entertained of him by many worthy citizens of this country. Nothing but *repentance* for the insult which he has offered by his unjustifiable conduct, can be an atonement to them, and reinstate him in their good opinion. As far as depends upon myself, I shall be ready to forgive him. Though the shaft was aimed at my heart, and at the same time could not fail to wound every native of this country ! yet my forgiveness shall not be the last obtained, as implacability forms no part of my character.

Doctor farewell.

William Smith.

Charleston, November 25, 1788.

The final shot in the broadside war in the Charleston district— "A Dose for the Doctor"—was fired by William Loughton Smith on November 25, 1788, the last day of the two-day election period.

Rare Book and Special Collections Division, Library of Congress, Washington, D.C.

Credentials of Pierce Butler, Senator from South Carolina. National Archives, Washington, D.C.

low-country planter who had been the spokesman for the Antifederalists in the Assembly, was asked to be a candidate but declined because of age and infirmities. Without apparently considering any other names, the legislature on January 22 chose Pierce Butler and Ralph Izard (q.v.). Butler, the third son of a baronet, sold his British army commission after his marriage in 1771 to Mary Middleton, an heiress to a vast South Carolina acreage. In his own right the owner of large plantations in both Georgia and South Carolina, Butler had become active in the political life of the low country. At the Constitutional Convention Butler contended strenuously to protect the economic interests of his state.

The much-traveled Izard, whose chief residence, The Elms, was at the head of Goose Creek not far from Charleston, was the owner of five plantations — totaling over 4,000 acres — and 500 slaves. He was currently serving in the South Carolina House of Representatives and had previously served in the Confederation Congress.

"Our Senators," Charles Pinckney informed Rufus King, "are Pierce Butler and Ralph Izard, esquires — both strong Federalists, and will I trust do credit to their appointment."

NEW HAMPSHIRE

Once the New Hampshire legislature completed the drafting of its election law on November 5, 1788, it speedily elected John Langdon (q.v.) to the United States Senate. Langdon, who had made it possible for New Hampshire to be represented at the Constitutional Convention when he offered to pay not only his own expenses but also those of his colleague, Nicholas Gilman (q.v.), was currently president of New Hampshire. Langdon's merits and qualifications aside, his political enemies welcomed the opportunity to get him out of the state. William Plumer, a member of the state legislature, recalled in 1826 that Langdon was elected without opposition, *but in electing the other Senator we were much divided. Samuel Livermore and Nathaniel Peabody were the principal candidates. The former was a Federalist, and the latter an Antifederalist; but the members did not in the election all vote according to their political creed other considerations governed some of them. John Taylor Gilman, who was then treasurer and a zealous Federalist, used the whole weight of his influence, and it was considerable, in support of Peabody. I was in favor of Livermore, and decidedly opposed to Peabody, whom I knew was an artful, cunning, intriguing man, destitute of moral principle, and an inmate with infamous characters. I thought his election would reflect disgrace on the state, and I opposed him from principle.*

The spirited debate over the proper men for the Senate was carried on in the public press. One who signed himself "A Friend to the People" lauded Samuel Livermore (q.v.) as chief justice of the state, but then went on to say, *I do not think His Honor the Chief Justice is a suitable person to represent us in Congress at this time as a Senator. I do not wish to hurt his feelings, for I love and respect his abilities, but the call of my country is more extensive than my feelings for a bosom friend. The amendments to the new Constitution is the most important object we are looking for, at the settling of the new Congress. . . . The voice of the people cry aloud for it.* The writer pointed out that Livermore at the ratifying convention had said, *with a great degree of firmness,* that the Constitution was now complete without any amendments. *If so, why should we send him to Congress to be an instrument to withhold from us the amendments so ardently wished for, and at the same time deprive us of a gentleman on the superior bench that time will scarce ever replace?* The writer concluded, "Were I to recommend any person for the office of Senator, I should be careful to avoid any character who had a hand in framing the Constitution, as it is, in some measure, a child of their own making. Consequently, they would wish to support it at any rate." He added, "On the other hand, I should avoid those who wish to destroy the whole. But take the middle path and choose some gentleman who wishes well to the whole

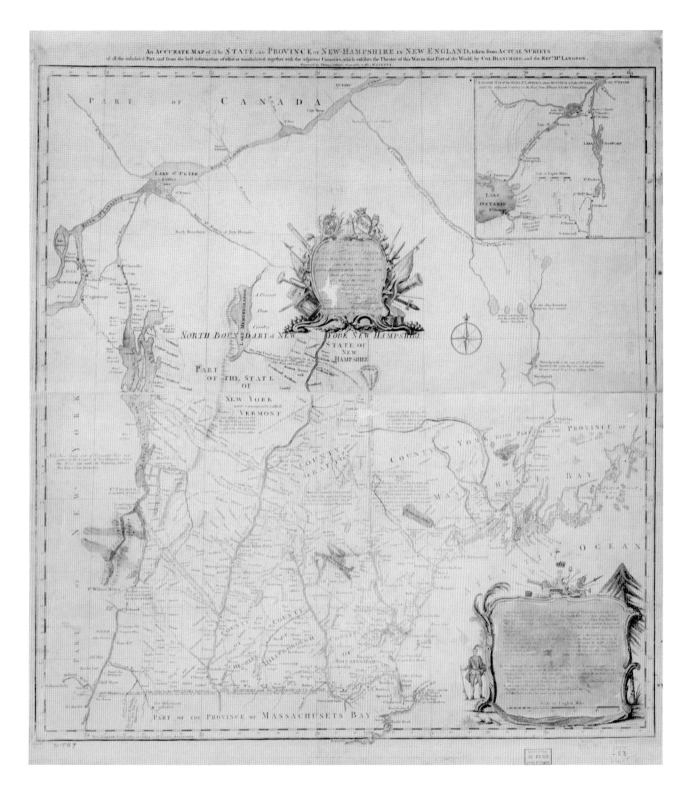

Map of New Hampshire; engraved by Thomas Jefferys, Boston, 1784. Geography and Map Division, Library of Congress, Washington, D.C.

community, and whose acquaintance and extensive knowledge will be serviceable in bringing about the amendments."

A correspondent who signed himself "Friend to Amendments" answered, "I cannot fall in with the notions of the *friend to the people* in your last with regard to the unfitness of our worthy President [Langdon] and Chief Justice [Livermore] for Senator in the new Congress." Of Livermore, the writer observed, *I know he holds an office of importance and fills it as nicely as a man can do, for I have been on the jury and heard him talk as glibly as ever I heard a minister read a sermon in the pulpit without having a word writ. But if there is another office of greater importance that he is better qualified to fill than any other man, it seems to me good policy would not oppose his being hoisted into it. And such an office is that for which he is a candidate.* The Federalist "Friend to Amendments" rebutted the assertion that "amendments to the new Constitution *is the most important object to be looked at in settling the new Congress.* In this I cannot agree with him. I think there is a number of much great importance, but will mention only two of them, viz., the *establishing a system of revenue and revenue laws* — which will require the very wisest heads we have among us — and the *appointment of a number of very important officers."* He concluded, "The business that must be done by the first Congress requires longer heads and honester hearts than we can find united in the same person among the opposers of the Constitution."

In the end the New Hampshire House settled on Antifederalist Nathaniel Peabody, only to have him be rejected by the Senate, who proposed instead the name of Federalist Josiah Bartlett. Dr. Bartlett, signer of the Declaration of Independence, was a venerated political institution, and the members of the House found no difficulty in agreeing to the nomination. The appointment made, Bartlett declared that he would not serve.

On January 3, 1789, the legislature substituted the name of Paine Wingate, who was a member of the old Congress. A Harvard graduate and Congregational minister, Wingate had resigned his pulpit in a dispute with his congregation and thereafter devoted himself to farming and politics. He was a Federalist.

In elections for New Hampshire's three seats in the House of Representatives, the candidates were to run at large, and if no one received more than one sixth of the votes, the six who topped the list would stand for a second go-round. Just as it took New Hampshire two conventions to ratify the Constitution, it took two elections to choose the state's delegates to Congress. And before the business was concluded, a special election was called for.

The elections were held on December 15, 1788, and the *New Hampshire Spy* reported that at the Portsmouth town meeting "not more than one quarter of the inhabitants, qualified by law to vote, attended." No one was elected.

Eliminated in the first round of voting were Joshua Atherton of Amherst, leader of the opposition to the Constitution at the 1788 ratifying convention, and Nathaniel Peabody.

The six survivors were Benjamin West, Samuel Livermore, Paine Wingate, Abiel Foster, John Sullivan, and Nicholas Gilman. Before the second election was held, Wingate had been chosen for the Senate, and Sullivan, former president of New Hampshire, had declared "that his intention was not to serve the state in that capacity, and that any votes given for him would be thrown away." Thus elected on February 2, 1789, were Gilman with 1,697 votes, West with 1,578, and Livermore with 1,500. Gilman, a delegate at the Confederation Congress, was a signer of the Constitution; West and Livermore had supported the document at the state ratifying convention. Gilman confessed to Tench Coxe that his election to Congress was *owing to a general partiality for my family & to the particular favor of my friends, who have some confidence in my integrity & love of Country rather than in my political information — for as I have spent but a small part of the last twelve years in that State & have declined a seat in the General Court.*

In May Benjamin West, who had previously refused to serve in Congress or as attorney general of the state, declared that he would not go to Congress. He was replaced at a special election held on June 22 by Abiel Foster, judge of the Rockingham County Court of Common Pleas. Foster, a former minister, had been active in politics since 1775, when he served in the provincial Congress. As a delegate to Congress, Foster was present at Annapolis on December 23, 1783, when George Washington resigned his commission. He was described then as "tall lank, 50 yrs. a Farmer, sunburnt."

On July 16, 1789, the New Hampshire returns were declared official, and the *New Hampshire Gazette* proclaimed, "This choice completes the organization of the federal government by the ratifying states."

Early in the first session of the Congress, a visitor to New York reported that the "lower House of Congress seems to abound with able speakers from the Southern States, but the voice of New Hampshire is not heard amongst them. This surely does not proceed from a deficiency of talents, for the abilities of our Representatives are very respectable." The anonymous author complained in the *New Hampshire Spy*, "But a gentleman without the powers of elocution in a popular assembly, is like a figurante on the stage, he serves to fill up the number, and count one, this is the extent of his influence."

VIRGINIA

James Madison had bested Patrick Henry at the Virginia ratifying convention, but when it came time to select the Old Dominion's delegates to the United States Congress, Henry was, as Madison expressed it, "omnipotent."

"Our Assembly is *weak*," Federalist Richard Bland Lee reported to Madison. "Mr. Henry is the only orator we have amon[g] us—and the friends to the new government, being all young & inexperienced—form but a feeble band against him."

Henry himself declined to be nominated for the United States Senate because he was unwilling, he proclaimed, to take the oath to support the Constitution. At George Washington's insistence, the Federalists placed Madison's name in nomination, but any slight chance he might have had evaporated when his friend and supporter, Alexander White, acknowledged that it was doubtful that Madison would obey instructions that should direct him to vote against direct taxation. Whereupon Patrick Henry declared, "The secret is out: it is doubted whether Mr. Madison will obey instructions." Madison was told, "Mr. Henry on the floor exclaimed against your political character & pronounced you unworthy of the confidence of the people in the station of Senator. That your election would terminate in producing rivulets of blood throughout the land."

Patrick Henry looked with favor upon the candidacy of Richard Henry Lee (q.v.). If Lee had gotten his way at the Confederation Congress, the Constitution would have been submitted to the states with a declaration calling for a bill of rights, elimination of the vice-presidential office, and an increase in the size of the House of Representatives. Lee had campaigned openly for the Senate appointment, asking his friends to get it about that he was willing to "exert my faculties for obtaining such amendments in the senate of the new legislature, if it shall please the Assembly to send me there." He wanted this information circulated, he added, "because I know it is a common art, in these times, to prevent elections by asserting that persons proposed will not serve, if elected." To another friend, Lee, who was the same age as George Washington, protested "that nothing but the reverence I have for the liberties of my country, and a thorough conviction of the danger these will be exposed to by the unamended state of the new constitution, could have induced me to consent again to become a public man."

William Grayson, Lee's colleague at the dying Congress, was also a candidate for the Senate. At the state ratifying convention Grayson had been

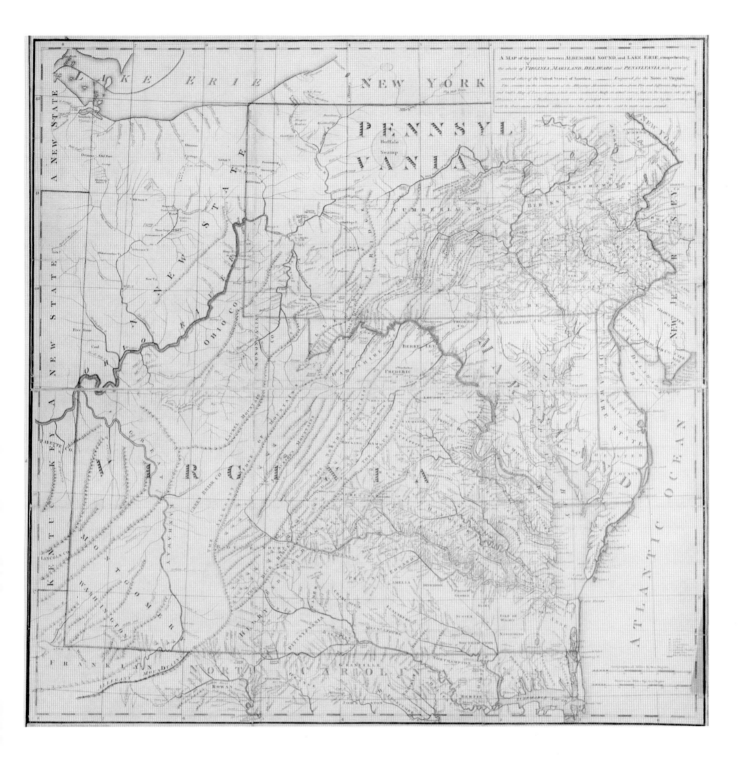

Map of Virginia compiled by Thomas Jefferson, Paris, 1786–1787. Geography and Map Division, Library of Congress, Washington, D.C.

Although Patrick Henry (1736–1799) disdained a place in the First Federal Congress, his control over the Virginia legislature insured the selection of two Antifederalist Senators and very nearly denied James Madison a seat in the House of Representatives.

By James Barton Longacre (1794–1869), after Lawrence Sully; watercolor on artist board, circa 1835. National Portrait Gallery, Smithsonian Institution, Washington, D.C.

eclipsed only by Patrick Henry in powerful amplification of the defects of the Constitution — frightening most of the Kentucky delegates into unswerving opposition when he warned that the New England states acting together might be able to negotiate a treaty with Spain that would close the Mississippi to American commerce. Madison's friend Edward Carrington observed that Grayson "is indeed the devoted Servant of Henry."

When the vote was taken by joint ballot on November 9, 1788, Richard Henry Lee's total stood at 98, William Grayson's at 86 and James Madison's at 77.

The outcome did not especially dismay Madison, who was inclined toward the House of Representatives, where he would owe his election directly to the people and not to the legislature. But Madison and his friends received a shock when the Henry forces drew up an election ordinance that set up ten districts and stipulated that all candidates be residents for at least twelve months of the district they strove to represent. "Mr. Henry," wrote an alarmed Federalist, had taken care "to arrange matters so as to have the County of which Mr Madison is an inhabitant thrown into a district of which a majority were supposed to be unfriendly to Govt. and by that means exclude him from the Representative body in Congress."

Federalist James Duncanson summed up, *In short the Assembly, or rather Henry by whose influence they were directed, took every step they could think of, that would have a tendency to obstruct, & prevent, as far as was in their power, the new Constitution being put in motion, in laying of the Districts, which were to choose our 10 Representatives in the new Congress.* He charged, "They pack'd the Counties so as to give as little chance as possible, for any Federalists to be elected."

Elections for delegates to the House of Representatives were held on February 2, 1789. Information on most of the races is meager, and returns are complete only from the "Henry-mandered" fifth district, where James Madison and James Monroe went head to head.

District 1: Berkeley, Frederick, Hampshire, Hardy, Harrison, Monongalia, Ohio, Randolph, and Shenandoah counties. Alexander White, whom Horatio Gates described as "a Staunch Fed.," had no competitor for the seat in the northern valley counties. White, who represented Frederick County in the Assembly, had been educated at the University of Edinburgh, studied law at the Inner Temple, and, testified Gates, "has long been at the Head of the Barr in this County. & much esteem'd in his profession."

District 2: Bourbon, Fayette, Jefferson, Lincoln, Madison, Mercer, and Nelson counties. In the district comprising the Kentucky counties, John Brown (q.v.), a delegate to the Confederation Congress and former western Virginia representative in the state Senate, was elected. Brown, a friend of Madison's, had exerted himself — if to little avail — to persuade Kentucky delegates to support the Constitution at the Virginia ratifying convention. "I pointedly gave it as my Opinion," he reported from New York, "that it ought

Andrew Moore (1752–1821), who had been one of James Madison's closest allies in the Virginia legislature, could generally be counted on to vote Madison's way at the First Federal Congress, although the interests of his constituents would cause him to oppose a duty on salt and the excise on whiskey.

From a photograph of a miniature illustrated in Clarence Winthrop Bowen's *The Centennial of Washington's Inauguration*

to be adopted without hesitation as the only Means left to prevent Anarchy & Confusion & to insure Safety & importance to the United States."

Brown seems to have been unopposed, although James Wilkinson, the arch-schemer who sought to separate Kentucky from Virginia and perhaps the union, boasted to the Spanish governor at New Orleans, "The place in Congress having been offered to me by the People, I rejected it for I judged my presence in Kentucky was more necessary to our projects, hence it was conferred on Mr. John Brown."

District 3: Augusta, Botetourt, Greenbrier, Hancock, Montgomery, Pendleton, Rockbridge, Rockingham, Russell, and Washington counties. Federalist Andrew Moore appears to have had some competition from one Hancock, but the election returns have not survived. Of Scotch-Irish descent, Moore had fought in the Revolution and studied law under George Wythe.

He had been elected to the House of Delegates in 1788.

District 4: Fairfax, Fauquier, King George, Loudoun, Prince William, and Stafford counties. This northern Virginia district, the home of both George Washington and George Mason, was the scene of a fair amount of electioneering. A number of candidates — both Federalist and Antifederalist — presented themselves, but the contest seems to have come down to Federalist Richard Bland Lee (q.v.), who had represented Loudoun County in the legislature since 1784, versus one John Pope, to whom James Madison referred as the likely winner. An Alexandria merchant reported to Horatio Gates, "We choose a very contemptible character by the name of Pope set up by the Anti's in opposition to Mr. Richd. B. Lee of Loudoun." A Falmouth merchant offered the tantalizing observation that "Two Gentlemen offers to represent this division in Congress & as one only is wanted on the occasion I understand one makes very free with the other's Reputation & by wch. I should not be surprized to hear of their having Exchanged a few dry blows." Returns from Fairfax County show that the victor, Lee, garnered 227 votes there against Pope's 61.

District 5: Albemarle, Amherst, Culpeper, Fluvanna, Goochland, Louisa, Orange, and Spotsylvania counties. Here was the battleground that James Madison (q.v.) was forced to contest — and he could be confident of carrying only Louisa and his home county of Orange. Madison's friends thought the outcome to be "extremely doubtful," and became increasingly worried as Patrick Henry's allies bruited it about that Madison had declared "that the Constitution required no alteration whatever."

In December Madison, who was with the Congress at New York, was advised that his friend James Monroe (q.v.) had been put up by the Antifederalists, "and the most active unceasing endeavours will not be wanting among his friends to secure his election. It therefore becomes indispensably necessary that your return to Virga. should be hastened as much as possible." Monroe, then serving in the House of Delegates from Spotsylvania County, had voted against the Constitution at the ratifying convention. He later told Thomas Jefferson that, although he would have been concerned to have excluded Madison from the Congress, he had been pressed "to come forward in this govt. on its commencement, and that I might not loose an opportunity of contributing my feeble efforts, in forwarding an amendment of its defects."

By mid-January, Madison was back in Virginia, traveling throughout Culpeper and Louisa — sometimes appearing in tandem with James Monroe — suffering from frostbite as he addressed the voters at open-air meetings. Madison took pains to deny that he was dogmatically opposed to any additions to the Constitution. "Amendments, if pursued with a proper moderation and in a proper mode," Madison said in a letter meant to be circulated in his district, "will be not only safe, but may serve the double purpose of satisfying the minds of well meaning opponents, and of providing additional guards in favour of liberty." To quiet the fears of the Baptists, faithful supporters who owed him a debt of gratitude because of his long stance in defense of freedom of conscience, Madison made a clear campaign promise: *It is my sincere opinion that the Constitution ought to be revised, and that the first Congress meeting under it, ought to prepare and recommend to the States for ratification, the most satisfactory provisions for all essential rights, particularly the rights of Conscience in the fullest latitude, the freedom of the press, trial by jury, security against general warrants etc.*

"The Freeholders of several religious denominations" were reminded in the Fredericksburg *Virginia Herald* that Madison had led the fight against the bill that would have forced all residents to pay a tax for the support of religion, "which received the patronage and support of Mr. Henry."

In the February election, Madison carried Orange County with a vote of 200; Monroe received but 9. Monroe carried Spotsylvania by 189 to 115 and Amherst by 246 to 145. Madison's attention to Culpeper County was rewarded with a vote of 256 against Monroe's 103. When all the ballots were counted, Madison had a victory margin of 336 votes.

Back at New York, Madison reported to Jefferson: *It was my misfortune to be thrown into a contest with our friend, Col. Monroe. The occasion produced considerable efforts among our respective friends. Between ourselves, I have no reason to doubt that the distinction was duly kept in mind between political and personal views, and that it has saved our friendship from the smallest diminution.*

District 6: Bedford, Buckingham, Campbell, Charlotte, Franklin, Halifax, Henry, Pittsylvania, and Prince Edward counties. In the sixth district Isaac Coles, "a Kinsman of Mr. Henry," James Madison related, "was but barely preferred to a young gentleman of good sense, and great moderation." The Antifederalist Coles was a planter and former member of the House of Delegates. His young opponent has not been identified.

District 7: Caroline, Essex, Gloucester, King and Queen, King William, Lancaster, Middlesex, Northumberland, Richmond, and Westmoreland counties. Several Antifederalists entered the fray here, including Arthur Lee, the brother of Richard Henry Lee, who issued a broadside proclaiming, *there is every Reason to hope, that the new Constitution — so amended as to remove the Apprehensions and secure the Confidence of the People — will promote our Interests at home, and our Respectibility abroad. But this will very much depend upon the Laws and Regulations of the first Congress, and the Train of Administration in which they place the new Government.*

Another of the "Antis" was Meriwether Smith, a longtime officeholder who had been among the dissenting delegates at the Virginia convention.

On the Federalist side Francis Corbin, a representative from Middlesex County since 1784, declared that he had intended to pay his personal respects to all the freemen in his district, *But my duty in the Assembly, added to the short interval between its final adjournment and the election of Members to Congress, together with the badness of the weather, and my own indisposition, have unfortunately frustrated my intentions. Therefore it is, that I am under the painful necessity of following the example of those who have addressed you by a PUBLIC LETTER.* He assured his constituents, "I am a friend to the Federal Constitution, but no enemy to general amendments."

Corbin added wryly, "Several respectable characters have made a tender of their services to represent you in Congress; I could say much in praise of some of them; — but I understand all have said enough in praise of themselves."

The Federalist field threatened to become all too crowded. John Page (q.v.) of Rosewell, whose political experience went back to the House of Burgesses, had entered the lists; and when Washington heard that Henry "Light Horse Harry" Lee, a Westmoreland County Federalist, seemed disposed to get into the race, he warned, "Whether Mr. Page's interest, or yours is best in the district I am not sufficiently informed to decide." But he advised that the two should consult rather than split the Federalist vote. Thereupon, Lee withdrew, saying that "otherwise the election may take an improper turn."

A completed count for the seventh district has not been discovered, but Page related in a letter of February 7, "If I am elected as I suppose I am (having lost but 23 votes in 3 Counties & having a great Intt. in the Northern Neck) I must set out for N. York [in?] ten Days."

District 8: Accomack, Isle of Wight, Nansemond, Norfolk, Northampton, Princess Anne, Southampton, and Surry counties. Three candidates stood for election in the Norfolk-area district — Colonel Josiah Parker (q.v.), whose count was 976; Colonel Thomas Mathews, 805; Colonel Isaac Avery, 204.

Mathews, the Federalist candidate, represented the borough of Norfolk in the House of Delegates and was elected speaker in 1788. Avery was sheriff of Northampton County. Parker, the naval officer at Portsmouth, claimed that he had not solicited any votes.

The Richmond *Independent Chronicle* noted that news of Parker's election was celebrated with "a discharge of 11 heavy cannon from the Town Point of Portsmouth, and 5 guns from the ship Le Contaeux."

Subsequent to the congressional election, a writer to the *Portsmouth Journal* explained that Parker *first declared himself Anti — Ushering forth to assist in preserving the rights and privileges of a free and independent people, in support of which it is well known he had in the course of the late war boldly risqued his life and fortune; but now that the Federal Government is ratified by a great majority, it was his prudence and good sense alone that directed him to avow himself a steady and faithful friend to the Constitution (as Federal), that he may still have it in his power to be of more material service to his country.*

Madison listed Parker among the Antifederalists but added to Jefferson that "Col. Parker appears to be very temperate."

District 9: Amelia, Brunswick, Cumberland, Dinwiddie, Greensville,

Mecklenburg, Lunenburg, Powhatan, Prince George, and Sussex counties. Raising high the Antifederalist banner was longtime Madison enemy Theodorick Bland, colonel of the Virginia Light Dragoons during the Revolution and lately Prince George's representative to the Virginia Assembly. "The district being wholly poisoned with enmity agst. the Constitution," Madison explained, "the Federalists thought it vain to put forth a candidate." Federalist Edward Carrington thought some of offering his candidacy, but, "Knowing that it would be impossible to stem the torrent upon direct federal principles," he decided instead to concert with others to support "a less obstinate anti than Bland." They fixed upon Samuel Goode, who had represented Mecklenburg in the House of Delegates, as the only man in the district who could answer their purposes, but he declined the service. After the ballots were cast, Bland declared that he had won 619 votes from five counties, and the remaining 27 votes cast were divided between eight or ten different candidates.

Bland would be the first member of the federal House of Representatives to die in office. Interestingly, the thoroughly Federalist William Smith of South Carolina commented after his colleague's death that Colonel Bland "was a truly honest good man—candid, open & fair—quite the gentleman & man of education & by far the best man in the whole Delegation—tho not the ablest."

District 10: Charles City, Chesterfield, Elizabeth City, Hanover, Henrico, James City, New Kent, Warwick, and York counties. Three candidates were voted upon in the tenth district—Benjamin Harrison, Sr., Miles Selden, Jr., and Samuel Griffin. Harrison, a longtime officeholder, had served in the Congress, in the House of Delegates, and as governor of Virginia. He had voted against the Constitution. Miles Selden had represented the Henrico district in the state Senate and was also in the Assembly. Samuel Griffin (q.v.), a planter who practiced law in Williamsburg, was in the Virginia House of Delegates. Madison told Washington in January that a Harrison victory was "probable, tho' great expectations are entertained in favor of Mr. S Griffin." In the end, the Federalist Griffin prevailed. John Marshall, who had represented Fauquier County in the House of Delegates, recalled in 1827, "I was pressed to become a candidate for Congress; and, though the district was unequivocally antifederal I could have been elected because that party was almost equally divided between two Candidates who were equally obstinate and much embittered against each other." Personal considerations caused the future Chief Justice to decline the contest, "after which the federalists set up and elected Colonel Griffin, who obtained rather more than one third of the votes in the district which constituted a plurality."

In the beginning the Antifederalists had high hopes that their arguments would carry the day. George Mason, who had declared that he would rather cut off his arm than sign the Constitution as it then stood, said confidently, "It

Twenty-eight-year-old Antifederalist William Branch Giles (1762–1830) was elected to the vacancy caused by the death of Theodorick Bland. William Maclay, upon meeting Giles for the first time recorded, "The Frothy Manners of Virginia were ever uppermost. Canvasbacks ham & Chickens, old Madeira, the glories of the Antient Dominion, all *amazing* fine, were his constant Themes."

From a miniature illustrated in Clarence Winthrop Bowen's *The Centennial of Washington's Inauguration*

is thought the Elections will go, very generally in favour of Men, who are for calling a federal Convention, to make Amendments." After the elections had been decided, George Lee Turberville, a member of the House of Delegates from Richmond County, exulted to James Madison, *The sense of the People so conspicuously manifested in favor of the New Government as it has been by the Election of seven Federalists (perhaps indeed of Eight, for Colo. Bland counts Josiah Parker a Federalist) out of ten Representatives must strike dumb the bold declamers of the last unfortunate session.* "Four-fifths of the state" said the boldest of the bold ones "are opposed in Conscience to this new project."

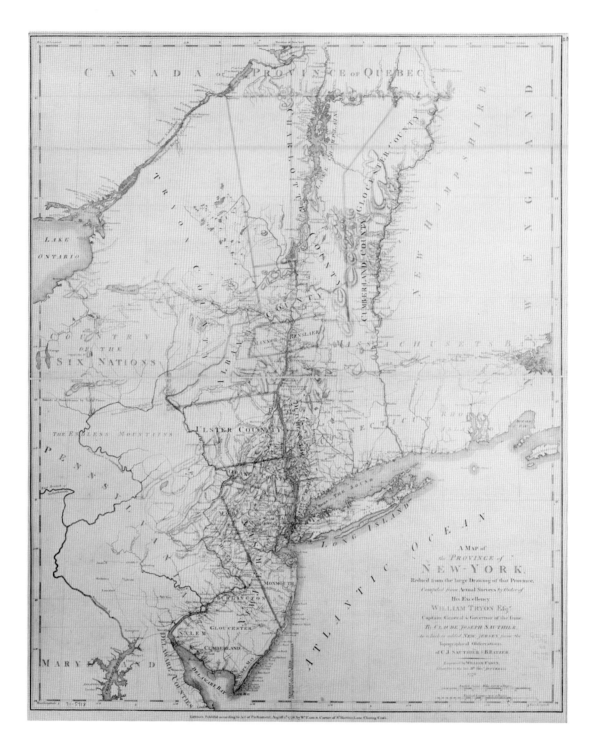

Map of New York by Claude Joseph Sauthier; engraved by William Faden, 1776.
Geography and Map Division, Library of Congress, Washington, D.C.

NEW YORK

New York, which was, outside of the city, the fiefdom of Antifederalist Governor George Clinton, had come hard and late to acceptance of the Constitution, and when it came to electing its congressional delegation the pattern was repeated.

With the Senate controlled by the Federalists and the Antifederalists dominant in the Assembly, agreement on an electoral law could not be reached. "Our Legislature are sitting at Albany & have been almost 2 Months," wrote Federalist Richard Platt on January 19, 1789, "without making any appointment of Senators, or devising any mode for chusing Electors & representatives to the new Congress & from all appearances we shall not be represented in the first Congress." Platt, a New York merchant, had his suspicions: "This is thought to be a Plan of Clinton's & his antifoederal friends, in order to get Congress removed from New York, notwithstanding all the Skill, Exertion & address exhibited last Summer by Col Hamilton & our Eastern [New England] friends to get established here."

The New York legislature, scoffed the Philadelphia *Federal Gazette* on February 3, "totally forgetting their own dignity, have been for some time past, playing at the *childish* amusement of *cross-purposes* with each other; and have not hesitated to sacrifice the interests of New-York and the union, at the accursed shrine of party spirit and political intrigue."

"The Genl: Assembly of this State after spending near 2 months in pure wrangling," Hugh Williamson of North Carolina reported on January 24, "have at length agreed to divide the state into six Election Districts for the choice of Representatives in the new Congress. They cannot yet agree about the mode of chusing Senators." The Assembly wanted to make sure that both Senators were Antifederalist, whereas the Senate maneuvered for the election of at least one Federal man. After passing a resolution calling on the Congress to convene a second Constitutional Convention, the New York Assembly adjourned on March 3, leaving the selection of Senators in abeyance.

Congressional elections took place on March 3–6, but the winners could not take their seats until after the official canvass by the legislative committee on April 11.

The Antifederalists, who were weak in the southern part of the state, did not offer a candidate in the Long Island-Staten Island first district. At a public nominating meeting held in mid-February, the participants agreed on Federalist Ezra L'Hommedieu, a member of the state Senate. But for some reason — perhaps because he hoped to be chosen for the United States Senate — L'Hommedieu stepped aside in favor of his brother-in-law, William Floyd. Floyd, signer of the Declaration of Independence, was elected with 894 votes.

District two — New York City and vicinity — was a Federalist stronghold. Alexander Hamilton would most certainly have been chosen had he not declined to be put forward. John Laurance (q.v.), a lawyer, was nominated at a public meeting on February 23, but support was soon agitated — fueled by the Antifederalists — for another Federalist, Jacob Broome, president of the New York City Chamber of Commerce. The great issue of the campaign was whether the constituency would be better served by a lawyer or by a merchant. Both sides filled the newspapers with their arguments. "BEWARE OF LAWYERS!!!" proclaimed one who signed himself "A true Antifederalist, and No LAWYER," reminding that, "Of the men who framed that monarchical, aristocratical, oligarchical, tyrannical, diabolical system of slavery, the *New Constitution, one half* were Lawyers!" Alexander Hamilton, as chairman of the Federalist committee of correspondence, led the fight on behalf of Laurance and reminded the voters that commercial arrangements would not be the only matter to come before the new Congress. "The preservation of the government itself, in its due force and vigor, is an object of the first consequence — and the establishment of the temporary residence of Congress in this city is another point in which we are deeply concerned."

When the ballots were counted on April 7, Laurance was handily elected with a vote of 2,418 against the 372 received by Broome.

The third district joined Dutchess County, which had sent seven Antifederalist delegates to the state ratifying convention, with Westchester County, whose six delegates had favored the Constitution. Antifederalists had great expectations here. The Federalists, however, nominated a strong contender in the person of the state attorney general, Egbert Benson (q.v.), a man who had been active in the political affairs of the state since 1775. Theodorus Bailey, the Antifederalist candidate, was a thirty-year-old lawyer yet to be elected to political office, but he had the advantage of touting his determination to see to it that the Constitution was amended. Benson mustered 584 votes, which gave him a majority of ten. Credit for the victory was claimed by Margaret Beekman Livingston, the grand old lady of the manor of Clermont, who wrote to her son, Chancellor Robert R. Livingston, "I think I have been the means of getting in Benson by my Exertions."

Orange County and Ulster, the home county of Governor George Clinton, were so adamantly against the Constitution that the Federalists thought it futile to put forth a candidate. Two Antifederalists contested for the seat. It was explained, "A party from Orange were obstinate for the nomination of Genl. Hathorn to the important office — Others were equally strenuous for Cornelius C. Schoonmaker Esqr." Hathorn, longtime representative from

Margaret Beekman Livingston (1724–1800), matriarch of the Clermont branch of the Livingston family who exerted herself in the Federalist cause in 1789, no doubt was disappointed when her son, Chancellor Robert R. Livingston, received no appointment in the Washington administration.

By Gilbert Stuart (1755–1828); oil on canvas, circa 1795. Museum of the City of New York

Orange County to the Assembly, was currently a member of the state Senate. Schoonmaker represented Ulster in the Assembly. The majority of the votes went to Hathorn.

District five — Clinton, Washington, and Columbia counties, and Albany County east of the Hudson River — was considered another hotbed of Antifederalism, and it was anticipated that Antifederalist assemblyman Matthew Adgate would easily defeat Federalist Peter Silvester. Silvester, who was a judge of the court of common pleas and assemblyman from Columbia County, signified that he did not wish to become a candidate — related his brother-in-law, Peter Van Schaack — "but at the same Time declared that he conceived it the Duty of every Citizen to give up his own Inclinations to the Voice of the People." Van Schaack added, "If he succeeds in this Antifederal District, I shall be much deceived." The proprietors of the Columbia County manors turned out their tenants for Silvester, however, and he was elected by 127 votes.

District six — including that part of Albany County lying west of the Hudson River, and the counties of Montgomery and Ontario — had sent a delegation to the ratifying convention who were unanimously opposed to the Constitution. Antifederalist assemblyman Jeremiah Van Rensselaer tied his campaign to the reelection of Governor George Clinton and was given a victory margin of 241 over the Federalist candidate Abraham Ten Broeck, former mayor of Albany and county judge of the court of common pleas.

By the time Governor Clinton called a special session of the state Assembly to make another attempt at electing United States Senators, the April elections had given the Federalists control of both the Assembly and the Senate.

"The Legislature assemble at Albany tomorrow," William Smith of South Carolina observed on July 5, 1789, "for the sole purpose of electing Senators — the Candidates are General Schyler, Duane, Judge Yates — King — the Chancellor — Morris — Schyler & Yates have the best prospect of success — many speak of L'Hommedieu as having a good chance." Alluding to constitutional framer Rufus King's (q.v.) recent removal from Massachusetts to New York, Smith went on to note that King "has the Interest of Hamilton on this occasion, but he is too young in the Country in the opinion of a great many."

On July 12 Federalist members of the legislature met and "judged it most prudent to consolidate their strength to prevent division." They unanimously decided to offer a Senate seat to Judge Robert Yates, who, although a dissenter at the Philadelphia convention, had finally come around to support the Constitution and had been picked by the Federalists to undertake the unsuccessful race against Governor George Clinton. The judge declined the offer, feeling that it would be more prudent for him to continue on the state bench. Chancellor Robert R. Livingston also let it be known that he would not be a candidate.

The Federalists in caucus unanimously agreed to support their Senate leader, General Philip Schuyler (q.v.), Alexander Hamilton's father-in-law, for one of the Senate places. In the voting for the second seat, James Duane, mayor of New York, received 24 ballots and Rufus King, 20. King immediately withdrew, and the Federalists thought that the matter was settled. But Ezra L'Hommedieu and another state Senator, Lewis Morris, signer of the Declaration of Independence, declared that they would not be bound by the vote and insisted upon maintaining their candidacy. If it were not for the defection of L'Hommedieu and Morris — as Robert Troup, an assemblyman from New York City, told Alexander Hamilton — Schuyler and Duane would have been appointed without difficulty; but now it was uncertain if Duane would succeed. Troup concluded, "Nothing but delicacy to Duane as an old inhabitant has prevented King from being unanimously supported by all the members of the Southern district except L'Hommedieu & Morris." Hamilton immediately set about circulating rumors that if Duane should leave the mayor's office for the Senate, "the probability was, that some very unfit character would be his successor."

On June 11 Governor Clinton had called on Rufus King. King, who made careful notes on all political dealings, detailed the conversation that took place when the two met on the following day. Clinton observed that, at the last session of the legislature, the Antifederalists had not been able to unite on a candidate for United States Senator. Melancton Smith, the Antifederalist legislative leader, was in disfavor because he had seen the expediency of voting for the Constitution. The choice of Smith, Clinton confessed, "would have been difficult." John Lansing, who had early left the Constitutional Convention and opposed ratification, would decline the post, Clinton said, since his legal practice was flourishing, and "he owed it to a numerous young family, not to go into public life." Clinton dismissed Judge Robert Yates with the comment "that he thought it an important Question, whether any Gentleman in the State Judiciary ought to take a share in the national Legislation, that this might be Confounding the judiciary and Legislative Departments." The governor "observed that Mr. Duane had considered it as his right to be appointed a senator — but that it was not a right of any man." Then he noted that he had heard King's name mentioned, and the New Englander replied "that I was but lately an Inhabitant of the State, that probably many of the old and very respectable Citizens wd. claim it as their right, and that I had no Disposition to enter into any Controversy on the subject." To this the governor responded that King "was a member of the Assembly, and that he had ever considered that appointment as sufficient authority for him to appoint any person to an Office for which he might in his Judgement appear capable."

In the news from New York printed in the *Massachusetts Centinel* on July 29, a correspondent noted, "In one of my last letters, I mentioned that Messrs. SCHUYLER and DUANE were elected Federal Senators for this State — This was a mistake. — Mr. DUANE was chosen by the House but the Senate did not concur therein. — The second choice was concurred in." There followed the announcement of Rufus King's election by unanimous vote in the House and a large majority in the Senate.

Thus New York, the state that had ratified the Constitution by a margin of only two votes, ended up sending two stalwart Federalists to the Senate and four Federalists, out of the delegation of six, to the House of Representatives.

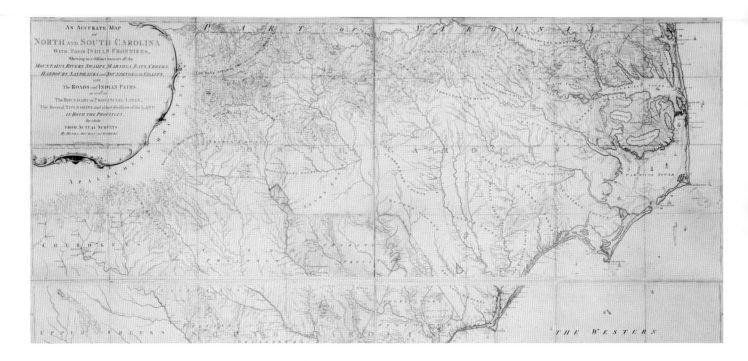

An Accurate Map of North and South Carolina (detail of North Carolina) from Henry Mouzon *et al.*; published by Robert Sayer and John Bennett, London, 1775. Geography and Map Division, Library of Congress, Washington, D.C.

The North Carolina ratifying convention, held at Hillsborough in the summer of 1788, rejected the Constitution, and the state remained outside the union during the first session of the federal Congress. A second convention, held at Fayetteville, finally accepted the document on November 21, 1789.

Two days after ratification, Governor Samuel Johnston, who, even though a Federalist had been chosen to preside over both state conventions, informed his brother-in-law James Iredell, "I have been very earnestly solicited by a number of members, and particularly by the anti-Federal party, to take a seat in the Senate, which I have agreed to."

Since members of the state legislature were ready to convene at Fayetteville, no time was lost in getting down to the business of choosing Senators. Eleven names were placed in nomination.

In a joint session, the North Carolina legislature elected Johnston on the

"It was fitting," wrote Samuel Johnston's (1733–1816) early biographer, "that he who, for more than twenty years, had stood among the statesmen of North Carolina as the very personification of the spirit of union and nationalism should be the first to represent the state in the Federal Senate."

From a miniature illustrated in Clarence Winthrop Bowen's *The Centennial of Washington's Inauguration*

first ballot, but it was reported in the press that "the appointment of the other Senator had not been made, as there was not a majority of the Houses in favor of any person." The Antifederalists, unable to unite behind any one person, scattered their votes in more than four directions.

After four ballots, the legislature — which was inclined to balance Edenton's Johnston with an inland man — settled on Benjamin Hawkins from Warren County. Hawkins, a Federalist, was a graduate of the College of New Jersey and had served in the Confederation Congress. Elkanah Watson, who was in North Carolina when "the State was strongly convulsed by the agitation of the question of adopting the Federal Constitution," observed that Colonel Hawkins's mother "was a great politician; and I was assured, that she has more political influence, and exerted it with greater effect, than any man in her county."

Antifederalists at the first convention had charged that all five members of the House of Representatives would likely be from the coastal areas. Young John Steele (q.v.) from inland Salisbury had answered then, "The time, place, and manner, of holding elections are to be prescribed by the legislature. . . . They may, and most probably will, lay the state off into districts." This proved to be the case, and five divisions were made — Roanoke, inland to the north; Edenton-New Bern, the upper coast; Cape Fear, the lower shore; Yadkin, stretching to the Alleghenies; and Western, beyond the mountains. Elections were scheduled for February 4 and 5, 1790, except for the Western district, where they were delayed until March 8 and 9. Almost nothing is known about any of the contests in North Carolina.

The Roanoke division, with a population of 108,000, was the largest constituency in the nation. John Baptista Ashe — member of a prominent North Carolina family, Revolutionary War colonel, and former member of Congress — won election over Nathaniel Macon and William Moore. Married to the sister of the militant Antifederalist Willie Jones, once considered the most influential politician in the state, Ashe was an Antifederalist. Macon, his

John Baptista Ashe (1748–1802), taking his seat in Congress just in time to vote against the assumption, wrote from New York on April 10, 1790, "I feel a Satisfaction in N. Carolina's having stept into the Union at the Moment She did; for her Delagation I hope will give a favorable turn to this impending Cause of evil."

From a miniature illustrated in Clarence Winthrop Bowen's *The Centennial of Washington's Inauguration*

main opponent, a planter and former member of the state Assembly, was likewise an Antifederalist. When a new congressional district was created in 1791, Macon won election and served in Congress for a quarter of a century. Ashe, who pleased his constituents by opposing the increasing costs and power of the national government, was reelected from the truncated original district.

In the Edenton-New Bern division, Dr. Hugh Williamson (q.v.) was chosen over another Federalist, Stephen Cabarrus, speaker of the North Carolina House of Commons. Williamson, a framer of the Constitution, had been in attendance at the old Congress until the last day — October 10, 1788 — on which the dying body was able to muster a quorum. He had remained at New York as his state's "Confidential Servant" and had done yeoman work in getting North Carolina an exemption from foreign tonnage duties in August 1789. According to the *State Gazette of North Carolina*, Williamson received 2,150 votes against 757 for Cabarrus.

Cape Fear, the most Antifederalist area in the state, elected Timothy Bloodworth, who had tried for a seat in the United States Senate. Bloodworth, a Wilmington blacksmith and member of the state legislature and briefly of the old Congress, had proclaimed the Constitution to be a dangerous document and predicted that its adoption would lead to either "autocratic tyranny, or monarchical monarchy." Bloodworth was opposed by Benjamin Smith, a wealthy planter of Brunswick County who had voted for the Constitution at the Hillsborough convention.

There is no known portrait of Bloodworth, but he has been characterized by Griffith J. McRee, writing in 1858, as *Preacher, smith, farmer, doctor, watchmaker, wheelwright and politician; if his brain was a receptacle of ideas somewhat ill-assorted, and his learning so ill-digested as sometimes to excite ridicule, and expose him to the charge of quackery, his manifold services, his unheralded charities, his gentle offices, had been received by his neighbors as testimonials of a mission almost divine. In the social circle, good-humored, gay, and full of racy anecdotes, as a politician he was resolved almost to fierceness, and almost radical in his democracy.* Bloodworth, born in poverty, was by 1790 the owner of 4,266 acres of land and nine slaves.

The Yadkin division sent John Steele of Salisbury, a member of the state legislature, to Congress. Steele, a young merchant, had been an articulate supporter of the Constitution at both ratifying conventions. Steele was opposed by Antifederalist Joseph McDowall, also a member of the legislature and one of those mentioned for the Senate seat. In elections for the Second Congress, held in early 1791, McDowall was again unsuccessful against Steele, but he succeeded to the seat after Steele's retirement in 1793.

The division west of the Alleghenies sent John Sevier (q.v.), famed Indian fighter and governor of the aborted state of Franklin, to the Congress. Sevier had been a delegate to the Fayetteville convention and had voted in favor of the Constitution.

RHODE ISLAND

Rhode Island, controlled by the paper-money country party, had declined to send delegates to the Constitutional Convention and subsequently resisted more than a half-dozen attempts to call a convention to consider the document. Nonetheless, no one doubted that sooner or later "that shameless Prostitute" would become part of the union. In the distribution of congressional seats at the Grand Convention, a seat had been designated for "that little trollop of a sister."

In September of 1789 Governor John Collins, a Federalist convert, called a special session of the Assembly to consider the liquidation of the public debt

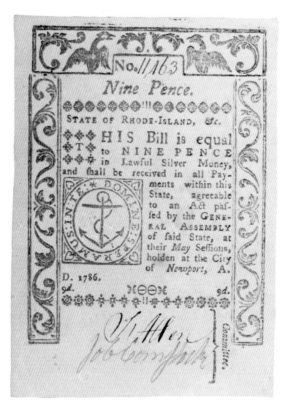

The pro-paper money country party, taking control of the Rhode Island legislature in 1786, placed the state on a course that kept her out of the union until May 1790.

Rhode Island paper money, 1786. National Numismatic Collection, National Museum of American History, Smithsonian Institution, Washington, D.C.

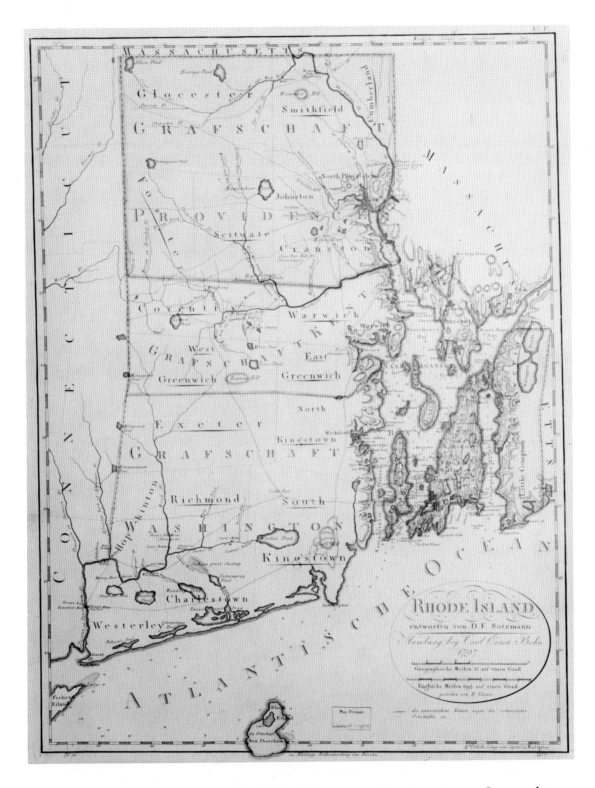

Map of Rhode Island by Daniel Friedrich Sotzmann, Hamburg, 1797. Geography and Map Division, Library of Congress, Washington, D.C.

and the ratification of the Constitution. He reminded the legislators that although the federal Congress had thus far refrained from imposing foreign duties on the trade from Rhode Island, the threat that they might do so was very real. Many delegates, however, were bound by instructions from their town meetings to vote against a convention, and the proposal to consider ratification was rejected 39 to 17. But the Assembly, liquidating the state debt by means of their almost-worthless paper money, made it practical for Rhode Island to come to terms with a Constitution that prohibited state emissions of paper money.

Outside Newport and Providence, public opinion remained unconvinced of the merits of ratification. What was a central government but a monster that would impose heavy taxes and threaten individual liberties besides? Offensive to the state's large Quaker population was the constitutional sanction given to the slave trade. Providence merchants Nicholas and John Brown calculated that "about two thirds of the Freemen of this state are opposed to the new Constitution."

But when North Carolina came into the union in late November, the pressure on Rhode Island increased. Although even the Antifederalist leaders had now come to recognize the inevitability of ratification, it was not finally accomplished until May 29, 1790 — more than a year after Washington's inauguration — and by a very close vote of 34 to 32.

Within a week the state legislature was called into session, and it passed legislation for the election of Senators and members of the House of Representatives.

Although the country party controlled the General Assembly, the election of Senators did not proceed altogether according to the wishes of the Antifederalists. "The Candidates for Senators were at first numerous," wrote Federalist Henry Marchant, "but like the weaker Blossoms they fell off at length to four." Two were Antifederalists — Jonathan Hazard and Joseph Stanton, Jr. — and two were Federalists, Theodore Foster and Jabez Bowen.

Jonathan Hazard, reported Federalist William Ellery, "finding that Constitution must be adopted sooner or later, and desirous of being a Senator he became a trimmer." Hazard assumed that his long and faithful services to the country party guaranteed him the support of the Antifederalists and reasoned that, by adopting a more moderate stance, he might pick up some Federalist support. But, explained Ellery, "the Feds were not strong enough to give him any effectual aid if they were disposed to do it."

"By his trimming," Hazard "incurred the enmity of his old friends," and they had nothing to lose by turning to Joseph Stanton, Jr., who, William Ellery declared, is "a Violent paper-money man, and was an obstinate Anti to the last." Stanton, as a delegate from Charlestown, had stood himself in good stead with his party at the ratifying convention when he voiced apprehensions about the central government's taxing authority, warned against the exten-

Theodore Foster (1752–1828), noted one Rhode Island Federalist, "is so distinguished for an amiable Moral Character— that he is very Popular." Another remarked that Rhode Island's new Senator was "a Gentleman of Highest Honor and good Sense, and a good Fed:— but under some Restraint from his Connection with Our Gov. Fenner, having married his Sister, and being appointed by His Influence."

From a portrait illustrated in Clarence Winthrop Bowen's *The Centennial of Washington's Inauguration*

sive powers given to the executive, and particularly attacked the Constitution as encouraging the slave trade.

Of the two Federalist candidates, Jabez Bowen, former deputy governor of the state, was perceived as extreme in his sentiments and consequently especially offensive to the Antifederalists. Theodore Foster, a Providence lawyer, was viewed as a more moderate man and was seemingly without enemies. Moreover, he had distinguished himself during the Revolution. But most importantly, Foster was the brother-in-law of the newly elected country party governor, Arthur Fenner. Fenner, aware that his faction was in decline and seeing advantage in cultivating the Federalists, sacrificed Hazard and threw his support to Foster. On June 12, 1790, the legislature in joint session elected Joseph Stanton, Jr., and Theodore Foster.

A few days later, a Newport Federalist reported to Henry Knox, *Our Senators will be on their Way (in a few Days) to New York; Mr. Stanton you'l find to be a man highly tinctured with Anti principles, and filled with the most exalted Ideas of the*

Landholders Consequence — but as he is a man of much Modesty & Condecension, I flatter myself he will do (after Spending Some time with you) right. Mr. Foster will do all in his power to promote the Interest of the Union, with a proviso that he does not deviate from any of the determined plans of his Brother Fenner, our present Governor, by whose Influence he obtained his appointment. This Gentleman possesses a good heart, has genuine Federal Sentiments, a full Share of Sensibility, and is a man of Liberal Education.

Three county party leaders — Simon Potter, Job Comstock, and James Sheldon — entered the lists for the August election of a delegate to the House of Representatives. Comstock and Sheldon had voted against the Constitution. Both men were charter members of Providence Abolition Society, and at the state convention Comstock, who was a Quaker, openly voiced his suspicions that Congress would allow the slave trade to continue after 1808. The Federalists put forth a single candidate, Benjamin Bourn (q.v.), a Harvard-educated Providence lawyer. Bourn drew opposition because of his anti-paper-money reputation and was criticized for his opposition to the ratifying convention's antislavery amendment. In the country Bourn did not do well, but by carrying Newport and overwhelming Comstock at Providence with a vote of 303 against 21, he was elected by a majority of 239.

Credentials of Theodore Foster, Senator from Rhode Island. National Archives, Washington, D.C.

"A COLLECTIVE BODY OF MEN"

The elections have been hitherto vastly more favorable than we could have expected," a relieved George Washington reported to the Marquis de Lafayette on January 29, 1789. "Did it not savour so much of partiality for my Countrymen I might add, that I cannot help flattering myself the new Congress on account of the self-created respectability and various talents of its Members, will not be inferior to any Assembly in the world."

At the start of the First Congress, William Grayson and Richard Henry Lee of Virginia were the only Antifederalists in the Senate. After Rhode Island joined the union, another "Anti" was added in the person of Joseph Stanton, Jr., who took his seat in June 1790.

In the House of Representatives, the Antifederalist contingent was initially but ten — Elbridge Gerry and Jonathan Grout from Massachusetts; John Hathorn and Jeremiah Van Rensselaer from New York; Theodorick Bland (and his replacement, William Branch Giles), Isaac Coles, and Josiah Parker from Virginia; Aedanus Burke, Thomas Sumter, and Thomas Tudor Tucker from South Carolina. The arrival of the Representatives from North Carolina would add John Baptista Ashe and Timothy Bloodworth to the Antifederalist ranks.

Ninety-five men served in the First Federal Congress — the number augmented beyond the twenty-six Senators and sixty-five Representatives because of one resignation and two deaths. Senator William Paterson resigned in November 1790 to become governor of New Jersey and was replaced by Philemon Dickinson. Senator William Grayson died on March 12, 1790, as he was on his way to the second session of Congress. His place was filled on an interim basis by John Walker and finally by Antifederalist James Monroe. Representative Theodorick Bland of Virginia died on June 1, 1790, and William Branch Giles took his place in December.

"There are few shining geniuses," noted Fisher Ames shortly after he took his seat as a Representative from Massachusetts; but "there are many who have experience, the virtues of the heart, and the habits of business." He added, "The Senate will be a very respectable body."

Above all, the members of the First Congress brought with them a depth of political experience. Roger Sherman of Connecticut, the oldest among them, had been for forty years on the public stage; John Steele of North Carolina, the youngest of the group, a lad of twelve when Sherman put his name to the Declaration of Independence, had been seasoned by two terms in his state legislature as well as by participation in two ratifying conventions.

William Samuel Johnson of Connecticut had a political career that extended back to the Stamp Act Congress of 1765. George Read of Delaware, Charles Carroll of Maryland, Elbridge Gerry of Massachusetts, George Clymer and Robert Morris of Pennsylvania, as well as Richard Henry Lee of Virginia had all signed the Declaration of Independence.

Eleven members of the Senate had been delegates to the Constitutional Convention — John Langdon of New Hampshire, Caleb Strong of Massachusetts, Oliver Ellsworth and William Samuel Johnson of Connecticut, Rufus King of New York, William Paterson of New Jersey, Richard Bassett and George Read of Delaware, Robert Morris of Pennsylvania, Pierce Butler of South Carolina, and William Few of Georgia.

In the House of Representatives, nine men had been at the Philadelphia convention — Nicholas Gilman of New Hampshire, Elbridge Gerry of Massachusetts, Roger Sherman of Connecticut, George Clymer and Thomas Fitzsimons of Pennsylvania, Daniel Carroll of Maryland, James Madison of Virginia, Hugh Williamson of North Carolina, and Abraham Baldwin of Georgia.

Almost without exception those elected to the First Federal Congress had served in their state legislatures, some of them beginning their careers in the colonial assemblies. A goodly number had been delegates to the Continental and Confederation Congresses. Most of them had taken part in their state ratifying conventions.

A great share of the Congress had been educated at the handful of colleges then flourishing in America. From Harvard came the entire Massachusetts delegation, save for Theodore Sedgwick, who had left Yale after an altercation, and Jonathan Grout, who came to the law by way of apprenticeship. In addition, Paine Wingate and Abiel Foster of New Hampshire, Benjamin Bourn of Rhode Island, Rufus King of New York, and Jonathan Trumbull of Connecticut all were Harvard men. Yale educated William Samuel Johnson (as did Harvard), Benjamin Huntington, and Jonathan Sturges of Connecticut, as well as Abraham Baldwin of Georgia. College of New Jersey (Princeton) alumni included Samuel Livermore of New Hampshire, Oliver Ellsworth of Connecticut, Jeremiah Van Rensselaer of New York, John Henry of Maryland, William Paterson of New Jersey, William Branch Giles and James Madison of Virginia, as well as Benjamin Hawkins of North Carolina. Lambert Cadwalader, Jonathan Elmer, and Philemon Dickinson of New Jersey, Joshua Seney of Maryland, William Grayson of Virginia, and Hugh Williamson of North Carolina all studied at the College of Philadelphia (University of Pennsylvania). John Brown, Isaac Coles, Richard Bland Lee, James Monroe, John Page, and John Walker of Virginia matriculated at William and Mary College. King's College, which since had become Columbia, graduated Egbert Benson of New York; Queen's College,

North-West Prospect of Nassau Hall, with a Front View of the Presidents House, in New Jersey.

The College of New Jersey, which had the distinction of educating more framers of the Constitution than any other institution, was superseded at the First Federal Congress by Harvard.

North-West Prospect of Nassau Hall by Henry Dawkins (active in America circa 1753–1786); engraving, 1764. The Library Company of Philadelphia, Pennsylvania

subsequently Rutgers, graduated James Schureman of New Jersey. Theodore Foster of Rhode Island was educated at Rhode Island College (Brown University).

Among those educated in Europe were the Maryland Carrolls, who had been sent to the Jesuit College of St. Omer in France, and the Pennsylvania Muhlenbergs, who traveled to the center of Lutheran learning at the University of Halle in Germany. Theodorick Bland of Virginia, Hugh Williamson of North Carolina, and Thomas Tudor Tucker of South Carolina had pursued medicine at the University of Edinburgh. Others who studied abroad included South Carolinians Ralph Izard — at Christ College, Cambridge — and William Loughton Smith, who read law in the Middle Temple at London and went on to additional studies in Geneva. Alexander White of Virginia first attended the University of Edinburgh and then went on to the English courts of law.

More than half of the members of the First Congress had shouldered arms during the Revolution — either in the Continental army or in their state militias. Six in the Senate belonged to the Society of the Cincinnati — Philip Schuyler of New York, William Grayson and James Monroe of Virginia, Benjamin Hawkins of North Carolina, James Gunn of Georgia, and honorary member Robert Morris of Pennsylvania. In the House of Representatives the Cincinnati numbered seventeen — Nicholas Gilman of New Hampshire, Jonathan Trumbull and Jeremiah Wadsworth of Connecticut, John Laurance and Jeremiah Van Rensselaer of New York, Thomas Hartley and John Peter Muhlenberg of Pennsylvania, John Baptista Ashe of North Carolina, Theodorick Bland and Josiah Parker of Virginia, Thomas Tudor Tucker of South Carolina, Abraham Baldwin and George Mathews of Georgia, plus honorary members Elias Boudinot of New Jersey, William Floyd of New York, John Sevier of North Carolina, and James Jackson of Georgia.

Predominantly, the members of the First Federal Congress were Anglo-Saxon in descent. William Maclay of Pennsylvania, William Paterson of New Jersey, Andrew Moore of Virginia, and Hugh Williamson of North Carolina came from Scotch-Irish stock. Of German ancestry were the two Muhlenbergs and Daniel Hiester of Pennsylvania. Elias Boudinot of New Jersey,

General Peter Muhlenberg (1746–1807) of Pennsylvania was among the members of the First Congress who had fought in the Revolution from the start to the finish — seeing action at Brandywine and Germantown, suffering through the winter at Valley Forge, and participating in the battle of Monmouth, the capture of Stony Point, and the Yorktown campaign.

National Portrait Gallery, Smithsonian Institution, Washington, D.C.

William Floyd (1734–1821) of New York, among the members of the First Congress who had long participated in Continental politics, might have been James Madison's father-in-law, had not his daughter Catherine spurned the young Congressman's affections at Philadelphia in 1783. Defeated for reelection in 1790, Floyd was portrayed by Ralph Earl back at his family estate, Brookhaven, in Mastic, Long Island.

By Ralph Earl (1751–1801); oil on canvas, circa 1793. Independence National Historical Park Collection, Philadelphia, Pennsylvania

Daniel Huger of South Carolina, as well as John Sevier of North Carolina came from French Huguenot stock; Philip Schuyler, Jeremiah Van Rensselaer, and Egbert Benson of New York and Henry Wynkoop of Pennsylvania were members of old Dutch families; Thomas Sinnickson of New Jersey descended from early Swedish settlers. Aedanus Burke, William Paterson, and Thomas Fitzsimons were all born in Ireland — Fitzsimons to a Catholic family.

Debate had ensued in some of the states over whether lawyers or merchants were best equipped to deal with the manifold problems that would face the

First Congress. It was generally assumed that both would be needed — although there were those who were prejudiced either in favor of or against the gentlemen of the law. Lawyers dominated, but the mercantile element was well represented in the Senate by Robert Morris of Philadelphia, John Langdon of Portsmouth, and Tristram Dalton of Newburyport, and in the House of Representatives by Jeremiah Wadsworth of Hartford, Thomas Fitzsimons and George Clymer of Philadelphia, William Smith of Baltimore, and Benjamin Goodhue of Salem, as well as Elbridge Gerry, recently retired from the Marblehead trade.

Almost all of the southern members were plantation owners. John Page of Virginia and Pierce Butler and Ralph Izard of South Carolina were notable for vast landholdings and hundreds of slaves.

Four members of the First Congress were physicians — although all of them had some time since given up medicine for politics — Jonathan Elmer of New Jersey, Theodorick Bland of Virginia, Hugh Williamson of North Carolina, and Thomas Tudor Tucker of South Carolina. Two in the Congress — Paine Wingate and Abiel Foster of New Hampshire — had abandoned their Congregational pulpits in favor of politics; and the Muhlenberg brothers, Frederick and John Peter, had left the Lutheran ministry for the same purpose.

They were — most of them — married men who had fathered many children. Among the eligible, romance indeed flowered, and several members of Congress made alliances with New York ladies. Widower John Page of Virginia married Margaret Lowther in March of 1790. Joshua Seney of Maryland wed Fanny Nicholson, the sister of Mrs. William Few, three months later. Just before he departed New York for Philadelphia, John Vining of Delaware married Mary Seton, daughter of prominent New York merchant William Seton. But the most talked-about match was that of Isaac Coles with Catherine Thompson, the sister of Mrs. Elbridge Gerry. Coles, a forty-two-year-old widower with grown sons, was reported to be older than the bride's father. "Tell Isaac Coles," wrote a friend from Virginia to Congressman John Brown, *I thought him a little out of his head when he joined Cousin Patrick in his opposition to the government, but that if he marries a young wife I will apply for a statute of lunacy against him. It would divert me — to see him take up the lady's fan before a large room full of company, or follow her carrying her muff.*

As the members of the First Congress got down to business, William Smith of South Carolina was pleased to observe, "Our debates are conducted with moderation and ability extremely unusual in so large a body — consisting of men under the influence of such jarring interests coming from such different countries and climates and accustomed to such different manners." Soon enough there would be grumblings of "intrigue, cabals & combinations." But Paine Wingate of New Hampshire gave a realistic assessment of his fellows when he told a constituent, "You will remember that Congress is but a collective body of men, men of like passion, subject to local prejudices & those biases which in some measure are inseparable from human nature."

It turned out that Paine Wingate was the last survivor of the First Federal Congress. Robert C. Winthrop, in preparation for the bicentennial of Harvard, went to Stratham, New Hampshire, to interview Wingate as the oldest living graduate, and recorded: *On my alluding to the fact that he was a member of the first Senate of the United States, he told his wife to bring him the old original printed Journals of that Congress, the copies which he had received as a member, at New York, in 1789. He then asked me to read over to him the names of his colleagues in that memorable body. I read them to him accordingly. . . . I went through the whole list, and at the end of each name the old man repeated the name in a clear, ringing tone, and asked most eagerly, "Where is he?" On my saying that he was dead, he exclaimed, "Is he dead?" "And is he dead too?" It had escaped his enfeebled memory that he himself had long been the last survivor.* Alas, there is no portrait of Wingate. He never sat to an artist, it was said, because his wife objected to the expense.

Virginia Antifederalist Isaac Coles (1747–1813), united in political sentiment with Massachusetts's Elbridge Gerry, joined him also in a family relationship when he married Mrs. Gerry's sister. Coles, remembered Mrs. Royall Tyler, who as a young girl was a member of the Gerry household, "was reported to be immensely rich in land and negroes, and, though older than her father, and not so good looking, being lame from repeated attacks of gout, yet that beautiful girl accepted him at once."

From a miniature illustrated in Clarence Winthrop Bowen's *The Centennial of Washington's Inauguration*

No future session of Congress will ever have so arduous
and weighty a charge on their hands.
The business of legislation is always attended
with difficulties, and requires the combined exertions
of genius, talents, and experience;
but the present Congress have no precedents,
that apply to the circumstances of the United States,
to direct their footsteps — no examples to imitate,
and no striking historical facts on which
to ground their decisions — All is bare creation.
They have a constitution to unfold and display
that is original in its construction and design —
interests to attend to that never were before blended
and made cognizable by a legislative body —
an example to set original in its formation —
and anticipation to justify that are founded
upon the most exalted ideas of human perfections.
Added to these, their materials are few —
their objects numerous — and expectations boundless —
In such a situation, those that undertake the conduct
of our publick affairs upon right principles,
when time shall do them justice, will rank
with the first patriots and friends of mankind.

Georgia Gazette, July 30, 1789

PART TWO

THE

BUSINESS

OF

CONGRESS

THE FIRST SESSION
MARCH 4 TO SEPTEMBER 29, 1789

"A new Era in the Annals of the World"

The first Wednesday in March of 1789 was the day set for the convening of the First Federal Congress. Robert Morris, Senator from Pennsylvania — one of the few members in New York at the appointed time —sent his wife a description of the historic moment. *Last night they fired 13 cannon from the Battery here over the Funeral of the Confederation, and this morning they saluted the new Government with 11 Cannon, being one for each of*

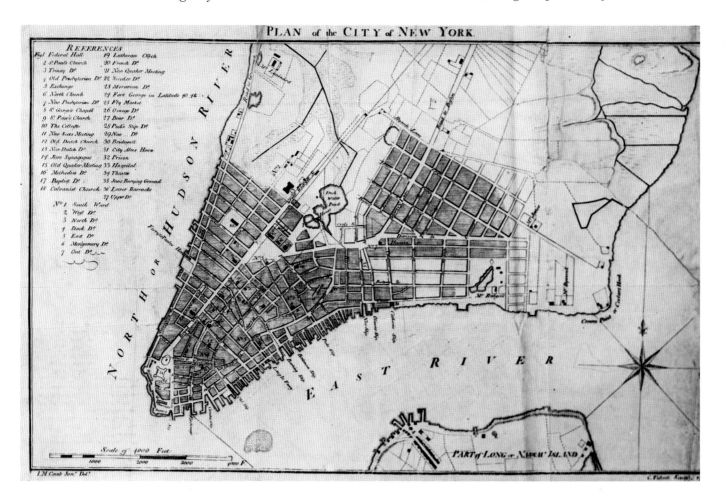

Plan of the City of New York from the *New-York Register* for 1789. American Antiquarian Society, Worcester, Massachusetts

the States that have adopted the Constitution. The Flag was hoisted on the Fort, and Federal Colours were displayed on the top of the New Edifice and at several other places of the City: this, with the ringing of Bells and Crowds of People at the meeting of Congress, gave the air of a grand Festival to the 4th of March, 1789, which no doubt, will hereafter be celebrated as a new Era in the Annals of the World.

But the flush of anticipation paled as the days passed and neither house of Congress achieved a quorum. No good omen this. It seemed as if the languor of the old Confederation — where states went unrepresented for months, or even years, at a time — was to carry over into the new government. "This is a very mortifying situation," fumed Fisher Ames. "We lose credit, spirit, every thing. The public will forget the government before it is born."

In part, tardiness could be blamed on conditions of travel. "The great quantities of ice with which the rivers to the southward have been filled," explained a correspondent in the *Massachusetts Centinel,* "have rendered the passage of boats across them impracticable or very dangerous." One of the arriving members "travelled near 100 miles up one of the rivers, before he could cross on the ice."

Weeks passed, and as the requisite twelve Senators and thirty Representatives failed to assemble, the Federalist *Centinel* on March 25 once more tried to explain away the embarrassment. "The warm weather we have lately had has broke up the ice in the rivers, and filled the roads with mire." A communication from New York informed, "So very bad is the travelling even from Philadelphia to this city, that a gentleman who came to town yesterday was *three days* on his journey from that place. This is the SOLE CAUSE of the members not attending." But another writer pointed out that "This extraordinary delay may, in part, be attributed to the badness of the roads, and the impracticability of crossing the rivers, but it is principally owing to the misconduct of the States of New York and New Jersey, respecting their elections." The New York legislature had not yet agreed on its Senators and had delayed the count for delegates to the House until April 10. In New Jersey a dispute raged over just when the polls should be closed.

"The Delay not only looks ill," pronounced the *Maryland Journal* on March 31, "but works ill, by preventing the Collection of Duties for the Union, which is a loss to the United States of near *One Hundred Thousand Dollars* per month."

New York's inconvenient location was viewed as a major reason that a quorum was so backward in assembling. "The southerners give this delay as an additional reason," it was noted in the press, "why a more central situation ought to be fixed on for the session of Congress."

For six years past, the national government had been in a state of peregrination. In June 1783 mutinous Pennsylvania troops in demand of back pay had marched upon the Supreme Executive Council of the state as they sat in Saturday session at the State House. Acting on the suggestion of Alexander Hamilton, who raised the fear that the soldiers might raid the

REGISTER,

For 1789.

CONGRESS *of the* UNITED STATES.

GEORGE WASHINGTON, *Esq.*
PRESIDENT OF THE UNITED STATES,
—*Commander in Chief of the Army and Navy thereof, when in actual Service,*—No. 3, Cherry street.
JOHN ADAMS, Esq. *Vice-President,* Greenwich road.

SENATORS OF THE UNITED STATES.

New-Hampshire— John Langdon, 37 Broad street.
                Paine Wingate, 47 Broad do.
Massachusetts. Tristram Dalton, 37 Broad do.
                Caleb Strong, 15 Great dock do.
Connecticut.   William Samuel Johnson, at the College.
                Oliver Ellsworth, 193 Water street.
New-York.   ————, ————,
New-Jersey.   Jonathan Elmer, 48 Great dock do.
                William Paterson, 51   all do.
Pennsylvania.   William Maclay, at Mr. Vandolsom's, near the Bear market.
                Robert Morris, 39 Great dock street.
Delaware.   Richard Bassit, 15 Wall do.
                George Read, 15 Wall do.
Maryland.   Charles Carroll, 52 Smith do.
                John Henry, 27 Queen do.
Virginia.   William Grayson, 57 Maiden lane.
                Richard Henry Lee, at Greenwich.
South-Carolina. Pierce Butler, 37 Great dock do.
                Richard Izard, Broad way, opposite the French ambassador's.

Georgia.   William Few, 90 William street.
                James Gunn, 34 Broad way.
                Samuel A. Otis, secretary, 5 Wall streets.
                James Mathers, door keeper, } 59 Broad
                Cornelius Maxwell, messenger, }   street.

REPRESENTATIVES *of the* UNITED STATES.

New-Hampshire—Nicholas Gilman, corner of Smith and Wall streets.
               Samuel Livermore, 37 Broad street.
               Benjamin West, [not returned.]
Massachusetts. Fisher Ames, 15 Great dock street.
               Elbridge Gerry, corner of Broad way and Thame's do.
               Benjamin Goodhue, 47 Broad do.
               Jonathan Grout, 47 Broad do.
               George Leonard, 15 Great dock do.
               George Partridge, do.
               George Thatcher, 47 Broad do.
               Theodore Sedgwick, 15 Great Dock do.
Connecticut.   Benjamin Huntington, 59 Water street.
               Roger Sherman, do.
               Jonathan Sturges, 47 Broad street.
               Jonathan Trumbull, 195 Water do.
               Jeremiah Wadsworth, do.
New-York.   Egbert Benson, cor. of King & Nassau do.
               William Floyd, 27 Queen do.
               John Hathorn, at Mr. Strong's near the Albany pier.
               Jeremiah Van Rensselaer, do.
               John Lawrance, 14 Wall street.
               Peter Sylvester, 45 Maiden lane.
New-Jersey.   Elias Boudinot, 12 Wall street.
               Lambert Cadwallader, 15 do.
               James Schureman, 47 Little dock do.
               Thomas Sinnickson, 47 do.   [do.
Pennsylvania. George Clymer, at Mr. Anderson's Pearl
               Thomas Fitzsimons, do.
               Thomas Hartley, 19 Maiden lane.
               Daniel Heister, do.
               F. A. Muhlenberg, speaker, Rev. Dr. Kunzie's, 24 Chatham row.
               Peter Muhlenberg, do.

Pennsylvania.   Thomas Scott, at Mr. Huck's, corner of Smith and Wall streets.
                Henry Wynkoop, at Mr. Vandolsom's, near Bear market.
Delaware.   John Vining, 19 Wall street.
Maryland.   Daniel Carroll, 52 Smith do.
                Benjamin Contee, 15 Wall do.
                George Gale, 52 Smith do.
                Joshua Seney, 15 Wall do.
                William Smith, 52 Smith do.
                Michael Jenifer Stone, 15 Wall do.
Virginia.   Theodorick Bland, 57 Maiden lane.
                John Brown, 19 do.
                Isaac Coles, 57 do.
                Samuel Griffin, at the white conduit house, near the hospital.
                Richard Bland Lee, 15 Wall street.
                James Madison, jun. 19 Maiden lane.
                Andrew Moore, 15 Wall street.
                John Page, 19 Maiden lane.
                Alexander White, do.
South-Carolina. Josiah Parker, 57 Maiden lane.
                Edanus Burke, Wall streets, at Mr. Huck's.
                Daniel Huger, do.
                William Smith, Broad way, next door to the Spanish minister.
                Thomas Sumpter, 40 Wall street.
                Thomas Tudor Tucker, at Mr. Huck's, corner of Smith and Wall do.
Georgia.   Abraham Baldwin, 193 Water do.
                James Jackson, 63 Broad way.
                George Matthews, do.
                John Beckley, clerk of the house of representatives, 19 Maiden lane.
                Joseph Wheaton, serjeant at arms, 16 George street.
                Gifford Dally, door keeper, back of the Trinity Church, North river.

☞ It was the intention of the editors to have here inserted the names of all the public officers appointed under the new constitution, but the different departments not being yet established, it is not in their power to insert them this year.

The *New-York Register* made haste to publish the local addresses of the members of the new Congress.

American Antiquarian Society, Worcester, Massachusetts

Bank of North America, Elias Boudinot, president of the Congress, hastily summoned his colleagues to an emergency meeting in their quarters just below the council chamber. No quorum gathered, but the Congress remained in the surrounded building until three o'clock — which was the usual time of adjournment — and then walked out between the soldiers. Although the protest was aimed at the state and not the national government, the Congress, affronted that Pennsylvania had refused to call out the militia to protect its dignity and authority, "decampt in the night." They moved first to Princeton, then Annapolis, and next Trenton, finally coming to New York in 1785.

Wrangling in the dying Congress over the initial meeting place for the new government was intense and protracted. Philadelphia, Wilmington, Lancaster, and Baltimore were all in contention, but members from New England, New Jersey, and South Carolina, adhering stubbornly to New York, exhausted the opposition into submission. James Madison, who along with George Washington envisioned the permanent seat of government on the

View of the FEDERAL EDIFICE in NEW YORK.

Federal Hall, which stood at the juncture of Broad and Wall streets in New York, was extensively described in the *Columbian Magazine* in August 1789. It was pointed out that the thirteen stars in the frieze, together "with the American Eagle and other insignia in the pediment, and the tablets over the windows, filled with thirteen arrows and the olive branch united, mark it as a building set aside for national purposes."

"The speaker's chair is opposite the great door, and raised by several steps," went an account of the interior published in the *Massachusetts Magazine* of June 1789, "the chairs for the members are ranged semi-circularly in two rows in front of the Speaker. Each member has his separate chair and desk." It was noted that "the curtains and chairs in this room are of light blue damask." In the Senate chamber, "the President's chair is at one end of the room, elevated about three feet from the floor, under a rich canopy of crimson damask."

View of the Federal Edifice in New York; published in the *Columbian Magazine*, August 1789. Fraunces Tavern Museum, New York City; gift of Stanley D. Scott

Potomac, looked upon the temporary expedient with unease.

"This Town is not half so large as Philadelphia; nor in any manner to be compared to it for Beauty & Elegance," wrote John Page of Virginia, arriving in New York on March 16. *Philadelphia I am well assured has more Inhabitants than Boston & New York together. The streets here are badly paved, very dirty & narrow as well as crooked & filled up with a strange Variety of wooden & stone & brick houses & full of Hogs & mud. The College, St. Paul's Church, & the Hospital are elegant Buildings.*

In a bid to keep the capital at New York, the citizenry subscribed more than $39,000 to fit up the hundred-year-old City Hall "to accommodate the Grand Congress of the United States, with a building suitable to their dignity." French military engineer Pierre L'Enfant was engaged to undertake the renovation. He designed an imposing meeting-room for the House of Representatives on the first floor and an equally grand room for the Senate on the second. "So that the common terms of upper and lower house," it was pointed out, "will be applicable here in a literal sense."

"No pains have been spared by the inhabitants of this place to provide for the reception of Congress & render their stay here agreeable," wrote Senator Oliver Ellsworth upon his arrival from Connecticut. Federal Hall, he declared, "does honor to the city & surpasses in elegance any building in the Country. I wish the business expected to be transacted in it may be as well done & as universally admired as the house is." The English-bred Senator Pierce Butler of South Carolina testified that the building "assuredly surpasses the Accommodations for the Lords and Commons of Great Britain."

Perspective View of the City Hall in New York taken from Wall Street by Cornelius Tiebout (circa 1773–1832); engraving, circa 1791–1793. The Metropolitan Museum of Art, New York City; the Edward W. C. Arnold Collection of New York Prints, Maps, and Pictures; bequest of Edward W. C. Arnold, 1954

Those who wished to see the seat of government moved elsewhere dubbed the federal edifice "Fool's Trap." Alexander White, a Representative from Virginia, wrote from New York on March 8, "The City of N. York have made wonderful exertions in erecting a Building for [our] Reception, it is nearly finished and will when completed contain some of the most elegant appoi[n]tments this some say is intended as a Trap to catch us Southern Men." Congress's meeting-place, joked Frederick Muhlenberg of Pennsylvania, was "really elegant & well designed — for a Trap — but I still hope, however well contrived we shall find Room to get out of it."

Pennsylvania Representative Daniel Hiester's (1747–1804) memorandum book affords a view of the everyday life of a member of the First Congress. He arrived at New York by carriage, where he arranged to board at Mr. Ellsworth's, agreeing to separate charges for firewood, wine, and porter. Immediately he subscribed to John Fenno's *Federal Gazette* and Thomas Lloyd's *Congressional Register.* On July 31, 1789, he recorded charges incurred when he met with the Pennsylvania delegation at City Tavern "abt. the permanent Seat of Congress." Hiester paid the tailor for making a suit of black clothes and the barber for "dressing and curling hair." His purchases included pomatum, visiting cards, an umbrella, black shoes and knee buckles, and a new hat, as well as Jedidiah Morse's *Geography.* Among other activities, Hiester attended "an American play," went to see the balloon ascension, enjoyed a game of nine pins, and jaunted about to Harlem, Flatbush, and Kingsbridge.

From a portrait illustrated in Clarence Winthrop Bowen's *The Centennial of Washington's Inauguration*

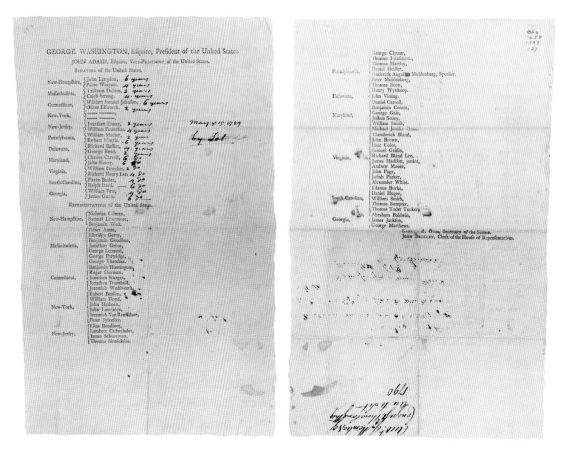

On May 15, 1789, members of the Senate drew lots to determine the length of their respective terms. Those in the first class were to serve for two years, in the second four, and the third, six, as noted in this broadside list of members.

John Carter Brown Library, Brown University, Providence, Rhode Island

Philadelphians, of course, who thought their city the only proper meeting-place, were not impressed by anything that New York had to offer. George Clymer declared sarcastically, "The people here presumptuously call their town the Capital. I don't suppose this folly will be suffered to last very long, the prevailing wish being to create a town for the permanent residence."

On April Fool's Day, with the arrival of Thomas Scott from western Pennsylvania, the House of Representatives at last had a quorum. Richard Henry Lee, arriving from Virginia, enabled the Senate to proceed to business on April 6. Frederick Augustus Muhlenberg of Pennsylvania was elected Speaker of the House of Representatives, and John Langdon of New Hampshire was chosen president pro tempore of the Senate.

The first business of the combined legislature was to count the votes cast by the electoral college for President and Vice-President. Messengers thereupon were sent to summon George Washington and John Adams — their "town

FEDERAL HALL

The Seat of CONGRESS

Printed & Sold by A. Doolittle New-Haven 1790.

The only contemporary rendering of the inauguration of George Washington as President of the United States was drawn by the visiting French artist Pierre Lacour and engraved on copper by Amos Doolittle of New Haven.

"This is the great important day," William Maclay wrote as Washington took the oath of office on April 30, 1789. *The President was conducted out of the middle Window into the Gallery and the Oath administered by the Chancellor. Notice that the Business was done, was communicated to the Croud by Proclamation &ca., who gave three Cheers, and repeated it on the Presidents bowing to them—as the Company returned into the Senate Chamber, the President took the Chair, and the Senate and Representatives their Seats. He rose & all arose also and addressed them.* Maclay noted that the President "was dressed in deep brown, with Metal buttons, with an Eagle on them, White Stockings a Bag and Sword."

Federal Hall, The Seat of Congress by Amos Doolittle (1754–1832); engraving, 1790. The Historical Society of Pennsylvania, Philadelphia

meeting majesties," as New Englanders jovially put it — to New York.

"We have Work enough before us," assessed Representative James Jackson of Georgia, "the Fabric it is true is raised, but the inside workmanship is yet to finish, the Rooms are yet to be aparted."

In the House of Representatives, members sat in the full glare of "two spacious galleries open to all." Samuel Davis, a young traveler from Massachusetts, went to observe the proceedings and noted in his journal, "Visit the gallery. Prayers performing. The members sit in semicircles covered; uncovered when speaking" (that is, with their hats off). John Fenno, who had come to New York in April to begin publication of the Federalist *Gazette of the United States,* was on hand and identified all of the members for Davis's benefit.

Other reporters also crowded the gallery, and summaries of the debates — which were viewed as highly interesting — were carried in newspapers throughout the nation. Thomas Lloyd, an enterprising shorthand writer who had endeared himself to the Federalists by his partisan reporting of the debates of the Pennsylvania and Maryland ratifying conventions, was given a convenient seat near the Speaker of the House, which, he advertised, "enables

Jeremiah Wadsworth sent on samples of broadcloth from his Hartford wool manufactory to Washington's secretary, Tobias Lear, in the hope that the President might order fabric for a suit of clothes and thus give "meaningful encouragement" to the infant industry. His wish was gratified when, at his New York inaugural, the President as well as the Vice-President and the entire Connecticut delegation appeared in suits made from material manufactured at Hartford.

Samples of wool broadcloth from the Hartford Woolen Manufactory. The Connecticut Historical Society, Hartford

him to assure the public the greatest degree of accuracy in detailing the words, sentiments and opinions delivered by the members." His transcribed notes, sold to the public weekly as the *Congressional Register,* provided the most complete account of the debates in the House of Representatives during the first session of Congress and into the second session until he inexplicably ceased publication on March 8, 1790.

James Madison was one of the many members who criticized Thomas Lloyd's reports as "defective, and desultory." In 1832 Madison recalled that Lloyd "was indolent and sometimes filled up blanks in his notes from memory or *imagination*" and added, "he finally, became a votary of the bottle and perhaps made too free use of it sometimes at the period of his printed debates." The little sketches grew more numerous as the sessions of Congress wore on, likely an indication that the members found it increasingly expedient to furnish the reporter with the text of their remarks, thus leaving Lloyd with time on his hands.

Cover and an inside page showing shorthand notes and sketches from volume one of Thomas Lloyd's notes of debates in the House of Representatives. Manuscript Division, Library of Congress, Washington, D.C.

Members of Congress made frequent complaint that reports of the debates were full of errors and distortions. And although mistakes could easily be attributed to the inadequacies of the shorthand systems of the time, some Representatives suspected that partisan motives were behind the misrepresentations.

In most quarters, however, publication of the proceedings of Congress was looked upon as a means of diffusing national ideas and acquainting the public with the new system of government. When the people "are informed of the reasons which actuate their representatives," wrote a correspondent to the *New York Journal*, "they will more readily place a confidence in their determination." The New York *Daily Advertiser* observed, "Under the old confederation the people of the United States now and then used to hear from Congress, by the way of a solitary straggling resolution in the newspapers: How altered is the state of things!"

Alexander White, returning to Virginia during the summer of 1789, apprised James Madison, "At the Inns on the Road I was surprised to find the knowledge, which the Land Lords, and Country People who were at some of them, had acquired, of the Debates and Proceedings of Congress." When he reached his home, Woodville, in Frederick County, he commented again, "The pleasure which our open Doors, and the knowledge of our Debates obtained by that means, has given the People, can hardly be conceived. The different conduct of the Senate must of course have a contrary effect."

The Senate sat behind closed doors. "There are certain foibles which are inseparable from men and bodies of men," pronounced Senator Paine Wingate of New Hampshire in defense of secrecy, "and perhaps considerable faults which had better be concealed from observation." He posed the question to his brother-in-law Timothy Pickering: "How would all the little domestic transactions of even the best regulated family appear if exposed to the world; and may not this apply to a larger body?"

Much of what we know about the activity of the Senate comes from an extraordinarily vivid — and opinionated — diary kept by Senator William Maclay of Pennsylvania. At the time of his election to the Senate, Maclay was described as "a decided Federalist," but not long after he came to Congress he wrote, "My Mind revolts, in Many instances, against the Constitution of the United States. Indeed I am afraid it will turn out the Vilest of all Traps that ever was set to ensnare the freedom of an unsuspecting People."

Maclay was hardly unbiased; nonetheless the blunt outspokenness of the man gives him a credibility on his own terms. "He does not always vote right," noted Maclay of one of his colleagues, "and so I think of every Man who differs from me."

The cantankerous Maclay looked around at his colleagues and decided that there was not a one of them he could trust, and in the course of his entire journal he has scarcely a good word to say for anyone — treating Federalists

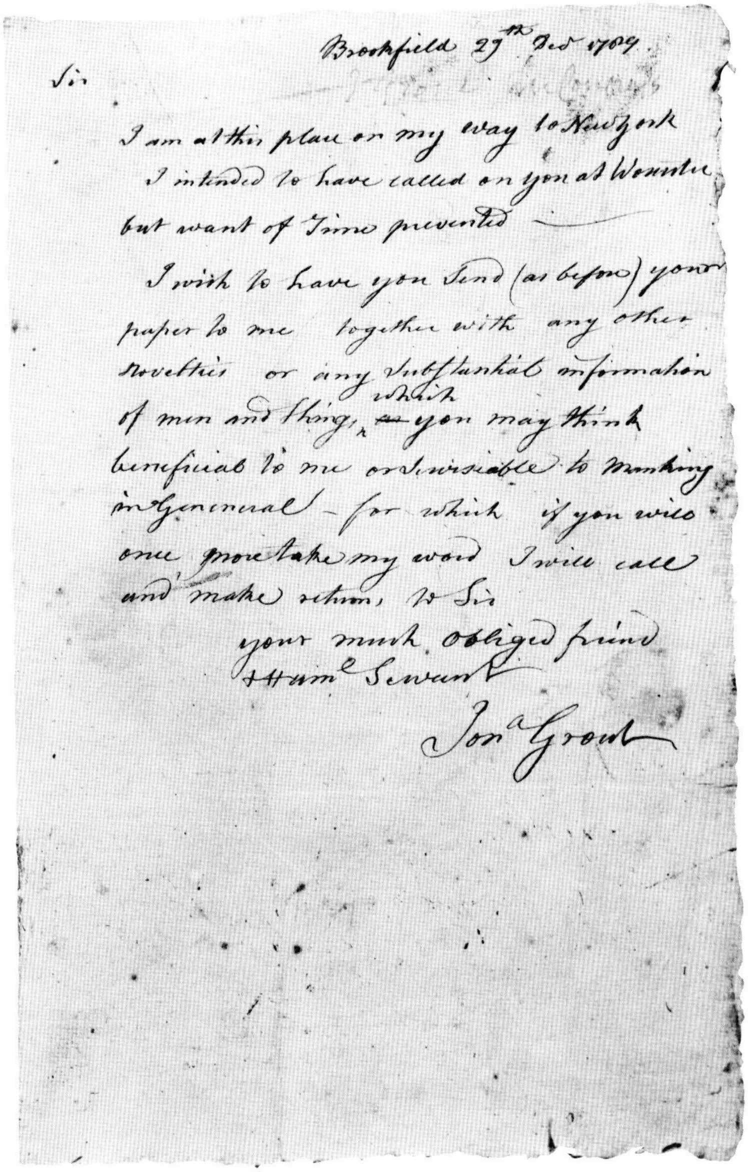

Brookfield 27th Decr 1789.

Sir

I am at this place on my way to New York

I intended to have called on you at Worcester but want of Time prevented —

I wish to have you Send (as before) your paper to me together with any other novelties or any substantial information of men and things, which you may think beneficial to me or serviceable to mankind in general — for which if you will once more take my word I will call and make return, so Sir

your much obliged friend
& Humle Servant

Jona Grout

Following the practice set by the old Congress, members of Congress were supplied with New York newspapers of their choice. Jonathan Grout, however, also called upon Isaiah Thomas, printer of the *Massachusetts Spy*, famed patriotic organ of the Revolution, to send him the news direct from Worcester.

Letter from Jonathan Grout to Isaiah Thomas, December 29, 1789. American Antiquarian Society, Worcester, Massachusetts

and Antifederalists with equal contempt. Who, save himself, was possessed of public virtue? Righteously he declared, "It is certainly a defect in my political character that I can not help embarking my passions and considering the interest of the public as my own."

William Maclay (1737–1804), who drew the two-year term in the first Senate, was not reelected and departed the national scene with a bitter heart and faded into obscurity. "As I left the Hall," he wrote as the Congress concluded, *I gave it a look, with that kind of Satisfaction which a Man feels on leaving a place Where he has been ill at Ease. Being fully satisfyed that many a Culprit, has served Two Years at the Wheel-Barrow, without feeling half the pain & mortification, that I experienced, in my honorable Station.* A century later his diary, a remarkable commentary on the political and social life during his tenure, was first published in its entirety.

Edgar S. Maclay, editor, *Journal of William Maclay* (New York, 1890). Dr. Robert Price, descendant of Senator William Maclay, and family

It was Maclay's habit to take notes in the Federal Hall and at the end of each day transcribe them in narrative form into his journal. "But all in the dumps again about the Residence," wrote Maclay on July 8, 1790. "It is time indeed that this Business should be settled, for all our Affairs are poisoned by it." Disappointed that the permanent residence would not be in Pennsylvania, Maclay reflected on July 22, "My consolation for going to the Potowmack is that it may give a preponderance to the Agricultural Interest" in the battle against the forces of commerce and industry. "Dire indeed will be the contest but I hope it Will prevail."

Diary of William Maclay, volume two. Manuscript Division, Library of Congress, Washington, D.C.

and endeavour to promote a ſweat by drinking warm liquors; and if he ſhould be troubled with a nauſea, or inclination to vomit, he may drink camomile-tea, or any thing that will make him vomit freely.

When the gout attacks the kidneys, and imitates gravel-pains, the patient ought to drink freely of a decoction of marſh-mallows, and to have the parts fomented with warm water. An emollient clyſter ought likewiſe to be given, and afterwards an opiate. If the pain be very violent, twenty or thirty drops of laudanum may be taken in a cup of the decoction.

Perſons who have had the gout ſhould be very attentive to any complaints that may happen to them about the time when they have reaſon to expect a return of the fit. The gout imitates many other diſorders, and by being miſtaken for them, and treated improperly, is often diverted from its regular courſe, to the great danger of the patient's life.

Thoſe who never had the gout, but who, from their conſtitution or manner of living, have reaſon to expect it, ought likewiſe to be very circumſpect with regard to its firſt approach. If the diſeaſe, by wrong conduct or improper medicines, be diverted from its proper courſe, the miſerable patient has a chance to be ever after tormented with head-achs, coughs, pains of the head and inteſtines; and to fall, at laſt, a victim to its attack upon ſome of the more noble parts.

OF THE RHEUMATISM.

THIS diſeaſe has often a reſemblance to the gout. It generally attacks the joints with exquiſite pain, and is ſometimes attended with inflammation and ſwelling. It is moſt common in the ſpring, and towards the end of autumn. It is uſually diſtinguiſhed into acute and chronic; or the rheumatiſm with and without a fever.

CAUSES.———The cauſes of a rheumatiſm are frequently the ſame as thoſe of an inflammatory fever; viz. an obſtructed perſpiration, the immoderate uſe of ſtrong liquors, and the like. Sudden changes of the weather, and all quick tranſitions from heat to cold, are very apt to occaſion the rheumatiſm. The moſt extraordinary caſe of a rheumatiſm that I ever ſaw, where almoſt every joint of the body was diſtorted, was in a man who uſed to work one part of the day by the fire, and the other part of it in the water. Very obſtinate rheumatiſms have likewiſe been brought on by perſons

Interjected among William Maclay's trenchant discourses on matters of state, ceremonies, and etiquette are notations concerning his health, a preoccupation he shared with most of his colleagues. Maclay, who suffered with a lameness in both knees, found "that my political Wrangles have affected my corporeal Feelings so as to bring on in degree my rheumatic indisposition." On July 12, 1789, he recorded "My swelld knee gave me great pain and prevented my rest. Put on Flannels and staid at home all day, had no book but Buchan's family Physician read a good deal in it."

English doctor William Buchan's *Domestic Medicine*, published in several American editions, was among the most utilized books in America. Looking beyond professional advice, Maclay jotted down every cure for rheumatism that came to his attention— among them "a Tea Spoonful of the Flour of Brimston taken every Morning before Breakfast," which had proved efficacious to General Arthur St. Clair, "Assa Foetida laid on burning Coals and held to the Nose," recommended by another acquaintance, as well as "Cyder in Which an hot Iron has been Quenched."

William Buchan, *Domestic Medicine* (Philadelphia, 1784). Rare Book and Special Collections Division, Library of Congress, Washington, D.C.

A perfervid advocate of republican simplicity, Maclay denounced the "foolerries fopperies finerries and pomp of Royal etiquette" instigated by those he called the court party. John Adams and his ilk, fumed Maclay, "cared for nothing else but . . . the creation of a new monarchy in America." To Maclay's great disgust, the Senate was preoccupied for almost a month with matters of ceremonies and titles. The Vice-President, who regarded proper form as integral to the respectability of the government, posed the question of just how the President should be addressed. Ralph Izard of South Carolina suggested "Excellency," and others mentioned "Highness" or "Elected Highness." Richard Henry Lee, who was of the opinion that "All the World, civilized and Savage called for titles," moved that a select committee be appointed to consider the possibilities. James Madison wrote confidentially to Thomas Jefferson, "J. Adams espoused the cause of titles with great earnestness. His friend R. H. Lee tho elected as a republican enemy to an aristocratic constitution was a most zealous second."

On May 9 the Senate select committee returned with the recommendation that the President should be addressed as "His Highness the President of the United States of America and Protector of the Rights of the Same." William Grayson of Virginia jested that the Vice-President might be dubbed "His Superfluous Excellency."

In the House of Representatives, "Not a soul said a word *for* titles," wrote Fisher Ames. "The antispeakers edified all aristocratic hearts by their zeal against titles. They were not warranted by the Constitution; repugnant to republican principles; dangerous, vain, ridiculous, arrogant, and damnable."

The House maintained its insistence upon republican plainness, and eventually the Senate was forced to agree that the Chief Executive should be addressed simply as "The President of the United States."

"We are obliged to avail ourselves of the Judgement and information of Every member present"

The essential first task undertaken by the House of Representatives was the raising of revenue to support the government. An impost was looked upon as the most eligible way to do this, although members from the plantation South, whose constituents found it cheaper to buy goods from Europe than they did from the North, had every inducement to keep the rates as low as possible. New Englanders, for other reasons, were in agreement that the tax must not be too great. "Experience has clearly proved that high duties will be evaded," Fisher Ames observed. "No people better understand smuggling than our's."

Initially it was hoped that a bill might be passed in time to tax the spring imports, but it soon became apparent that conflicting economic interests precluded speedy passage.

Nonetheless, business proceeded harmoniously. "We sit five hours daily," Fisher Ames recorded in July. "There have been few long speeches, a very punctual attendance, great good humour, and a common wish to expedite the bill in due season to be passed for the collection to begin on the first of August."

Michael Jenifer Stone of Maryland informed his brother at about the same time: *The House of Delegates is a wise Body and upon the whole very cool and Polite. There is a great Deal of Speaking because there are a great many Speakers but oratory is not much attended to — reason is the thing that is heard — The Speakers are —Ames, Madison — Sedwich — Lawrance, Smith (S. Carolina), Vining, Benson, White, Gerry, Boudinot, Page, Sherman (Roger) Livermore, Jackson, Fitzsimons — Stone (MJ) and a great many others who occasionally make remarks — I think you had better become a Subscriber to the Congressional register — We go Slowly but this is not owing to Idleness — The Subject is Extensive and new — No one Man can Grasp it. We are obliged to avail ourselves of the Judgement and information of Every member present. Time must be taken for this.*

James Madison, who undertook direction of the revenue bill, emphasized that income was the main object of the impost and that "commerce ought to be as free as the policy of nations will admit." But Thomas Fitzsimons of Pennsylvania had different ideas. He submitted an additional list of dutiable articles, which was frankly intended "to encourage the productions of our country and protect our infant manufactures; besides others tending to operate as sumptuary restrictions upon articles which are often termed those of luxury." His colleague Thomas Hartley agreed: "I think it both politic and just that the fostering hand of the general government should extend to all those manufactures which will tend to national utility."

One after another of the members spoke up in favor of increasing the tariff on articles manufactured in their home districts. Daniel Carroll, who represented Frederick County, Maryland, site of the Amelung glassworks, won protection for glassmaking. Roger Sherman from tobacco-growing Connecticut declared that he wanted tobacco taxed so high that a "prohibition on imports" would result. Benjamin Goodhue of Massachusetts, whose district included the shoe-manufacturing center of Lynn, moved for a tax on shoes — leather, silk, or stuff — and galoshes and slippers as well. George Clymer of Pennsylvania declared for duties on steel, noting that a furnace in Philadelphia "made three hundred tons in two years." But Thomas Tudor Tucker of South Carolina, whose constituents were dependent on foreign steel for their farm implements, voiced his opposition. Richard Henry Lee of Virginia "laboured with Spite and acrimony," charged William Maclay, against the Pennsylvania delegation's desire to protect the sugar houses of Philadelphia, swearing that "the loaf Sugar of America was bad it was lime and other vile composition, he had broke a Spoon in trying to dissolve and seperate it." He concluded pathetically, "And so I must go on breaking my spoons, and three Millions of People must be taxed to support half a Dozen People in Philada."

Generally Congressmen from the agricultural South stood ready to oppose protection of infant industries, but on occasion some of them saw fit to add to the list of taxable goods. South Carolina and Georgia, noted Aedanus Burke of South Carolina, had the potential for the manufacture of hemp, and therefore he proposed a tax on the imported item. Thedorick Bland and Josiah Parker of Virginia, who were of the opinion that their state's coal mines might supply the nation, argued for a duty on coal.

The proposed tax on rum brought morality into the debate. Elias Boudinot of New Jersey favored "taxing this article as high as there is a probability of collecting the duty," to discourage importation and thereby

The mechanics and manufacturers of the City of New York were among the several industrial groups to protest "the profusion of foreign articles, which has deluged the Country." They looked to Congress for relief, "convinced, that, as the united voice of America has furnished you with the means, so your knowledge of our common wants has given you the spirit to unbind our fetters."

Membership certificate from the New York Mechanick Society, 1791. The Henry Francis du Pont Winterthur Museum, Winterthur, Delaware

NEW-YORK AIR FURNACE.

PETER T. CURTENIUS, and Co.

HAVE repaired the New-York Air-Furnace, *and have procured the best Workmen, together with the necessary Apparatus to carry on the Manufacture of* Cast-Iron, *in the completest and best Manner, so that the Ware they make will be equal to any imported from Europe, and the Price less.*

The WARE manufactured at this Furnace, consists of the following Articles, viz.

Pots and Kettles of various sizes from one to fifteen gallons, Tea Kettles, Pye Pans, Skillets, Griddles, Pot-Ash Kettles and Coolers, Whaling Kettles, Boilers for Tallow-Chandlers and Sugar-Works, Stoves for Sugar-Bakers, Mill-Cases, Cast Bars for Sugar-Works and Distilleries, Rollers and Shears for Slitting-Mills, Hearth and Jamb Plates, cast agreeable to any pattern, Close Stoves for Work-shops, Franklin Stoves neatly decorated with carved work, Bath Stove-Grates elegantly ornamented with carvings, Chimney Backs, Ships Cabouses of the new construction, with bake ovens, in which the same fire that roasts and boils the meat bakes the bread, Mill Rounds and Gudgeons, Saw-Mill Cranks, Calcining Plates for making Pearl Ashes, Cast Iron Screws for Fulling and Paper Mills, Fullers Plates cast to any size, Sash Weights, Forge Hammers and Anvils, Plow Plates, Half Hundreds, Quarters, Fourteen and Seven Pound Weights; Cart, Waggon, Coach, Phaeton, Chair and Sulky Boxes, &c. &c. &c.——Also, **Bells** *for Churches, made of the best Bell Metal, from fifty to one thousand weight.*

N. B. Persons who want any Backs or other Ware, cast agreeable to particular Patterns, will please to send their Patterns to the **Furnace**, *near Mr. Atlee's Brewery, North-River, or leave them at the House of* **Peter T. Curtenius,** *No.* 48. *Great Dock-Street, near the Exchange.*

New-York: Printed by J. M'Lean, No. 41, *Hanover-Square,*

1787

Peter T. Curtenius, who operated a cast-iron manufactory in New York City, in this 1787 broadside advertisement exemplifies the many small enterprises that looked to the Congress for protection from foreign competition.

The New-York Historical Society, New York City

benefit the morals of the people. But Fisher Ames, whose constituents were much engaged in the rum trade, jumped up to say, "If any man supposes that a mere law can turn the taste of a people from ardent spirits to malt liquors, he has a most romantic notion of legislative power." John Laurance of New York concurred, declaring, "We are not to deliberate and determine on this subject as moralists, but as politicians, and endeavor to draw (if I may use the expression) from the vices of mankind, that revenue which our citizens must, in one form or another, contribute."

Nothing could exceed the hue and cry raised by Madison's proposal for a six-cent tax on molasses, which was, among other things, an ingredient essential to the manufacture of rum. "I have just heard that you have laid a duty on molasses," wrote an angry constituent to George Thatcher, who represented the Maine part of Massachusetts. "For heaven sake what motive, what inducement could you have for that for it is the meat and drink of this state. . . . For God's sake don't destroy the labors of the diligent." Another outraged New Englander noted, "Molasses is a necessary of life that cannot be manufactured in our Country — Why then should it be taxed at all?" The duty *never will be collected, unless it is done at the point of the sword!*

New England Representatives waxed eloquently and pathetically against the tax on molasses, but as Lambert Cadwalader of New Jersey wryly commented, neither the claim of the "attachment of the old and middle aged, nor that of the children crying for it, could soften the Hearts of the Opposition." The rate, however, was in the end reduced to two-and-a-half cents per gallon.

The impost bill was put into the hands of a select committee composed of John Laurance, who represented mercantile New York City, Thomas Fitzsimons, a Philadelphia merchant, and Elbridge Gerry, who had retired from active commerce shortly after his 1786 marriage to the daughter of a New York merchant. Senator William Maclay grumbled that "There could not have been selected within the Walls of the House two such improper Characters as Gerry & Lawrence. Gerry highly Antifederal married and intimately connected with the Trade of this place; Lawrence of New York a mere tool for British Agents & factors." Maclay heard talk that Thomas Fitzsimons was delaying the bill until his own ships should arrive from China.

On May 16 the tariff bill passed the House. When it reached the Senate, the members from New Jersey, Pennsylvania, Delaware, and Maryland, Maclay summed up, wanted the impost to be both productive of revenue and also effective for the encouragement of manufactures. This group considered the rates set by the House, with the exception of the tax on salt, as being too low. "But the members, both from the North, and still more particularly from the South, were ever in a flame when any articles were brought forward that were in any considerable use among them." Pierce Butler, related Maclay, "arraigned the Whole impost law, and then Charged (indirectly) the Whole

Congress with a design of oppressing South Carolina." Maclay went on, "Butler flamed away and threatened a dissolution of the Union with regard to his State, *as sure as God was in the firmament!*"

In addition to the tax on imports, the House bill also included a tax on the carrying capacity of all ships arriving from foreign ports. Tonnage duties bore most heavily on the agricultural South, and William Loughton Smith confided to a friend in South Carolina, "Had we not cried out lustily, the New England Delegates were disposed to make them much higher."

Over the objection of some southerners, a majority of the House was brought around to agree that American ships should pay lesser fees than foreign vessels. Accepted also by the House was Madison's proposal that there should be a discrimination in favor of nations with whom America had treaties of friendship and commerce, namely France. This was pointed retaliation against England's refusal to negotiate a commercial treaty with her late colony. "I wish to teach those nations who have declined to enter into

Pierce Butler (1744–1822), William Maclay declared, "has Words at Will, but scatters them the most at random of any Man I ever heard pretend to speak." He was, charged the Pennsylvanian, "ever and anon crying out against local Views and partial proceedings," while at the same time guarding South Carolina's important indigo trade. Butler was, pronounced Maclay, "the most local and partial Creature I ever heard open a mouth."

From an unlocated miniature illustrated in Clarence Winthrop Bowen's *The Centennial of Washington's Inauguration*

commercial treaties with us," said Madison, "that we have the power to extend or withhold advantages as their conduct shall deserve." John Laurance, whose New York City constituents were engaged heavily in trade with Great Britain, protested that Madison's measure would serve to decrease customs revenues in order to pay tribute to France.

Discrimination also evoked a vigorous debate in the Senate. Caleb Strong of Massachusetts proclaimed that "this discrimination was showing an inimical disposition to great Britain, it was declaring commercial War with her." William Maclay stood up to say "that if Commercial Treaties were of any Use at all, Nations in Treaty should stand on better Terms than those Who had kept at a Sulky distance. But if we now treated all alike, we need never hereafter propose a Commercial Treaty." Maclay asked "if we were not called on by Gratitude to treat with discrimination, those Nations who had given Us the helping hand in the time of distress." But Maclay found little agreement with this view. "It was echoed from all parts of the House that nothing but interest governed all Nations." When the vote was taken, Madison's proposition was killed. "The Senate, God bless them," observed Fisher Ames, "as if designated by Providence to keep rash and frolicsome brats out of the fire, have demolished the absurd, impolitic, mad discrimination of foreigners in alliance from other foreigners."

On July 1 a conference committee of both houses agreed to the final terms on tariff and tonnage duties, and the bill was enacted on July 4, 1789. Its purpose was not only to raise revenues "for the payment of the debts of the United States" but also to provide for "the encouragement and protection of manufactures."

"I am happy to find Congress have at last begun to make Progress in their Business," Benjamin Contee heard from a Maryland voter. "The People here began to clamor. They say you have too many Speakers who would rather harangue about this mode of drawing the Cork than let their Friends taste the Liquor contained in the Bottle."

"To 'live & move & have its being'"

While the House devoted its energies to the shaping of a revenue bill, the Senate began the task of setting up a federal judiciary — without which the collection of taxes could not be enforced.

On April 7, just one day after the Senate achieved a quorum, a select committee was appointed to bring in a judiciary bill. The members — one from each state — were Oliver Ellsworth of Connecticut, William Paterson of New Jersey, William Maclay of Pennsylvania, Caleb Strong of Massachusetts, Richard Henry Lee of Virginia, Richard Bassett of Delaware, William Few of Georgia, and Paine Wingate of New Hampshire. Ellsworth, Paterson, Strong, Bassett, and Few had all been delegates to the Federal Convention, but there

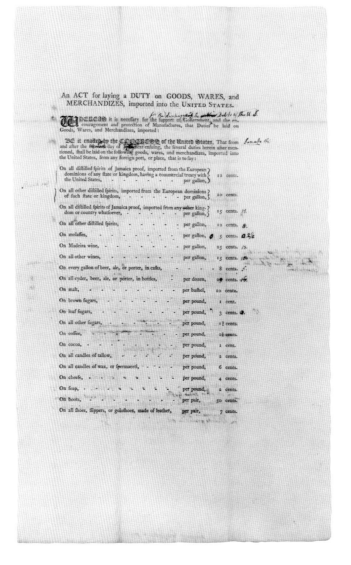

Shown here are the changes made by the Senate in the House bill for the raising of revenues by means of an impost.

Rare Book and Special Collections Division, Library of Congress, Washington, D.C.

had been almost no debate on the judiciary during that summer of 1787.

To implement the four-hundred-word constitutional authorization of the third branch of government, the Senate committee brought forth a bill for the establishment of a Supreme Court with a Chief Justice and five associate justices, as well as district courts for each state and the districts of Maine and Kentucky. Three traveling circuits, composed of two members of the Supreme Court and the district court judge of the particular state, were set up as courts of original jurisdiction and to handle appeals.

The Senate committee labored upon the bill, Fisher Ames testified, "with vast perseverance, and have taken as full a view of their subject, as I ever knew a committee take." The chief credit belonged to Oliver Ellsworth, but William Paterson and Caleb Strong also were major participants.

When the bill reached the Senate floor, the Antifederalists from Virginia, fearful that state courts would be undermined by a federal judiciary, stood in heated opposition to the system. Both Richard Henry Lee and William Grayson insisted that the jurisdiction of the federal courts be limited to admiralty and maritime measures. William Maclay, although he had major doubts about the bill, "rose and read over from the Constitution a number of the powers of Congress — Viz. collecting Taxes duties imposts, naturalization of Foreigners, Laws respecting the Coinage, punishing the counterfeiting of the Coin, Treason against the united States &ca." There was no way in which the Constitution could be construed, Maclay concluded, "to bring these cases within admiralty or maritime jurisdiction."

Others, such as Paine Wingate, objected to the cost of providing such a great number of judges with permanent salaries. "I think it will be a very expensive machine without deriving benefits to the public equal to the cost."

In the midst of the debate on the judiciary, the Senate was obliged to adjourn, Maclay noted in his journal, when "the Grand procession of the Free Masons came by, with much noise of Musick."

On July 17, 1789, the bill passed the Senate, with Lee, Grayson, Maclay, and Wingate, as well as John Langdon of New Hampshire and Pierce Butler of South Carolina, voting in opposition. Pronounced Maclay, "It certainly is a Vile law System, calculated for Expence, and with a design to draw by degrees all law business into the federal Courts." He reflected darkly, "The Constitution is meant to swallow up all the State Constitutions by degrees and thus to Swallow by degrees all the State Judiciaries."

In the House of Representatives, the Antifederalists from South Carolina — Aedanus Burke, Thomas Sumter, and Thomas Tudor Tucker — joined by Samuel Livermore of New Hampshire and Michael Jenifer Stone of Maryland, continued the fight against the judiciary bill.

Leadership in favor of the bill came from Fisher Ames and Theodore Sedgwick of Massachusetts, John Laurance of New York, and William Loughton Smith of South Carolina. It was the only time during the first session of the Congress that James Madison did not play a dominant role.

The judiciary bill, with some few changes from the Senate version, passed the House on September 21 and was signed by the President three days later. Such was the skill of its Senate drafters that the structure they created in 1789 has served to this day with only a few modifications.

With provision made for revenue and the judiciary, Oliver Ellsworth proclaimed to Noah Webster, "the Government will begin to 'live & move & have its being.'"

New York June 8, 1789.

Dear Sir,

I congratulate you & the city of Hartford on your settlement there in the practice of the law. Should you like a tenement of my house, by & by when you can see what the accommodations will be, I shall be glad to engage it to you. —

The business of Congress progresses slowly but not unfavourably. I hope, in a month or two more, to see the judiciary & revenue departments organized; when the Government will begin to "live & move & have its being."

I am Sir, with much esteem,
Your obedt. huml Servt.
Oliv Ellsworth.

Noah Webster Junr. Esqr.

Once the judiciary was established and the revenue bill passed, Connecticut Senator Oliver Ellsworth confidently declared that the government would truly be born.

Oliver Ellsworth to Noah Webster, June 8, 1789. The Pierpont Morgan Library, New York City

"We must cut our coat according to our cloth"

The rate of compensation to be paid to members of Congress and other officials stirred up a good bit of controversy.

Benjamin Goodhue, one of the House conferees meeting with Robert Morris and others from the Senate, fretted that his arguments against high salaries "have but a little avail with such Kind of characters who are ever talking of respectibility public tables parade etc." He complained to a Salem friend, *When I told Morris We must cut our coat according to our cloth and if We did not We should as certainly be ruined by such practices as any individual would (which perhaps he took to himself) he answered me by saying that We had but just put our thumb*

Mr Maclay's Compliments wait on the Vice President of the united States. begs leave to inform him, That he is in so ill a State of Health, That he cannot have the honor of dining, with him on Friday next ———

Septr 1st 1789

William Maclay, who might be expected to put forth any excuse to avoid dining with the Vice-President, was in fact on September 1 "exceeding ill, with a settled and acute pain in my loins particularly on my left side or hip." He added in his diary, "Dressed however and went to the Hall," where he sat in extreme pain through the debate on the salary bill, in order to give his vote in favor of the lowest sums.

William Maclay to John Adams, September 1, 1789. Louisa Catharine Adams Clement Hull

upon the latch of revenue and the next session We should open the door which would supply easily all our wants. Morris casually suggested "a stamp duty of paper, Excises and if necessary a land tax." An appalled Goodhue informed Morris that "he would find himself mistaken if he supposed the people of America would submit to such impositions for the purpose of feasting a few Favourites in luxury and profusion."

John Adams, who felt himself much put upon by the niggardly five thousand dollars awarded the Vice-President, spoke up sharply when he broke a tie vote giving judges a five-hundred-dollar increase over the three thousand first proposed. "Somebody had said Judges could be had for less," William Maclay quoted him as saying, "That People must be abandoned and forsaken by God, who could speak of buying a Judge as you would an horse." But when the Chief Justice's salary was debated in the House of Representatives, Fisher Ames was of the opinion that the finest legal talent in New England could be had for fifteen hundred dollars, and he successfully moved a salary of three thousand. The compensation act finally awarded the Chief Justice four thousand dollars and the associate justices five hundred dollars less.

Maclay made a motion that members of Congress be paid five dollars a day, but he was supported only by Jonathan Elmer of New Jersey and Paine Wingate of New Hampshire. Robert Morris, according to William Maclay, "almost raged," told Maclay that "he cared not for the Arts people Used to ingratiate themselves with the public," and declared for eight dollars a day. Maclay responded that he "knew the public mind was discontented. I thought it our duty to attend to the voice of the public." Pierce Butler of South Carolina rose to declare *that a Member of the Senate should not only have a handsome income but should spend it all. He was happy enough to look down on these things; he could despise them, but it was scandalous for a Member of Congress to take any of his Wages home; he should rather give it to the poor.* Maclay continued, "Mr. Morris likewise paid himself some Compliments on his manner & Conduct in life his disregard of money; and the little respect he paid to the common Opinions of People."

In the House of Representatives Theodore Sedgwick moved to reduce the Representatives' pay to five dollars while keeping the Senators' rate at six. James Madison agreed with the distinction, observing that if there were no discrimination, "men of interprize and genius will naturally prefer a seat in the house, considering it to be a more conspicuous situation." Most members of the House, however, would brook no insinuation of inferiority, and salaries for both branches were ultimately set at six dollars a day.

A public clamor was raised about the "high compensations and Salaries given by the Congress," and members soon heard from their constituents. Robert Morris was among those who refused to be swayed by mail from home. "In spite of Doctor Logan, Centinel, & all other discontents," he wrote defiantly in September 1789, "I have voted for the highest Salaries well knowing that the Public are best served when they pay well."

"Our constituents, in complaining, forget the sacrifices we make of domestic happiness, time and even health, to their service," wrote an anonymous member of Congress in a letter that appeared in the *Pennsylvania Gazette.* If proper wages were not paid, "your government will be administered only by a few aristocratic nabobs, who can afford to live without wages upon the income of large states. Should this be case, then farewel to the liberties of our country."

Ralph Izard (1742–1804), whose taste for civilized living is epitomized in his portrait with his wife, Alice DeLancey, painted during their Italian sojourn, was insistent that members of Congress should be paid salaries that would enable them to live like gentlemen.

By John Singleton Copley (1738–1815); oil on canvas, 1775. Museum of Fine Arts, Boston; Edward Ingersoll Browne Fund

Frederick Muhlenberg declared that, while the Congress remained at New York, it was impossible to live for less than six dollars a day. "This proves fully that the good of the United States requires a removal from this place, & whenever this happens I shall chearfully vote to lessen the Salaries. You have no conception at what extravagant rates every thing is paid for in this place," he told his Pennsylvania correspondent, *and the general principle seems to be this,*

"That as the stay of Congress is doubtfull it is necessary to take time by the forelock." There is not a place within the State of Pennsylvania, where we could not live more comfortably on four Dollars than here on Six — it is in vain at this place to talk of frugality, Oeconomy, & a Republican Stile of Living.

"A tub thrown out to a Whale"

James Madison, under pressure from the Virginia legislature and in fulfillment of promises made during his election campaign, proposed on May 4, 1789, that debate on amendments to the Constitution should be opened at the end of the month. "Poor Madison," Robert Morris observed, "got so cursedly frightened in Virginia that I believe he has dreamed of amendments ever since." William Loughton Smith thought Madison's action ill-timed. "It must appear extremely impolitic to go into consideration of amending the Government, before it is organized, before it has begun to operate."

Madison insisted that if Congress delayed, the people "may think we are not sincere in our desire to incorporate such amendments in the constitution as will secure these rights, which they consider as not sufficiently guarded." John Vining of Delaware shot back, "The wheels of the national machine cannot turn until the impost and collection bill are perfected." He went on, "These are the desiderata which the public mind is anxiously expecting. . . . The most likely way to quiet the perturbation of the public mind, will be to pass salutary laws."

In his methodical way, Madison plowed ahead, sifting through the 210 recommendations for amendments that had been submitted to Congress by the state ratifying conventions, compiling them into eighty subjects. On June 8 he took the greater part of the session to outline the changes that he proposed.

Opposition came not so much from the Federalists, even though most of them saw no need for a bill of rights, but rather from the more extreme of the Antifederalists, who wanted no palliative that would head off the calling of a second convention. William Grayson of Virginia was convinced that the drive for amendments was a plot "to break the spirit of the Antifederalist party by divisions."

Elbridge Gerry recommended that the House be constituted as a committee of the whole to consider every single constitutional amendment proposed at each of the state ratifying conventions. "Seven out of thirteen," he reminded the House, "had thought the constitution very defective, yet five of them had adopted it with a perfect reliance on Congress for its improvement." Gerry asked, "Now, what will these states feel if the subject is discussed in a select committee, and their recommendations totally neglected?"

On July 21 the appointment of a select committee — one member from each of the eleven states — was agreed to by a vote of 34 to 15. Five of the members — James Madison, Abraham Baldwin, Roger Sherman, Nicholas Gilman, and George Clymer — were signers of the Constitution. They were joined by John Vining, Aedanus Burke, Egbert Benson, Benjamin Goodhue, Elias Boudinot, and George Gale. Antifederalist Burke of South Carolina was skeptical that "solid and substantil amendments" could be expected from such a group.

Just one week later, the committee report was made to the whole house. "It consisted of most satisfactory amendments indeed," a visitor in the gallery made haste to relay to North Carolina, where the Antifederalists proclaimed

REDEUNT SATURNIA REGNA.

On the erection of the Eleventh PILLAR of the great National DOME, we beg leave most sincerely to felicitate " OUR DEAR COUNTR

Rise it will.

The foundation good—it may yet be SAVED.

The FEDERAL EDIFICE.

ELEVEN STARS, in quick succession rise—
ELEVEN COLUMNS strike our wond'ring eyes,
Soon o'er the whole, shall swell the beauteous DOME,
COLUMBIA's boast—and FREEDOM's hallow'd home.
Here shall the ARTS in glorious splendour shine!
And AGRICULTURE give her stores divine!
COMMERCE refin'd, dispense us more than gold,
And this new world, teach WISDOM to the old—
RELIGION here shall fix her blest abode,
Array'd in mildness, like its parent GOD!
JUSTICE and LAW, shall endless PEACE maintain,
And the " SATURNIAN AGE," return again.

One of the main arguments for early consideration of amendments to the Constitution was the intelligence that North Carolina, in the words of one Antifederalist, "would never swallow the Constitution until it was amended."

On the erection of the Eleventh Pillar; published in the *Columbian Centinel,* August 2, 1788. Serial and Government Publications Division, Library of Congress, Washington, D.C.

that Congress never would take up the subject of amendments: "the rights of conscience — the liberty of the press — the trial by jury in all common law cases, and other things I do not so particularly remember, are all included, and guarded in the plainest manner."

But Aedanus Burke derided the proposals as "little better than whip-syllabub, frothy and full of wind, formed only to please the palate." They were "like a tub thrown out to a Whale, to secure the freight of the ship and its peaceable voyage."

The Antifederalists intended more radical alterations. "Gerry is not content with those alone," George Clymer of Pennsylvania wrote, "and proposes to treat us with all the amendments of all the antifederalists in America." Elbridge Gerry and Thomas Tudor Tucker presented a long string of additional proposals. "There was a curious medley of them," Frederick Muhlenberg told Benjamin Rush, and of a nature that even the radical party in Pennsylvania would "have pronounced dangerous Alterations [rather] than Amendments."

Heated debate was engendered by the recommendation that the people should have the right to instruct their Representatives. "I contend Sir," declared Gerry, "that our constituents have not only a right to instruct but to *bind* this Legislature."

Madison argued that the existence of this right was problematical. "I wish that the amendments may consist of an enumeration of simple and acknowledged principles: The insertion of propositions that are of a doubtful nature, will have a tendency to prejudice the whole system of amendments."

On August 24 the House approved seventeen of Madison's amendments and sent them to the Senate. George Clymer and Thomas Fitzsimons told Robert Morris "that the business of Amendments was now done with in their House & advised that the Senate should adopt the whole of them by the Lump as containing neither good or Horrid being perfectly innocent." Morris rejoined, "The Waste of precious time is what has vexed me the most, for as to the Nonsense they call Amendments I never expect that any part of it will go through the various Trials which it must pass before it can become a part of the Constitution."

Morris proved to be mistaken. After the conferees from both houses agreed on the final form for twelve amendments, they were submitted to the states at the close of the first session of Congress, and by December 15, 1791, ten of them had become part of the Constitution.

THE GREAT DEPARTMENTS
OF GOVERNMENT

"The creation of a vast number of offices and officers"

Speculation as to who would fill the posts in the new government had long been rife. "Everybody here is occupied to dispose of the offices according to his inclination," wrote Baron Steuben from New York on December 12, 1788. "For the great chair are the candidates G. W. or God Almighty. for the second Great Adams or Big Mistris Knoks. She allone disputes this place to the first of men." If she failed in her attempts, "the Big Bookbinder," as Steuben called her nearly three-hundred-pound husband, would be appointed secretary of war — a post to which the Baron himself aspired. John Jay, Steuben opined, would be Chief Justice, and Alexander Hamilton, minister of finance. "Of Foreign Affairs perhaps Madison, perhaps King."

In the debate leading to the establishment of the first of the three great departments of government — Foreign Affairs — a fundamental matter of executive authority was raised. Since confirmation of appointments required the advice and consent of the Senate, did removal call for the same procedure? "This has been the most important question & the most solemn debate we have had since the meeting of Congress," wrote William Loughton Smith on June 21, 1780. He added, "Tho' the house was nearly divided on the subject & the arguments were generally warm & animated, yet I never saw a debate conducted with so much temper & good humour."

Smith spoke against giving the President exclusive power of removal and quoted from the *Federalist* to buttress his arguments. The next day Egbert Benson of New York sent him a note saying that, "upon more mature reflection," Publius (that is Alexander Hamilton) *"had changed his opinion & was now convinced that the President alone should have the power of removal at pleasure."*

James Madison, in a carefully reasoned speech, pointed out that the Senate had *expressly* been given the right to advise and consent but had *not* been given the right of removals. Therefore, since this power had not been taken away from the President, it fell under general grant of power to the executive. William Maclay cynically observed that Madison took this position "in Order to pay his Court, to the President, whom I am told he already affects to Govern." Maclay sputtered with indignation, "But for the House of Representatives, by a side Wind, to exalt the President above the Constitution and depress the Senate below it, is — but I will leave it without a name."

On July 15, as the bill was under discussion in the Senate, Maclay recorded, "I have seen more caballing and meeting of the Members in knots this day, than I ever observed before." Partisan politics was unmistakable. "It seems as if a Court party was forming, indeed I believe it was formed long ago."

In describing the debate on the Senate floor, Maclay noted that, after William Paterson from New Jersey had argued that the executive held removability as a matter of course, Tristram Dalton of Massachusetts declared that his mind had been changed by Paterson's arguments. "Mr. Izard was so provoked," detailed Maclay, "that he jumped up, declared nothing had fell from that Gentleman that possibly could convince any Man — that Man might pretend so, but the thing was impossible." Thereupon, Robert Morris, red of face, "rose hastily. He threw Censure on Mr. Izard; declared that the recanting Man behaved like a Man of honor; that Mr. Patterson's Arguments were good and sufficient to convince any man."

When the vote was taken, the sides were precisely drawn: Ralph Izard and Pierce Butler of South Carolina, John Langdon and Paine Wingate of New Hampshire, William Few and James Gunn of Georgia, William Grayson and Richard Henry Lee of Virginia, William Samuel Johnson of Connecticut, and William Maclay of Pennsylvania came down on the side of senatorial concurrence; George Read and Richard Bassett of Delaware, Caleb Strong and Tristram Dalton of Massachusetts, William Paterson and Jonathan Elmer of New Jersey, John Henry and Charles Carroll of Maryland, Oliver Ellsworth of Connecticut, and Robert Morris of Pennsylvania favored the sole authority of the executive. The Vice-President broke the tie by deciding the question in favor of the "court party."

Abigail Adams was annoyed that some Massachusetts newspapers charged her husband with looking forward to his own presidency and "voting power into his own Hands." Mrs. Adams wrote indignantly to her sister, *His Rule through life has been to vote and act, independant of Party agreeable to the dictates of his conscience, and tho on that occasion he could have wisht on account of the delicacy of his situation not to have been obliged to have determined the Question, yet falling to him, he shrunk not.* She sputtered, "Not a word did any of our state say when his vote reduced the duty upon molasses. All was silence then."

The Department of Foreign Affairs was established on July 27. In September, after Congress had on the basis of economy rejected the idea of a Home Department, a variety of leftover functions, such as conducting the census and granting patents and copyrights, were placed there. The name was then changed to the Department of State.

In considering the creation of the Department of the Treasury, the question arose as to whether the agency should be headed by one man or by a board of three. Both had been tried under the old Confederation. Elbridge Gerry orated vigorously in favor of a triumvirate. But Abraham Baldwin of Georgia, remembering the chaotic days before Robert Morris had been named superintendent of finance, expressed the general opinion when he wrote, "experience has wrought a very general conviction that a board of commissioners will not answer for that duty."

The treasury bill was signed by the President on September 2, 1789. To ensure congressional control over the purse strings, it was stipulated that the secretary should submit his reports directly to the Congress and respond to that body without presidential intervention. It proved to be an arrangement made to order for the man appointed to head the Treasury, Alexander Hamilton.

On August 7 the War Department was authorized. As an indication that Congress considered this agency not quite the co-equal to the other two departments, the secretary's salary was set at three thousand dollars — five hundred dollars less than those authorized for State and Treasury.

William Maclay was sure that this would lead to no good. During the second session of the Congress, when the secretary of war asked that additional regiments be raised for the protection of frontier settlers, Maclay fumed, "The first Error seems to have been the appointing of a Secretary at War [Henry Knox] When we were at Peace, & now we must find Troops, least his office should run out of employment."

Maclay, in full blast against the burgeoning of the national government, wrote in April 1790, *The first thing done under our new government, was the Creation of a Vast number of Offices and Officers. A Treasury dilated into as many branches, as invention could Frame. A Secretary of War with an Host of Clerks; and above all a Secretary of State, and all these Men labor in their several Vocations. Hence We must have a Mass of National Debt, to employ the Treasury; an Army for fear the department of War should lack Employment. Foreign engagements too must be attended to keep Up the Consequence of that Secretary. The next Cry will be for an Admiralty.*

GEORGE WASHINGTON

1732–1799

President of the United States

When I saw Washington," wrote the generally cynical Fisher Ames, describing the President-elect's arrival at New York, "I felt very strong emotions. I believe that no man ever had so fair a claim to veneration as he."

Louis-Guillaume Otto, chargé d'affaires of France, in January 1790 sent a lengthy report to his government, detailing the beginning of the Washington administration. *I cannot refrain from observing that the success which the President has had up to now is unique in its own way and that never has the citizen of a free country enjoyed among his compatriots a confidence as pure and as universal. In more than one hundred gazettes, often very licentious, published daily in the United States, his name has constantly been respected; in an assembly composed of so many heterogeneous individuals as is that of Congress, he has always been spoken of with veneration.*

"Our August President is a singular example of modesty and diffidence," Abigail Adams remarked to her sister. "He has a dignity which forbids Familiarity mixed with an easy affibility which creates Love and Reverence." She added, "He never rides out without six Horses to his Carriage, four servants, & two Gentlemen before him." Irritated by the reverential treatment accorded Washington in the press contrasted with the ridicule heaped on her husband's penchant for ceremonies and titles, she could not forbear remarking, *This is no more state than is perfectly consistant with his Station, but then I do not Love to see the News writers fib so. He is Perfectly averse to all marks of distinction, say they, yet on the 4th of July when the Cincinnati committee waited upon him he recieved them in a Regimental uniform with the Eagal most richly set with diamonds at his Button.*

William Maclay, exasperated that the administration was having its way with the Congress and particularly irritated by being obliged to attend one of the President's Tuesday-afternoon levees, exploded, *Republicans are borne down by fashion And a fear of being charged with a want of Respect to Genl. Washington. If there is Treason in the Wish I retract it, But would to God, this same Genl. Washington were in Heaven. We would not then have him brought forward as the constant cover to every Unconstitutional irrepublican Act.*

The Italian sculptor Giuseppe Ceracchi has portrayed the President in the guise of a Roman statesman, an approved style of the day and one that

George Washington by Giuseppe Ceracchi (1751–1801/2); marble, circa 1816 after the 1792 original. National Portrait Gallery, Smithsonian Institution, Washington, D.C.

particularly appealed to a society that considered itself attuned to the virtues of the Roman Republic. Ceracchi had come to the United States in 1791 to campaign for the commission to execute the equestrian statue of George Washington authorized by the Confederation Congress in 1783. The President agreed to sit for his bust, and the artist took the terra-cotta model back to Italy in order that it might be carved in marble. Upon his return to Philadelphia in 1794, Ceracchi insisted upon leaving the marble bust with Washington, even though the President said that it would be improper for him to accept it as a gift. The bust remained on view at the President's house for several months, until the sculptor, incensed at his lack of success in gaining patronage for a grandiose "Monument to American Liberty," demanded that he be paid for the work. While Washington, awaiting an appraisal, hesitated, Ceracchi retrieved the work and sold it to the Spanish minister.

THOMAS JEFFERSON
1743–1826
Secretary of State

Thomas Jefferson, on leave from his duties as minister to France, found upon his arrival in Virginia that the President had nominated him as secretary of state. At the urging of James Madison, Jefferson put aside his personal preference for a return to France and accepted the appointment. He arrived at New York in March 1790. Abigail Adams, who thought Jefferson "one of the choice ones of the earth," reported to her sister, "Mr. Jefferson is here, and adds much to the social circle."

William Maclay met Jefferson for the first time on May 24, when the secretary appeared before the committee concerned with determining diplomatic grades and salaries. "Jefferson is a slender Man; has rather the Air of Stiffness in his manner," observed Maclay. "His cloaths seem too small for him. He sits in a lounging Manner on one hip, commonly, and with one of his shoulders elevated much above the other. His face has a scruny aspect. His Whole figures has a loose shackling Air." The Pennsylvanian went on, *He had a rambling Vacant look & nothing of that firm collected deportment which I expected would dignify the presence of a Secretary or Minister. I looked for gravity, but a laxity of Manner, seemd shed about him. He spoke almost without ceasing. But even his discourse*

Thomas Jefferson by Mather Brown (1761–1831); oil on canvas, 1786. Charles F. Adams *partook of his personal demeanor. It was lax & rambling and Yet he scattered information wherever he went, and some even brilliant sentiments sparkled from him. The information which he gave Us respecting foreign Ministers &ca. was all high Spiced. He has been long enough abroad to catch the tone of European folly.*

During his first months in office, Jefferson — although tortured by daily migraine headaches — busied himself with fulfilling the House of Representatives' request that he draft a plan for establishing a uniform system of weights and measures. The report was submitted on July 4, 1790, but the Congress never acted upon it.

Patent applications, rather than foreign affairs, occupied the greatest share of Jefferson's time. Under the law enacted in 1790, a three-man board composed of the secretaries of state and war, together with the attorney general, examined all inventions. To Jefferson fell the task of determining whether or not a patent was justified. "Many of them indeed are trifling," Jefferson wrote on June 27, 1790, "but there are some of great consequence which have been proved by practice, and others which if they stand the same proof will produce great effect."

In London, Thomas Jefferson commissioned his portrait from the young Massachusetts artist Mather Brown and ordered this replica for presentation to John Adams.

ALEXANDER HAMILTON
1755/57–1804
Secretary of the Treasury

Alexander Hamilton had deftly turned aside all suggestions that he pursue a seat in the Senate or House of Representatives, in the hopes that he might receive the Treasury appointment. When it was offered, Hamilton readily accepted, although with a large brood of children to support, he could scarcely afford to give up his flourishing law practice.

Six days after Hamilton assumed office, the House of Representatives abolished its committee on ways and means, thus giving the secretary of the treasury the initiative in formulating financial policy and recommending sources of revenue.

Hamilton submitted his first report on public credit to the House of

Alexander Hamilton by John Trumbull (1756–1843); oil on canvas, 1792. Donaldson, Lufkin & Jenrette

Representatives on January 14, 1790. In it he proposed to fund the consolidated debts of the nation, including the war debts of the states, by establishing permanent funds for paying the national debt and for converting the various debt certificates into interest-bearing government bonds. "A national debt if it is not excessive will be to us a national blessing," Hamilton had written to Robert Morris in 1781. "It will be a powerfull cement of our union. It will also create a necessity for keeping up taxation to a degree which without being oppressive, will be a spur to industry."

During the third session of Congress, Hamilton submitted two further reports. To finance his funding and assumption scheme — which Congress had agreed to during the second session — he advocated additional duties on imported spirits and an excise on domestic spirits. In his second report the secretary called for the establishment of a national bank, another fiscal concept that he had shared with Robert Morris in 1781. *The tendency of a national bank is to increase public and private credit. The former gives power to the state for the protection of its rights and interests, and the latter facilitates and extends the operations of commerce among the individuals. Industry is increased, commodities are multiplied, agriculture and manufactures flourish, and herein consist the true wealth and prosperity of a state.*

To Hamilton the attachment of the moneyed interest to the national government was crucial to the survival and growth of the republic. Hamilton's vision of America went far beyond the agrarian view espoused by supporters of Madison and Jefferson; in his recommendations to the Congress Hamilton set the nation on the course toward industrial greatness.

The French traveler Jacques Pierre Brissot de Warville, meeting Hamilton in 1788, recorded, "He looks thirty-eight or forty years old, is not tall, and has a resolute, frank, soldierly appearance." James Madison, not long hence to become Hamilton's great philosophical rival, was also present, and Brissot compared the two men. "Mr. Hamilton had the determined appearance of a republican; Mr. Madison, the thoughtful look of a wise statesman."

At the end of December 1791, Hamilton was apprised that a number of citizens of New York, "desirous of expressing the sense they entertain of the important Services you have rendered your Country," had commissioned his portrait by John Trumbull to be "placed in one of our public buildings." It was the subscribers' desire that the representation should "exhib[it] such part of your Political Life as may be most agreeable to yourself." Hamilton replied that he would "chearfully obey their wish as far as respects the taking of my Portrait; but I ask that they will permit it to appear unconnected with any incident of my political life. The simple representation of their fellow Citizen and friend will best accord with my feelings."

HENRY KNOX
1750–1806
Secretary of War

Henry Knox, secretary at war under the Articles of Confederation, was appointed to head the new Department of War in September 1789.

The January following, the President delivered to a closed session of the House of Representatives Knox's report calling for an increase in the military establishment. The secretary pointed out that the United States had only one battalion of artillery of 240 men and one regiment of infantry, which numbered 560. This force, said the secretary, was utterly inadequate "To prevent the usurpation of the lands of the United States — To facilitate the surveying and selling of the same, for the purpose of reducing the public debt

Without doubt the most formidable of the official wives was Lucy Flucker Knox (1757–1824), who was described as "a lively and meddlesome but amiable leader of society, without whose co-operation it was believed, by many besides herself, that nothing could be properly done, in the drawing-room or ball-room, or any place indeed where fashionable men and women sought enjoyment." The only depiction of the enormous Mrs. Knox is this silhouette cut by one of the young sons of Robert Morris.

Ink on cardboard, not dated. Massachusetts Historical Society, Boston

— and for the protection of the frontiers from Georgia to Lake Erie." The Congress responded by passing the Military Establishment Act of April 30, 1790, which authorized the raising of a regiment of infantry consisting of "one thousand two hundred and sixteen non-commissioned Officers, privates, and Musicians," who would be in the service of the United States for three years. During the third session of the Congress — in response to Indian depredations in the Northwest Territory and cries from Georgia for more protection along her frontier — Knox was authorized to raise an additional regiment. "It is essential to show all lawless adventurers," Knox had told the Congress, "that notwithstanding the distance, government possess the power of preserving peace and good order on the frontiers."

"It has been my anxious desire to devise a national system of defence adequate to the probable exigencies of the United States," the secretary declared in his report for the regulation of the militia, "and at the same time to erect a standard of republican magnanimity independent of, and superior to, the powerful influences of Wealth." Knox held that every able man between eighteen and sixty "is firmly bound by the social compact to perform his proportion of military duty for the defence of the State." However, after a bill was drawn up by the House, so many amendments for exemption from militia duty were proposed that action was deferred until the Second Congress.

General Henry Knox was originally portrayed by Charles Willson Peale for his gallery of American heroes. The portrait here was done by the artist's nephew, Charles Peale Polk, who made a practice of duplicating his uncle's work. Knox is shown wearing the badge of the Society of the Cincinnati, the fraternal organization of Continental army officers that had been formed at Knox's instigation in 1783, when Washington's army was about to disband.

William Maclay, dining with Thomas Jefferson, Alexander Hamilton, and Henry Knox, compared the three secretaries and concluded that "Knox is the easiest Man, and [has] the most dignity of Presence." Maclay added, "Knox staid longest. As indeed suited his Aspect best, being more of a Bachanalian Figure."

Henry Knox by Charles Peale Polk (1767–1822), after Charles Willson Peale; oil on canvas, circa 1783–1790. National Portrait Gallery, Smithsonian Institution, Washington, D.C.

ABIGAIL SMITH ADAMS
1744–1818
Lady of the Vice-President of the United States

I ndeed I have been fully employd in entertaining company," Abigail Adams declared to her sister in August 1789. *In the first place all the Senators who had Ladies & families, then the remaining Senators, and this week we have begun with the House, and tho we have a room in which we dine 24 persons at a Time, I shall not get through them all, together with the publick Ministers for a month to come.* She complained, "It is next to impossible to get a servant from the highest to the lowest grade that does not drink, male or Female. I have at last found a footman who appears sober, but he was born in Boston."

Mrs. Adams protested, *If one was to Credit the Clamours of the Boston papers, we should imagine that there was nothing going forward but dissipation, instead of which, there is nothing which wears the least appearance of it, unless they term the Presidents Levee of a tuesday and Mrs. Washingtons drawing of a fryday such.* She herself received company on Monday evenings, and "All other Ladies who have public Evenings give Tea, Coffee & Lemonade." Only Mrs. Knox "introduces cards, and she is frequently put to difficulty to make up one table at whist." Abigail asked her sister, *Pray is not this better than resorting to Taverns, or even having supper partys? Some amusement from the Buisness of the day is necessary and can there be a more Innocent one than that of meeting at Gentlemens Houses and conversing together? But faction and Antifederalism may turn every Innocent action to evil.*

Disturbed by reports circulating in Massachusetts that an animosity existed between the Adamses and the Washingtons, Abigail begged her sister to make public such parts of her letters "as would contradict such idle stories." Mrs. Adams proclaimed, *Mrs. Washington is a most amiable Lady, polite affable and Friendly. She does me the honor of frequently visiting me, and the more I know her the more I esteem her. I usually attend her drawing rooms, but as these are* sessions of ceremony only, *it is not from those visits that I derive the greatest satisfaction or pleasure.*

Mrs. Adams could not hold back from expressing her satisfaction with the appointments made by President Washington, but confided to her sister, "I know that I stand in a delicate situation. I am fearful of touching upon political subjects yet perhaps there is no person who feels more interest in them."

Pleased with her situation at Richmond Hill, a country house a mile

Abigail Smith Adams by an unidentified artist; oil on canvas, circa 1785–1788. New York State Historical Association, Cooperstown

outside of New York City, and happy to be close to her daughter and grandchildren, Abigail Adams looked with dread upon the government's move to Philadelphia. "I feel low spirited and Heartless," she wrote on October 3, 1790. *I am going amongst an other new set of company, to form new acquaintances, to make and receive a hundred ceremonious visits, not one of ten from which I shall derive any pleasure or satisfaction, obliged to leave Mrs. Smith behind, and the Children to whom I am much attached.* Ill as the time of her departure drew near, she sighed, "I have a journey before me which appears like a mountain & three Ferries to cross."

At Philadelphia she settled down in another country place, Bush Hill, but declared, "The Schuylkill is no more like the Hudson, than I to Hercules." Even though the house was still in the process of being painted, she was obliged to see the throng of Philadelphia ladies who came to call on her. "Gentlemen and Ladies solicitous to manifest their respect were visiting us every day from 12 to 3 oclock in the midst of Rooms heepd up with Boxes, trunks, cases etc."

By spring she allowed to her sister, Elizabeth Shaw, "There is much more society than in New York, and I am much better pleased and satisfied than I expected to be when I was destined to remove here."

In a letter of February 6, 1791, Mrs. Adams described the ceremonial life of the Washington administration. "On tuesday from 3 to 4 the president has a Levee," at which time he was visited by members of Congress and "such of the inhabitants as chuse attend." She went on, *On Thursdays he usually gives a Dinner, and a very handsome one too, to such company as he invites individually, and they are always proper chosen. On Friday evenings Mrs. Washington has a drawing room which is usually very full of the well born and well bred. Sometimes it is as full as her Britannick Majesties Room, & with quite as Handsome Ladies, and as polite courtiers. Here the company are entertained with coffee tea cake Ice creams Lemonade, etc & they chat with each others swish about, fine Ladies Shew Themselves, and as candle Light is a great improver of beauty, they appear to great advantage: this Shew lasts from seven till nine o'clock. When comeing & going during those Hours, as it is not Etiquette for any person to stay Long.* Mrs. Adams concluded, "As to visits many must be of the ceremonious kind, but then there is this satisfaction that one can make 20 in a forenoon."

Abigail Adams's portrait seems likely to have been painted when her husband was minister to England.

THE PEOPLE PETITION

*"The Duty of the legislature to attend to subjects
brought before them by their constituents"*

The right of the people to petition their government was taken with the utmost seriousness by the members of the First Congress, and rarely was a memorial or petition rejected without committal to a committee. Only when the Quakers prayed for an amelioration of the slave trade was there a major row over consideration. Large slaveholder John Page of Virginia, differing with Representatives from South Carolina and Georgia, voted for commitment, he explained, "because it was the duty of the legislature to attend to subjects brought before them by their constituents."

By way of petition all manner of problems — both general and personal — came to the attention of Congress. For example, public creditors of Philadelphia petitioned that "measures may be taken to fund the debts of the United States"; Winthrop Sargent, secretary of the Northwest Territory, prayed that the Congress would increase the sum allowed for his services and expenses.

Special-interest groups throughout the country were heard from. Tradesmen and manufacturers of Baltimore, who looked to the new government for protection against the flood of English imports, asked that Congress impose "such duties on all foreign articles which can be made in America, as will give a just and decided preference to the labors of the petitioners." Artisans from the city of New York filed a like petition, enclosing "a list of such articles as can be manufactured in the state of New-York." A group from Boston directed "the attention of Congress to the encouragement of manufactures, and the increase of American shipping," and shipwrights from Baltimore pleaded "the increase of American shipping and tonnage." Merchants and traders of the town of Portland prayed that molasses "may remain entirely free from all imposts and duties whatever." The manufacturers of mustard in Philadelphia prayed "the patronage of Congress to that manufacture, and that an additional duty may be imposed on imported mustard." Proprietors of the Beverly Manufactory in Massachusetts asked for the "patronage of government to their undertaking, and that an additional impost may be laid on the importation of cotton goods." Manufacturers of tobacco and snuff in Baltimore also looked to Congress for encouragement and prayed that "no duties may be imposed on manufactured snuff and tobacco exported." The coachmakers of Philadelphia urged the "patronage of Congress to that

More than seven hundred tradesmen and manufacturers of Baltimore petitioned Congress in April 1789 for "the Encouragement and Protection of American Manufactures," and appended a list of more than thirty items manufactured in Baltimore and in other parts of Maryland.

National Archives, Washington, D.C.

manufacture and that a tax on carriages manufactured in America may not be imposed."

Petitions asking for the enactment of copyright laws early poured into the Congress. Nicholas Pike of Newburyport prayed "an exclusive privilege may be granted him for a limited time" for "a new and complete System of

Arithmetic." Hannah Adams of Boston, the first woman in America to make her living by her pen, petitioned for a copyright "to protect and vend an alphabetical compendium of Christian sects."

Inventors made claims for patent protection. John Fitch of Pennsylvania, professing to be "the original discoverer of the principle of applying the power of steam for the purposes of navigation," asked for exclusive rights to his invention of a steamboat. Similar assertions were made in petitions submitted by John Stevens and James Rumsey. Samuel Briggs of Philadelphia prayed that "an exclusive privilege may be granted him for a limited time, to construct and vend a machine which he has invented for making nails by mill-work." Christopher Colles of New York asked protection for an invention for counting "the number of revolutions or vibrations of any wheel or other part of any mechanical engine or machine." Aaron Putnam of Medford, Massachusetts, wanted exclusive privilege for an improved method of distilling. Jacob Isacks of Newport, Rhode Island, petitioned that "some adequate reward or gratuity may be made for the discovery of an art or secret which petitioner possesses of converting salt water into fresh." John Macpherson wanted an exclusive privilege "to make and vend lightning rods, upon an improved construction; also, conductors and umbrellas, upon a model which he has invented, making them certain preservers from lightning."

The Baptist Stonington Association prayed that Congress "will adopt measures to prevent the publication of any inaccurate editions of the holy bible." Likewise, the Congregational clergy of Massachusetts asked that Congress take such measures "as in their wisdom may be thought proper, to secure the public from impositions by inaccurate editions of the holy scriptures."

A petition from some citizens of the United States being held captive in Algiers asked "the interposition of Congress in their behalf, and that effectual measure may be adopted for liberating them from slavery, and restoring them to their country."

Mary Katherine Goddard, superseded by a man after fourteen years of faithful service as keeper of the post office at Baltimore, prayed the Senate for redress after a petition signed by more than two hundred of the leading citizens of Baltimore had failed to sway Postmaster General Samuel Osgood.

A memorial was presented from citizens of the states of New Jersey and Pennsylvania "praying that the future Seat of Government might be established on the Banks of the Delaware, and proposing a cession of a tract of land ten miles square." Similar prayers came from the inhabitants of Carlisle, Lancaster, York, Reading, and Germantown, Pennsylvania. The citizens of Baltimore submitted a petition declaring their town "to be exceedingly commodious and eligible for the permanent seat of government of the United States."

Very many of the petitions came from disabled Revolutionary War soldiers, their distressed widows, and orphaned children. Others involved compensation for wartime services or losses to the enemy. Certain citizens of Westchester County, New York, for instance, asked to be reimbursed "for considerable quantities of wheat, rye, corn, oats and hay, cattle, sheep and hogs, which were taken from them during the late war, for the use of the army." Tristram Coffin of Nantucket prayed for compensation for the loss of a schooner burned by the British. Joseph Henry asked for payment for the "wood furnished the British prisoners at Winchester." Christian Knipe called for "payment for a wagon impressed into the service of the United States during the late war."

Altogether, memorials and petitions took up a substantial amount of the Congress's time. Many were tabled. Some of them, referred to the appropriate department secretary for a report, came back to be debated and voted upon. A number were carried over to be acted upon by future Congresses. Still others never came to resolution. Those, however, that were a reflection of public concerns often had an impact upon legislation.

Disabled veteran Albert Roux presented his memorial to Congress on January 26, 1791. National Archives, Washington, D.C.

"ADDRESS OF THE
PEOPLE CALLED QUAKERS"

In February of 1790 the House of Representatives was thrown into an uproar by several petitions submitted by the Quakers, and one signed by Benjamin Franklin on behalf of the Pennsylvania Society for the Abolition of Slavery. The Quakers meant, as archivist and former Postmaster General Ebenezer Hazard later explained, "no more than to request Congress to lay the African Trade under such Restrictions as the Constitution allowed." However, "one of the Petitions mentioned *Abolition,* & this alarmed the Southern Members, & excited violent opposition."

William Loughton Smith and his South Carolina colleagues Thomas Tudor Tucker and Aedanus Burke, as well as James Jackson of Georgia, were immediately on their feet. "We protested in the strongest terms against even committing them because the prayer was unconstitutional." In a jab at Benjamin Franklin, Tucker observed that he was surprised to see such a memorial "signed by a man who ought to have known the Constitution better."

For his part, Elias Boudinot expressed surprise at the argument "that the Quakers have no right to interfere in this business . . . after it has been so lately contended, and settled that the people have a right to assemble and petition for redress of grievances." Said Boudinot, who had a large Quaker constituency, "It is not because the petition comes from the Society of Quakers that I am in favor of the commitment, but because it comes from citizens of the United States, who are as equally concerned in the welfare and happiness of their country as others."

By a vote of 43 to 14 the memorials were referred to a special committee, whose report affirmed that Congress had the right to lay a tax or duty of no more than ten dollars on every slave imported, and also the authority "(so far as it is or may be carried on by Citizens of the United States for supplying foreigners) to regulate the African Trade, and to make provision for the humane treatment of Slaves." The report concluded "that the Memorialists be informed that in all cases, to which the authority of Congress extends, they will exercise it for the humane objects of the Memorialists."

An acrimonious debate ensued, with some members speaking for up to three hours. Fisher Ames of Massachusetts related, *Language low, indecent and profane has been used; wit equally stale and wretched has been attempted. . . . The southern gentry have been guided by their hot tempers, and stubborn prejudices and pride in regard to southern importance and negro slavery; but I suspect the wish to appear in the eyes of their own people, champions for their black property, is influential—*

To the President, Senate, and House of Representatives of the United States.——

The Address of the People called Quakers in their annual Assembly convened.——

Firmly believing that unfeigned righteousness in public as well as private stations is the only sure ground of hope for the divine blessing, whence alone rulers can derive true honour, establish sincere confidence in the hearts of the people, and feeling their minds animated with the ennobling principle of universal good will to men, find a conscious dignity and felicity in the harmony and success attending the exercise of a solid uniform virtue; short of which the warmest pretensions to public spirit, zeal for our country, and the rights of men, are fallacious and illusive.——

Under this persuasion as professors of faith in that ever blessed all perfect Lawgiver, whose injunction remains of undiminished obligation on all who profess to believe in him; "whatsoever ye would that men should do unto you, do ye even so unto them," we apprehend ourselves religiously bound to request your serious christian attention to the deeply interesting subject whereon our religious society in their annual assembly in the Tenth month 1783, addressed the then Congress, who, though the christian rectitude of the concern, was by the Delegates generally acknowledged, yet, not being vested with the powers of legislation, they declined promoting any public remedy against the gross national iniquity of trafficking in the persons of fellowmen; but divers of the legislative bodies of the different states on this continent, have since manifested their sense of the public detestation due to the licentious wickedness of the African trade for slaves, and the inhuman tyranny and blood guiltiness inseparable from it; the debasing influence whereof most certainly tends to lay waste the virtue, and of course the happiness of the people.——

Many are the enormities abhorrent to common humanity and common honesty, which under the faederal countenance given to

this

an election this year makes it the more probable.

William Loughton Smith, recounting the scene to the influential Charleston legislator Edward Rutledge, wrote, *The galleries were thronged with the Quakers who had presented the Petitions — they had the impudence to express a wish to be admitted within the house, but were told it would not be granted. Their appearance had a manifest influence on those members who apprehended the loss of their Election if they displeased the Quakers who vote* [as a bloc] *by System.* Smith told his colleagues, "We took each other, with our mutual bad habits and respective evils, for better, for worse; the Northern States adopted us with our slaves, and we adopted them with their Quakers."

Aedanus Burke, pointing to the audience, protested that "the men in the gallery had come there to meddle in a business with which they had nothing to do; they were volunteering in the cause of others, who neither expected nor desired it."

Elias Boudinot of New Jersey, Thomas Scott of Pennsylvania, John Vining of Delaware, and Elbridge Gerry of Massachusetts sprang to the defense of the Quakers and, according to press reports, "advocated the cause of the memorialists, and vindicated their characters, with great ability, eloquence, and liberality."

William Maclay looked in on the debate and declared, "The house have certainly greatly debased their dignity, using base invective indecorous language, 3 or 4 up at a time, manifest signs of passion, the most disorderly Wandering, in their Speeches, telling Stories, private anecdotes &ca."

"For ten days past," noted George Thatcher of Massachusetts on March 21, "the house of representatives, in Congress, have suspended all business, merely to attend to the Ravings of the South Carolina & Georgia Delegates, in attempting to prove the Lawfullness and good policy of Slavery." He added, "A stranger would be led to imagine that Slavery is the only sacred thing in the United States — whilst Religion, Law & Liberty are only of consequence as they are made subservient to the establishment of the most odious Slavery & despotism."

The committee of the whole house amended the report to declare "that the migration or importation of such persons as any of the States now existing shall think proper to admit, cannot be prohibited by Congress, prior to the Year one thousand eight hundred and eight." It was further stated "that Congress have no authority to interfere in the emancipation of Slaves, or in the treatment of them within any of the States, it remaining with the several States alone to provide any Regulations therein, which humanity and true policy may require."

Memorial "In behalf of the Yearly Meeting for Pennsylvania, New Jersey, Delaware, and the Western parts of Maryland and Virginia." National Archives, Washington, D.C.

DAVID RAMSAY
1749–1815

Dr. David Ramsay of Charleston, South Carolina, who had been defeated by William Loughton Smith in the congressional elections, petitioned the House of Representatives on April 15, 1789, to investigate Smith's eligibility to serve. It was Ramsay's contention that Smith had not been a citizen of the United States for seven years at the time of his election.

The petition, presented by Thomas Tudor Tucker, was referred to the committee on elections, which considered the evidence. On May 22, 1789, with only Massachusetts Antifederalist Jonathan Grout dissenting, the House of Representatives voted 36 to 1 that Smith was eligible to retain his seat.

Ramsay submitted a second petition, also on April 15, "Praying for the sole and exclusive right of vending in the United States" his *History of the Revolution of South Carolina from a British Province to an Independent State* and his forthcoming *History of the American Revolution*. This was submitted to a committee consisting of Tucker of South Carolina, Alexander White of Virginia, and Benjamin Huntington of Connecticut. Five days later the report was made, and after a debate the House ordered that a bill or bills be brought in, "making a general provision for securing to authors and inventors the exclusive right of their respective writings and discoveries." Huntington, Lambert Cadwalader of New Jersey, and Benjamin Contee of Maryland were given the assignment. The bill was presented on June 23 and considered by the committee of the whole House on August 17. Final passage of a copyright act, however, was postponed until the second session of the Congress.

Dr. Ramsay, connected to the Peale family though his brother Nathaniel's marriage to Charles Willson Peale's sister, was among those who sat to Rembrandt Peale during the seventeen-year-old artist's painting foray into South Carolina.

David Ramsay by Rembrandt Peale (1778–1860); oil on canvas, circa 1795–1796. The Gibbes Art Gallery, Carolina Art Association, Charleston, South Carolina

JEDIDIAH MORSE
1761–1826

On May 12, 1789, Jedidiah Morse, a Congregational clergyman from Connecticut who had authored *Geography Made Easy*, the first geography to be published in the United States, submitted a memorial praying that the Congress "pass such a General or particular Law as shall secure to him the exclusive benefit that may arise" from publication of his new book, *The American Geography, or A View of the Present Situation of the United States of America.*

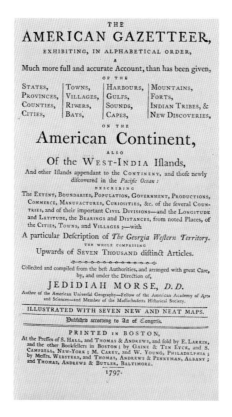

Quick to take advantage of the copyright law, Jedidiah Morse published several popular texts on American geography, including *The American Gazetteer.*
The Library Company of Philadelphia, Pennsylvania

Jedidiah Morse by Samuel Finley Breese Morse (1791–1827); oil on panel, circa 1810. Yale University Art Gallery, New Haven, Connecticut; gift of Miss Helen E. Carpenter

Morse affirmed that he had *with much labour & expense, & wholly at his own Risque, Compiled & published, a Geographical political & historical Treatise of the United States, entitled "The American Geography, or A View of the present Situation of the United States of America," embellished by two original maps, one of which was purchased by your Petitioner of the Compiler for a large sum of money,* and pointed out that "provision is made in the 4th section of the first Article of the Constitution of the United States, for Securing to Authors the exclusive right to their respective Writings." He expressed the hope that "Should a Statute or law be passed, it might be so Expressed as effectually to secure your Petitioner against all mutilations, alterations & abridgments of Sd book & maps, as may operate to his injury."

Congress on May 31, 1790, passed a copyright act, which provided the authors and proprietors of maps, charts, and books with protection for fourteen years and the privilege of renewal for an equal time thereafter.

The portrait of Morse was executed by his son Samuel who, against his father's advice, had adopted art as a profession.

FREDERICK WILLIAM AUGUSTUS BARON VON STEUBEN
1730–1794

No personal petition engendered more controversy than did Baron von Steuben's claim for his wartime services. In 1777, when he came to America from Prussia, Steuben entered into an agreement with the Continental Congress that he would seek no compensation if the British proved victorious. But if America prevailed, he would expect "such compensation as Congress would grant." Steuben, who had drawn some $26,000 from the Treasury on orders from the old Congress, submitted his memorial for additional payment to both houses of Congress on August 25, 1789.

Two weeks after Alexander Hamilton was appointed to head the Treasury Department, the House of Representatives resolved to refer the memorial to him. On March 29, 1790, Hamilton — long a champion of the Baron — recommended a sum of $7,396 to cover Steuben's debts and further to grant him an annuity for life. The House passed a bill on May 10 granting Steuben $7,000 and an annuity of $2,000.

Frederick William Augustus, Baron von Steuben, by Charles Willson Peale (1741–1827); oil on canvas, 1780. The Pennsylvania Academy of the Fine Arts, Philadelphia

"All appeared to be of opinion that he had rendered great Services to the United States by introducing discipline & oeconomy into the Army and therefore were willing to provide for his comfortable Support for the remainder of life," commented Roger Sherman on May 12, "but it was thought by a number of the members that the United States were not indebted to him by contract, and that a less annuity would have been Sufficient."

So, too, thought the Senate committee headed by William Maclay, which reduced the annuity to $1,000; but the full Senate, by a vote of 16 to 8, rejected the committee recommendation. A motion to raise the sum back to $2,000 resulted in a tie vote. Next, a motion was made to strike out the $7,000, and again the vote was even. In both instances the Vice-President decided the matter in the Baron's favor. Wrote Maclay in disgust, "Bonny Johnney Adams took uncommon pains, to bias Us without effect. I voted uniformly against allowing him [Steuben] one farthing, as I was convinced nothing was due to him." Those opposing the higher sums were the six New England Senators, the New Jersey and North Carolina contingents, William Few of Georgia, and Maclay of Pennsylvania. Maclay was indignant. "The World turned upside down only could Justify the determinations. But the Cabals of the Secretary [Hamilton] were successful, and the Baron's bill was triumphant."

Finally, agreement was reached to eliminate the outright payment but to raise the annuity by $500 to $2,500. The House accepted the Senate's amendments, and the act was approved by the President on June 4, 1790.

Friends of George Thatcher made haste to dispel rumors that he had voted for the Steuben pension. A correspondent told the *Cumberland Gazette* on January 24, 1791, "The publick may rest assured that Mr. Thatcher was opposed to the Steuben pension, in every stage of it." He had only voted to commit the report to a committee "to save the feelings of the Barron," and "this was supposed to be the most easy and delicate mode of getting rid of the business."

"I shall not be disappointed or displeased if the annuity given to the Baron should excite general disgust," wrote Paine Wingate. "I think it is an inexcusable abuse of the public money." He declared, "I hope the conduct of this business will be generally known and not soon forgotten."

Criticism in the press was forthcoming. A satirical card from a "distressed officer," addressed to the House committee that recommended the Steuben pension — Jeremiah Wadsworth, Elbridge Gerry, William Loughton Smith, and John Vining — *begs to interest the same feelings and eloquence, which they lately exercised in Congress in behalf of Baron Steuben, in his favor. He served his country faithfully for seven years during the late war. A year after the peace he sold his certificates for 3/9 in the pound, to pay some debts he contracted for the support of his family. He now humbly solicits the charity of a few dollars to pay his house-rent. The honor of Congress he conceives is concerned in relieving his wants, for they never can suffer one of those men, to whom they owe the existence of the government, from which they derive their power and consequence, to end his days in a gaol, or a poor house.* The writer concluded, *Will the man whose family is beggared by the loan of his money to the public, or will the soldier, who is now compelled to labour twenty-four hours to earn half a dollar, consent to pay their proportion of compensations so manifestly partial and unjust?*

One who signed himself "A Republican" pointed out that, of the inhabitants required to contribute to the Baron's $2,500 a year, "not one third are individually possessed of as much property as this pensioner receives annually."

With the funding and assumption bills still in abeyance, a letter published in *Freeman's Journal* of July 21, 1790, asked, *Is not every man who has furnished the public with property, entitled to his stipulated reward? And can Congress, without a blush, shut their ears against one class of creditors and extend relief to another? If the public are unable to perform* all *their contracts, they should give no preference.* The piece went on, *But the Baron Steuben rendered us most signal services — so have many others. But he has beggared himself in the American cause — so have thousands of others. But Congress made him the most positive and unequivocal promises of an adequate reward — so have they to every individual to whom they were indebted. But humanity and compassion would induce Congress to relieve him from his necessities. And is he* alone *the object of their humanity? Where is the whole class of public creditors who lent their property or afforded their services to the United States?*

In the spring of 1780, while Baron Steuben was in Philadelphia as military adviser to Congress, he commissioned Charles Willson Peale to paint his portrait. The artist, who charged his sitter ten guineas, noted on July 27 that the likeness "is now highly approved of, or I am most egregiously flattered." Suspended from a ribbon around the Baron's neck is the medal of the House Order of Fidelity, which he had received from Margraf Karl Friedrich of Baden. The star of the same order is displayed on his coat.

CATHARINE LITTLEFIELD
GREENE MILLER
1755–1814

During the war years, Mrs. Nathanael Greene had joined her husband at winter encampments, where she became General Washington's favorite dancing partner — upon one occasion the two danced "upwards of three hours without once sitting down." Now the pretty, sprightly Kitty Greene had fallen upon hard times. General Greene had died in 1786,

leaving her with four small children and a mountain of debts. Her petition to Congress, submitted on March 5, 1790, sought that Congress indemnify the Greene estate for the indebtedness that her husband had incurred when he stood surety for the bankrupt contractor whom he had engaged to supply his army. Her petition was referred to the secretary of the treasury.

"I Should have written You some time Since," Mrs. Greene wrote to Alexander Hamilton from her Georgia plantation on January 26, 1791, "but a dangerous fit of Illness has prevented Me and I am Still too weak to write more than Just to intimate my Wishes, that You may loose no time in bringing my affair before Congress." She went on, "I will only say that my independance, and of course happiness entirely depend on the Justice which Congress may please to do me. I pray You therefore my Dear good friend to *Report*."

Hamilton replied on March 8, "But my dear friend, I love you too well not to be very candid with you. I am afraid my report will not promote your interest." He explained that it appeared that General Greene had "stepped aside from the *authorised path*" without giving proper notification and the reasons for so doing. Hamilton said as much in his report but went on to add, *How far, the peculiar merit of the officer, or the peculiar hardship and misfortune of the case, may render advisable a deviation from that rule, are points, which the Secretary begs leave to submit, without observation, to the contemplation of legislative discretion.*

The secretary's report was considered by the committee of the whole House. But despite Mrs. Greene's many friends in the Congress, particularly Jeremiah Wadsworth of Connecticut, who was executor of her husband's estate, there was no resolution. Five times between 1790 and 1800 would Mrs. Greene renew her petition, but her claim was never satisfied. In the forefront of those resistant to her claim was Thomas Sumter of South Carolina, who maintained that General Greene should have applied instead to the state government for funds to maintain his troops, and furthermore that the general had been amply compensated through handsome grants awarded him by North Carolina, South Carolina, and Georgia.

"Gen. Greene's Case has been frequently before us," wrote William Loughton Smith on March 24, 1792, *but there is such persevering opposition to it & the members so nearly divided that the friends of the measure can't venture to take a final question without first counting noses, & the absence of one or two members or some other circumstance delays it from time to time.*

Mrs. Greene is shown here in her second widowhood, the portrait having been painted sometime between the death of her second husband, Phineas Miller, in 1803 and her own death in 1814.

Catharine Littlefield Greene Miller attributed to James Frothingham (1786–1864); oil on panel, circa 1803–1814. Museum Purchase. In the collection of the Telfair Academy of Arts and Sciences, Savannah, Georgia

JOHN FREDERICK
AMELUNG'S GLASSWORKS

John Frederick Amelung, coming from Germany in 1784, had established a glassworks at New Bremen, near Frederick, Maryland. On May 26, 1790, Amelung petitioned the Congress for financial help, explaining that losses sustained from a fire and other difficulties — the unforeseen high price of grain, the small demand for glass, the problems of collecting outstanding debts when cash had become so scarce — threatened the survival of his operation. "The Works, which bid fair to become of great and lasting Utility to the United States, are in danger of being rendered totally useless." It was pointed out that "between four and five hundred people now employed by him look up to him for their daily subsistence," and he begged leave "to solicit the Aid of the Government of the United States in this important Undertaking, either by granting him a loan of Money, upon the most undoubted and unequivocal Security, or by such other Means, as Congress in their Wisdom may see fit."

The petition was referred to a committee consisting of Daniel Carroll and George Gale of Maryland, Daniel Hiester of Pennsylvania, John Vining of Delaware, and Elias Boudinot of New Jersey. On June 2 the committee reported that they were of the opinion, "that a manufactory attended with so much difficulty in its commencement, so important in its' consequences to the United States, and of such general utility to the whole Union, ought to receive the assistance and protection of the United States." They recommended that a loan not to exceed eight thousand dollars be authorized. On June 3, when the report was debated, William Loughton Smith and Roger Sherman expressed doubts about the "Constitutional powers of Congress to loan money" and warned about establishing a precedent. A vote was taken, and the committee report was "disagreed to."

Case bottle made at the glass manufactory of New Bremen, Maryland, 1788. Division of Ceramics and Glass, National Museum of American History, Smithsonian Institution.

THE SECOND SESSION
JANUARY 4 TO AUGUST 12, 1790

"The Report of Mr. Hamilton"

During its "dreadful" — as Fisher Ames characterized it — second session, Congress came to grips with the two great divisive issues of its tenure: the management of the public debt and the location of the capital. "The business before them is a Herculian Labour," Abigail Adams commented. "The members of different states think so widely from each other that it is difficult to accommodate their interests to each other. What one member esteems the pillar the bulwark of the Constitution another considers as the ruin of his state."

On January 14, 1790, in keeping with his instructions, the secretary of the treasury submitted his report for the support of public credit. Alexander Hamilton proposed first of all that the debt be paid off via a long-term funding plan — a practice that had provided the British empire with liquid capital for the stimulation of business and industry — but a notion that went against the grain of those who felt that debt should be paid off entirely as quickly as possible. William Maclay, stunned by the secretary's report, exclaimed, "I feel so struck of an heap, I can make no remark on the Matter." Once he had recovered himself, the Pennsylvanian protested, "With all our Western Lands for Sale & purchasers every day attending at the Hall begging for Contracts. What Villany to Cast the debt on Posterity."

"Congress is daily engaged on the Report of Mr. Hamilton," wrote Aedanus Burke of South Carolina on March 3. *I know no man in either house, who is not totally at a Loss on this important subject. Funding the Debt is the Word at present, but no one can tell wh. way it will end. Funding the Debt may, or may not be, a blessing, or a curse to the people of America, for ought I dare say, at present.*

But the funding of the continental debt was not the half of it. Far more controversial was the secretary's proposal that the debts of the states — occasioned by the war for independence — be assumed by the national government and funded as part of the federal debt. All public creditors would be paid the specie value of their holdings.

Pronounced William Maclay, "The Secretarys People Scarce disguise their design, Which is to create a Mass of debt, which will Justify them in seizing all the Sources of Government, thus annihilating the State legislatures, and erecting an Empire on the Basis of Consolidation."

The various certificates of indebtedness — issued to supply and pay the army — had, to a very great extent, changed hands over the years as many

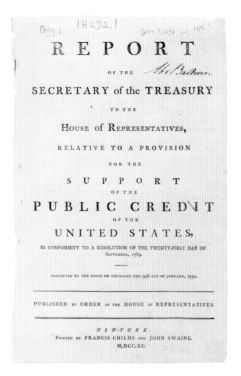

REPORT

OF THE *Mr. Baldwin*

SECRETARY of the TREASURY

TO THE

House of Representatives,

RELATIVE TO A PROVISION

FOR THE

SUPPORT

OF THE

PUBLIC CREDIT

OF THE

UNITED STATES,

IN CONFORMITY TO A RESOLUTION OF THE TWENTY-FIRST DAY OF
September, 1789.

PRESENTED TO THE HOUSE ON THURSDAY THE 14th DAY OF JANUARY, 1790.

PUBLISHED BY ORDER OF THE HOUSE OF REPRESENTATIVES.

NEW-YORK:
Printed by FRANCIS CHILDS AND JOHN SWAINE.
M,DCC,XC.

"The report of the Secretary of the Treasury has set curiosity in motion," wrote Fisher Ames on January 17, 1790. "It is allowed to be a masterly performance—is very long—is ordered to be printed." The Massachusetts Congressman explained, "The state debts are proposed to be assumed, and all the debts, except foreign, reloaned at four per cent. It is not to be presumed that any system, especially one so complex and important, can pass without great debate."

This copy of Alexander Hamilton's first report on the public credit, dated 1790, is inscribed with the name of Abraham Baldwin, the Representative from Georgia.

Rare Book and Special Collections Division, Library of Congress, Washington, D.C.

farmers and soldiers sold their holdings to speculators at a fraction of their face value. Once details of the secretary's plan became known, William Maclay recorded, "The speculation in certificates is in the mouth of every one." James Jackson of Georgia protested, "Since this report has been read in this House a spirit of havoc, speculation and ruin, has arisen, and been cherished by people who had an access to the information the report contained." Jackson bellowed, "My soul rises indignant at the avaricious and immoral turpitude which so vile a conduct displays."

Benjamin Hawkins of North Carolina, arriving to take his seat in the Senate on January 13, told William Maclay that "as he came up he passed two expresses with very large sums of money on their way for North Carolina, for the purpose of Speculation in certificates." Maclay also heard that Congress-

171

The Continental Congress in 1780 asked the states to assume responsibility for providing back pay for their Continental army regiments and for augmenting previous payments made in depreciated currency. To settle with their troops, the states issued certificates that by the end of the war represented the largest part of the states' debts.

Warrant for military pay on the state of Connecticut, December 24, 1783. National Numismatic Collection, National Museum of American History, Smithsonian Institution, Washington, D.C.

By coincidence, this fine surviving example of a loan office certificate has been made out to James Wadsworth, Jeremiah Wadsworth's Antifederalist cousin.
National Numismatic Collection, National Museum of American History, Smithsonian Institution, Washington, D.C.

Dear Brother

We are warmly Engaged about dis
-crimination. and how it will termi
-nate I know not— But I believe
it will be found— Just— and—
Impracticable. I am tolerably well and Frederich is very
well —

I am yr. aff.

M. J. Stone
Febuy— 17th 1790

James Madison's scheme for discriminating between original and subsequent holders of debt certificates astonished many of his colleagues and provoked questions and soul-searching debate among them, as Maryland Representative Michael Jenifer Stone noted.

Michael Jenifer Stone to "Dear Brother," February 17, 1790. William Briscoe Stone Papers, Manuscript Department, Duke University Library, Durham, North Carolina

man Jeremiah Wadsworth "has sent off Two small Vessels for the Southern States, on the Errand of buying up certificates." Abraham Baldwin noted, "packets are sent everywhere to buy state certificates." Maclay calculated that speculators were likely to make a profit of 300 percent.

Dismayed by the frenzied speculation, James Madison decided upon a radical course. "Mr. Madison made a strange Motion on Thursday," Thomas Hartley of Pennsylvania wrote on February 14, "which he inforced with a Speech of one hour and three Quarters length of the finest Language I almost ever heard." To the surprise of many of his colleagues, Madison proposed that a discrimination be made between original and subsequent holders of certificates. "To adopt his ideas," declared Theodore Sedgwick of Massachusetts, "would be a most violent breach of public faith, and would be impracticable in execution." Abraham Baldwin of Georgia called Madison's plan "a fanciful idea . . . a wild-goose scheme for so good and so sensible a man."

But General Peter Muhlenberg, a Representative from Pennsylvania, in describing nine subjects for John Trumbull to paint as part of his series on the history of the American Revolution, suggested that the artist portray "Mr. M–d — n pleading the cause of Justice and Humanity in Congress, an angel whispering in his ear, and a group of widows, orphans & decrepid soldiers,

173

contemplating him with ineffable delight."

What was particularly astonishing to his colleagues was that Madison had been the author of a resolution passed by the Continental Congress in 1783, which pledged that there would be no discrimination between original and later holders of public certificates. Challenged to explain why he now took ground so entirely different, he responded, "Until indeed the subject came close into view & the sacrifice of the soldiers was brought home to reflection, he had not sufficiently scanned and felt the magnitude of the evil."

William Maclay called on Madison at his lodgings and "told him plainly there was no chance of his Succeeding. It hurt his *Littleness*. I do not think he believed me." Maclay thereupon read resolutions he had drawn up — a scheme that included opening a land office for the sale of western lands to be paid for with debt certificates, but he continued, "I do not think he attended to one Word of them, so much did he seem absorbed in his own Ideas." Maclay attempted to hand Madison the resolutions, but "he offered them back without reading them. . . . His pride seems of that kind which repels all communication. He appears as if he could not bear the Condescention of it."

In the House of Representatives, reported Henry Wynkoop of Pennsylvania, the principal advocates for Madison's proposal were Richard Bland Lee and Alexander White of Virginia, as well as James Jackson of Georgia. Those in vigorous dissent were Fisher Ames of Massachusetts, Thomas Hartley of Pennsylvania, John Laurance and Egbert Benson of New York, Elias Boudinot of New Jersey, and Jeremiah Wadsworth of Connecticut.

Responding to lamentations from New Hampshire about the injustice of paying full value to those who bought certificates from the soldiers at the rate of two shillings and six pence on the pound, Abiel Foster shot back, *Where is the injustice in this case? Was not this the understanding between the parties at the time of the contract? Did not the seller obtain the market price? And did he not chuse to take this, rather than run the risque of keeping his security longer? And was there no hazzard to the purchaser, of loosing the whole of the purchase Money?*

Elbridge Gerry stood up to say that the speculators had performed a valuable function by keeping up the price of government securities. "But if their only crime is good fortune in their negotiations, if they have purchased the securities on the open market and honestly paid for them, treat them as good citizens, acquit them of fraud, and do them justice." Gerry himself was a large security holder, but he dissembled, "Being among those original holders who have transferred part of their certificates, and not replaced them, I can feel for myself as well as our brave soldiers."

The debate on discrimination aroused so much interest that for the first time ladies made an appearance in the gallery. Abigail Adams, along with Ruth Dalton, wife of the Senator from Massachusetts, and Sarah Jay, the wife of the Chief Justice, were present on February 21. Abigail Adams reported to her sister, *Mr. Smith of SC who married a Daughter of Mr Izard, is one of the first from that State, & I might add from the Southern States. Mr. Ames from our State & Mr. Sedgwick and Mr. Gerry are all right upon this Question & make a conspicuous figure in the Debates.* James Madison, she declared, "leads the Virginians like a flock of sheep."

William Maclay also looked in at the House proceedings and observed that Theodore Sedgwick, John Laurance, William Loughton Smith, and Fisher Ames "seemed to aim all at One point to make Madison ridiculous."

"The Proposition of Mr Madison on Discrimination has received a very lengthly, candid & dispassionate Discussion," Jonathan Trumbull of Connecticut wrote on March 20. Madison's proposal had been defeated by a vote of more than two-thirds of the House, and considering this great majority and the wide dissemination of this question in the newspapers, Trumbull hoped that "the public Mind will be quieted on the subject & that the immediate Sufferers will consider the Sacrifice as one part of the price of those Blessings which we have in prospect."

Richard Bassett of Delaware, advising George Read of the outcome of the vote in the House of Representatives, noted that their friend Madison *must be a little mortified thereat, as he labored the point in a most masterly manner, and appeared to have it much at heart, and I must own, in my poor opinion, had reason, justice, and every sentiment on his side, which ought to have acted as a stimulus to have induced a different decision.*

Although Hamilton and his "gladiators," as Maclay dubbed the secretary's supporters, achieved easy victory on the state discrimination motion, the

Continental loan certificate dated December 28, 1782, bearing 6 percent interest. National Numismatic Collection, National Museum of American History, Smithsonian Institution, Washington, D.C.

resistance to assumption of the state debts was unyielding. From the first, Theodore Sedgwick accurately predicted that opposition would come from those members "belonging to states whose debts are comparatively small & those who fear an excess of power in the national government." Particularly he had reference to Virginia, where great strides had been made in paying off the wartime debt, and whose citizens—not to mention political leadership—feared that the national government would be given the excuse for levying taxes that would infringe upon state powers of the purse.

It was on the question of assumption that James Madison came into decided conflict with the administration. In May, after Madison made a long speech against assumption, Fisher Ames reported, "He speaks of the assumption as increasing & perpetuating the *evil* of a debt. The word *evil* is always in his mouth when he speaks of our debt. He affirms that without assuming the debt may be paid more easily & speedily."

Theodore Sedgwick declared that Madison had become "an apostate from all former principles." Sedgwick went on in a private letter, *Whether he is really a convert to antifederalism — whether he is actuated by the mean and base motives of acquiring popularity in his own State that he may fill the place of Senator which will probably be soon vacant by the death of Grayson, or whether he means to put himself at the head of the discontented in America time will discover. The last, however, I do not suppose, because I have ever considered him as a very timid man.*

The Massachusetts delegation, with the exception of Antifederalist Jonathan Grout — and even he was eventually brought around — felt that assumption was vital to the continuation of the nation. "As our Debt is the largest in the Union," wrote Senator Caleb Strong, "and a considerable part of it was conceived for Services which tho' designed for the General Benefit, the Continent has been backward to recognize, perhaps the Measure will be as agreeable to . . . Massachusetts as to any of the States." It might also be added that in the wake of the 1786 revolt of the taxpayers, led by Daniel Shays and others, Massachusetts had no realistic possibility of raising revenues to pay off her state creditors.

Delegates from South Carolina, another state with a large unpaid debt, were strenuously in favor of assumption. The laggards from the back country were in time brought up smartly by the state legislature.

Connecticut likewise favored assumption. In the New York delegation, Hamilton's close associates — Senators Rufus King and Philip Schuyler and Representatives Egbert Benson and John Laurance — were strong supporters, as was Elias Boudinot of New Jersey.

Along with Virginia, Maryland and Georgia were fervent in resistance and would soon be reinforced by delegates from North Carolina.

Pivotal was Pennsylvania, where financial interests and public opinion were divided on the merits of assumption. That state was, opined Pierce Butler on April 23, 1790, "looking on to avail herself of an opportunity, by throwing

Typical of many original certificate holders was one George Garland, who was owed money for his service as a sail and tent maker.

National Numismatic Collection, National Museum of American History, Smithsonian Institution, Washington, D.C.

herself into either scale, to get Congress to Philadelphia."

William Maclay recorded that, when the Pennsylvania delegation met to consult on the adoption of the state debts, Robert Morris swore, "By G— it must be done!" George Clymer "expatiated on the growing Grandeur of Pennsylvania if it was done. Our Roads would be all made And our Communication all opened by land and water &c." Thomas Hartley warned that if the debts of the states were not assumed, "New England and [South] Carolina will fly off, and the Secretary's System is ruined." It was clear to Maclay which way the wind was blowing when Frederick Muhlenberg came back from the President's levee saying, *the State debts must be adopted. This I suppose, is the language of the court.*"

But the Pennsylvania delegation remained uncertain. Frederick Muhlenberg felt inclined to oppose it. Thomas Scott of western Pennsylvania was decidedly against it. Thomas Hartley, William Maclay shrugged, "is too giddy and unsettled for any One to determine how he will Vote, and, as his Judgment has no share in it the Presumption is that he will vote with Smith, of Carolina and those whose company he always keeps." George Clymer, Maclay reported, "had a proposal, to barter away the Pennsylvania Votes for an Assumption, for the Carolina & Massachusetts Votes for an adjournment to Philada."

On April 12 assumption was rejected by a committee of the whole House of Representatives with a vote of 31 to 29. Theodore Sedgwick could not contain his indignation. He stood up to say that the people of Massachusetts "have

177

demanded justice; we have implored the compassion of the Representatives of the people of America, to relieve us from the pressure of intolerable burdens; burdens incurred in support of your freedom and independence."

William Maclay gave full vent to his vein of sarcasm: *Sedgwick from Boston pronounced a funeral Oration over it. He was called to order, some confusion ensued. He took his hat & went out. When he returned his Visage to me bore the visible marks of Weeping. Fitzsimons reddened like Scarlet. His Eyes were brimful. Clymer's color always pale now verged to a deadly White. His lips quavered, and his neither Jaw shook with convulsive Motions. His head, neck & breast consented to Gesticulations resembling those of a Turkey or Goose, nearly strangled in the Act of deglutition. Benson bungled like a Shoemaker who had lost his End. Ames's aspect was truly hippocratic, a total change of face & feature. He sat torpid as if his faculties had been benumbed. Gerry exhibited the advantages of a cadaverous appearance. At all times Palid, and far from pleasing, he ran no risk of deterioration. Thro' an interruption of Hectic hems and consumptive coughs he delivered himself of a declaration, That the Delegates of Massachusetts would proceed no further, but write to their State for instructions. Happy Impudence sat enthroned on Lawrence's brow. He rose in puffing pomp, and moved that the Committee should rise, And Assigned the agitation of the House as a Reason. Wadsworth hid his Grief Under the rim of a round hat. Boudinot's wrinkles rose into ridges and the angles of his mouth were depressed, and their apperture assumed a curve resembling an horse Shoe.*

Assumption was too crucial a matter to be given up. "The debate on the assumption of state debts has been almost infinite," Abraham Baldwin wrote to his brother-in-law Joel Barlow on May 6. "The N Carolina members turned the scale against it, but they are still trying to cook the dish so as to make it more palatable, and intend to bring it forward again."

In June of 1790 New York was visited by an influenza epidemic. Richard Henry Lee was felled, and President Washington was reduced to a dangerous state. "We hear that Colo Bland is very ill," wrote Spotsylvania County Federalist John Dawson to James Madison. "Should he live I am realy apprehensive that he would not be reelected, there is such a clamour raisd against him because he voted in favour of this assumption." The Antifederalist from Virginia had declared for the assumption as "a demonstration to the World that our present Constitution aimed directly at consolidation, and the sooner every body knew it the better." Bland died on the first day of the month, further diminishing the chances for assumption. Bland's vote would also be missed by those who wished to keep the residence at New York, he being "the only gentleman from Virginia who prefers this place to Philadelphia."

In its report on the funding bill, the select committee of the Senate followed Hamilton's recommendation that 4 percent interest be paid on the government securities instead of the 6 percent originally promised by the old Congress. Robert Morris rose to protest the committee's decision. "His cholor fairly choacked him," recounted William Maclay. "He apologiz'd to the House that his agitation had deprived him of his Recollection on the Subject and he sat down." Maclay went on to say that when Morris rose again, he "mentioned his late confusion but declared it did not arise from the personal Interest he had in public Securities; That altho' he was possessed of some he was no Speculator."

The next day Maclay recorded, "Up rose Patterson with a lode of Notes before him. To follow him would be to write a pamphlet, for he was up near an hour." William Paterson contended that in justice, 3 percent or even 2 percent was as much as the holders of certificates could demand. "But what says law? — 6 per Cent." Philip Schuyler and Rufus King agreed that the 6 percent promised by the Continental Congress must be adhered to, but Oliver Ellsworth and Caleb Strong said that they could not agree to more than 4 percent. Robert Morris, among others, threatened that "if the gentlemen would not vote for six per cent, he would vote against the assumption and the whole Funding bill."

"It was seriously apprehended this morning early," wrote William Loughton Smith on July 14, *"that both assumption & funding would be thrown out altogether."* Hamilton, he reported, "was full of despondency." But as Smith and Ralph Izard approached Federal Hall, they "met Hamilton with a Smile on his countenance; he told us that a parly had taken place & that it was proposed that the *principal* of the public debt should be funded at 6 per cent, & the *interest* at 4—& the *State debts* at 4." It had been arranged "that the assumption

Massachusetts loan certificate engraved by Nathaniel Hurd in 1777.

National Numismatic Collection, National Museum of American History, Smithsonian Institution, Washington, D.C.

Indents—which derived their name from irregularly cut left-hand borders—were certificates of interest. They matched up with a receipt book kept by the government, thus protecting against counterfeiting.

National Numismatic Collection, National Museum of American History, Smithsonian Institution

should be taken up & agreed to, then the funding Bill — & then both committed to a committee of compromise." "The Assumption being carried," Smith related in a postscript dated July 17, "the funding Bill was taken up & both referred to a Committee of Compromise, viz. Butler, King, Morris, Elsworth, Strong, Read, R. H. Lee — the three first for 6 per cent — the three next for 4 — all six for the assumption; the last against the assumption." It was finally agreed that public creditors should be allowed a choice of three kinds of interest-bearing certificates — 6 percent certificates on the principal of the debt, 3 percent certificates on the arrears of interest thereon, or 6 percent certificates that would bear no interest for the first ten years.

The funding bill, with the assumption amendment attached, passed the Senate on July 21 by a vote of 14 to 12. Those voting for the bill were John Langdon of New Hampshire, Tristram Dalton and Caleb Strong of Massachusetts, William Samuel Johnson and Oliver Ellsworth of Connecticut, Rufus King and Philip Schuyler of New York, Jonathan Elmer and William Paterson of New Jersey, George Read of Delaware, Robert Morris of Pennsylvania, Charles Carroll of Maryland, and Ralph Izard and Pierce Butler of South Carolina. In opposition were Paine Wingate of New Hampshire, Theodore Foster and Joseph Stanton, Jr., of Rhode Island, Richard Bassett of Delaware, William Maclay of Pennsylvania, John Henry of Maryland, Richard Henry Lee and John Walker of Virginia, Benjamin Hawkins and Samuel Johnston of North Carolina, and William Few and James Gunn of Georgia.

In the House debate on the Senate bill only two members spoke at any great length—James Jackson, who was violently against it, and William Smith of South Carolina, who was enthusiastically in favor. Elbridge Gerry delivered a brief warning, that if the bill were postponed until the next Congress, "The Government will be in danger of convulsion — the revenue will probably be impaired or lost, and citizens attached to you will no longer be able to support your administration."

On July 26, 1790, the House of Representatives agreed to the bill by a vote of 34 to 28.

"The Act for making provision for the National debt and assuming of the State Debts was more than six Months on its passage through Congress," explained William Few of Georgia to his governor, "and in its progress assumed various shapes, and was opposed on various principles. . . . These clashing opinions were agitated in both Houses of Congress, until by a kind of compromise they produced the Act in its present form, with the assent of only a small majority of Congress."

But what Few does not here reveal is that Alexander Hamilton's financial program had carried the day only because the residence act had previously been passed. "The Assumption could never have been carried," related William Loughton Smith, *without the assistance of some new friends — Gilman and Livermore of New Hampshire have deserted us and Hartley of Pennsylvania. In lieu of these we have gained Lee and White of Virginia and Gale and Carrol of Maryland. This acquisition is the result of the Patowmac scheme — it seems there was an understanding between these gentlemen and some of the New England members that the latter would give no serious opposition to the residence bill if some of the Maryland and Virg. members would vote for the assumption.* The story unfolds in the discussion of the residence bill, which follows.

"Intrigues, cabals & combinations"

"The place of the seat of government," pronounced James Jackson of Georgia, "might be compared to the heart of the human body; it was the centre from which the principles of life were carried to the extremities, and from these it might return again with precision." In more prosaic terms, economic benefits were perceived as grandiose. "The seat of government is of great importance; if you consider the diffusion of wealth, that proceeds from this source," James Madison said in a speech of September 4, 1789. "I presume that the expenditures which will take place, where the government will be established, by them who are immediately concerned in its administration, and by others who may resort to it, will not be less than a half a million of dollars a year."

During the first session of the Congress, proposals were put forward for a permanent residence at sites on the Susquehanna River, adjacent to the falls of the Delaware at Trenton, and along the Potomac.

William Maclay had on August 25, 1789, nominated all of the places in Pennsylvania that aspired to have the seat of government: Lancaster, Wright's Ferry, Yorktown, Carlisle, Harrisburg, Reading, and Germantown. On September 8 Daniel Carroll presented a petition from the inhabitants of Georgetown, Maryland, "offering to put themselves and fortunes under the exclusive jurisdiction of Congress, in case that town should be selected as the permanent seat of the government of the United States." In mid-May both the Virginia and Maryland legislatures expressed a willingness to offer the federal government a ten-miles square that they could call their own.

Delegates from New York and New England connived to keep the government at New York until such time as a permanent capital might be built on the Susquehanna. But in the final days of the first session, Robert Morris maneuvered to have Germantown, just outside of Philadelphia, substituted for the Susquehanna, and although the House agreed, James Madison, in a hairbreadth escape, succeeded in attaching an amendment that sent the bill back to the Senate, where it was killed.

When the second session began, the question arose as to whether business left unfinished would be taken up *de novo*, that is, without regard to what had transpired during the first session. Oliver Ellsworth, wrote Maclay, "laboured long to show that this was a New Session, and concluded as the session was New Everything else should be new." And so it was decided that "the bills which had been in passage between the Two houses should be regarded as if nothing had passed in either respecting them." It was to be a fresh, although hardly straightforward or clear-cut, start for the residence bill.

As Congress, unable to reach agreement on the residence and embroiled in controversy over the management of the debt, came to a stalemate, the public made its dissatisfaction known. "The News papers, which are the mouths of the people are continually groaning with their complaints," George Thatcher observed. Dismissing objections that Congress was divided into parties, Thatcher wrote to a friend in Maine, "In this we only resemble the Christian world — they have been divided into angry parties for more than fourteen hundred years; and disputed with Gun, fire, & pamphlets about Dogmas of infinitely less consequence than the question of residence of Congress." Before the residence question was finally settled, the *New York Journal* calculated that "the yeas and nays have been taken upon it fifty times."

On May 24, 1790, Robert Morris moved that Congress should next meet in Philadelphia and was seconded by John Langdon. William Maclay remarked that "a dead pause ensued." The Vice-President asked if they were ready for the question. General Philip Schuyler of New York was quick on his feet to say that a matter of such great importance should not be decided in haste, and won a postponement.

The debate that took place on May 26 disgusted Maclay. Robert Morris, he said, *rose laughing heartily every time he got up. King laughed at him and he laughed back at King, and a number more joined in the laugh. This was truly ridiculous. Few, King & Butler rose. The amount of all they said was that a removal was inconvenient, that Philada. was not central. If we once got into it we would be accomodated in such Manner That we never could leave it &ca.* In the end the question was again postponed, and Morris withdrew his motion.

Maclay was indignant; Philadelphia's eligibility was manifest. "The Universal Consent of the Provinces before we were States and of the States since, was in favour of Philadelphia. This was veryfyed by every publick assembly Which had been called, from the Meeting of the first Congress, down to the late Meeting of the Cincinnati."

On May 31 the House of Representatives voted that the next session of the Congress should meet at Philadelphia, but in June they changed their mind and substituted Baltimore.

Back in the Senate, on June 8 Richard Henry Lee moved for a postponement of the permanent seat in order to take up a resolution for the next session being held in Philadelphia. It was, noted Maclay, a day of confusion. "Now it was That Izard flamed and Butler bounced & both seemed to rage with madness." The vote was tied, and the Vice-President voted against the postponement. "Now all was hurry and Confusion." Ralph Izard and Pierce Butler actually brought the ailing North Carolina Senator, Samuel Johnston, "with his night Cap on, out of bed, and a bed with him." Maclay went on, "The Vote was taken. We had our 11 & they had 13 against the Resolution." But all was not over. "In the Mean While a Mob and noise was about the Hall, as if it had been a fish Market. The postponed bill and the report of the Committee on it were called for." After many motions, the Senate adjourned in the face of "confusion and irregularity."

"Congress are much embarrassed by the two questions of assumption and residence," Thomas Jefferson wrote on June 20. "All proceedings seem to be arrested till these can be got over." Expressing an apprehension that was widespread among the members of Congress, the secretary of state declared, "It is evident that if every one retains inflexibly his present opinion, there will be no bill passed at all for funding the public debts, and if they separate without funding there is an end of the government."

"The two houses are much divided about the assumption," Elbridge Gerry related to James Monroe on June 25. "Their embarrassments are increased by blending this with the permanent & temporary residence of Congress. Intrigues, cabals & combinations are the consequence."

John Walker of Virginia, the new Senator appointed in the place of William Grayson, confided to Maclay that the Pennsylvania delegation had "agreed to place the permanent Residence on the Potowmack, and the temporary residence to remain 10 Years in Philada." Maclay declared that he knew nothing of any such agreement.

The motion for Baltimore as the permanent seat of government was rejected by a vote of 15 to 10 on June 28. Neither of the Maryland Senators, who favored a Potomac residence, supported their home state. Charles Carroll confided to his daughter that Baltimore had been proposed in opposition to the Potomac, not with any "serious intention of moving the Seat of Government to it," but as a ploy to keep Congress in New York three or four years longer "at which time some thought would be impossible to effectuate the removal."

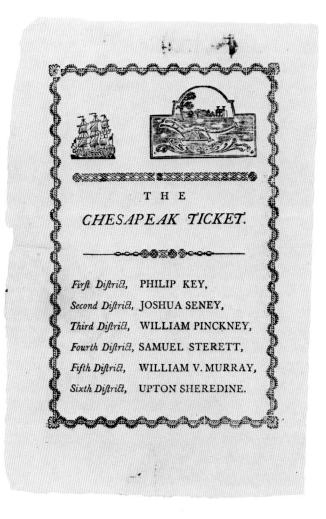

The passage of the residence bill caused a great turnover in the Maryland delegation. Baltimore voters, exercising vengeance against those who had voted for the Potomac site, saw to it that Daniel Carroll, Benjamin Contee, George Gale, and Michael Jenifer Stone were turned out. William Smith had declined to run for reelection; Joshua Seney was the sole incumbent to win reelection.

"Chesapeak Ticket" election broadside, 1790. Rare Book and Special Collections Division, Library of Congress, Washington, D.C.

Joshua Seney (1756–1798) (top), George Gale (1756–1815) (lower left), and
Benjamin Contee (1755–1815) (lower right), from miniatures illustrated in
Clarence Winthrop Bowen's *The Centennial of Washington's Inauguration*

On June 29 Ralph Izard's motion for a temporary residence of ten years for New York was carried by a vote of 13 to 12 but was rejected in a final vote on all the clauses. Charles Carroll was then back with a resolution for Philadelphia. New York Senators Schuyler and King tried for five years in each city. When they lost that motion, they tried for Baltimore and lost again. Pierce Butler's motion for two years in New York resulted in a tie vote, which the Vice-President decided in the negative.

On July 1, by a vote of 14 to 12, the Senate voted for a temporary residence of ten years at Philadelphia and a permanent residence on the Potomac. "Now King took up his Lamentation," related William Maclay. "He sobbed Wiped his Eyes and scolded & railed, and accused first every body and then nobody of bargaining contracting arrangements and engagements that would dissolve the Union. He was called on sharply. He begged pardon and Blackguard like raild again."

Anticipating a favorable vote in the House of Representatives that would move Congress southward, Richard Henry Lee wrote jovially on July 6 that the next day would probably decide whether Congress would leave New York for Philadelphia. *For every art that can be devised has been practised to overcome truth and public convenience—Stratagem in every shape—threats of Mob—Severance of the Union—And even beauty has condescended to aid a misjudged policy in this business. For this day the House has been crouded with Ladies, as much as to say, as you Vote, so will we smile—A severe trial for susceptible minds.*

The House agreed to the residence bill on July 12.

New Yorkers were understandably furious. "This measure has been carried by a compact in which the parties have sacrificed what many of them deemed national objects of prime magnitude, " wrote Philip Schuyler, "and on that account is very reprehensible, as well as because it has evinced a want of that decency which was due to a City whose citizens made very capital exertions for the accommodation of Congress."

The famous version of the Compromise of 1790 was first given by Thomas Jefferson in a document presumably penned in 1792. He related that, in order to mediate a crisis that threatened the very existence of the Union, he brought Hamilton and Madison together at a mid-June dinner, and out of the meeting came an understanding that would break the impasse over residence and assumption. Madison, although he could not himself go on record for assumption, agreed to use his influence to secure the necessary southern votes. Jefferson recalled, *It was observed, I forget by which of them, that as the pill would be a bitter one to the Southern states, something should be done to soothe them; that the removal of the seat of government to the Patowmac was a just measure, and would probably be a popular one with them, and would be a proper one to follow the assumption. It was agreed to speak to Mr. White and Mr. Lee, whose districts lay on the Patowmac and to refer to them to consider how far the interests of their particular districts might be a sufficient inducement to them to yield to the assumption. This was*

As part of the campaign to keep the capital at New York, the city began construction of an imposing presidential mansion on the site of old Fort George, where once the royal governors had held court. "The N. Yorkers are going on with their Government House," Daniel Hiester wrote at the end of March 1790, "confident that the Seat of the Gen. Government is theirs for a long time." Before the structure was completed, the government decamped.

Government House by C. Milbourne; watercolor on paper, 1797. The New-York Historical Society, New York City

done. Lee came into it without hesitation. Mr. White had some qualms, but finally agreed.

And, although Jefferson does not say it, Hamilton also agreed to make the terms of the assumption more palatable to Virginia and other southern states by agreeing to the assumption of additional amounts of state debts and an extension of the time for submitting claims.

"Lee & White from Virginia who had reprobated the Assumption on any terms or conditions declared that their objections were removed by the Bill for the Settlement of accounts having past, & by the limitation of the debts assumed," testified William Loughton Smith on August 8. "Gale & Carrol, who had been equally bitter against it, did not think it worth their while even to assign a reason for such an astonishing conversion & were as anxious for the measure as they had been to defeat it a month before." Richard Bland Lee, Alexander White, and Daniel Carroll all represented congressional districts along that portion of the Potomac River designated for the federal city, and George Gale had long been associated politically with the Potomac's promoters.

According to Smith's account, *In the Senate Read & Carrol who had been opposed to the assumption voted for it: thus, notwithstanding the accession of No. Carolina & R. Island, two States bitterly opposed to the assumption, we have by dint of perseverance obtained a majority for it in both houses. It is laughable to find the same members who a few weeks ago insisted on the absolute necessity of detaching the assumption from the funding Bill & declared they never would vote for them united, now gravely voting for an association because the residence bill is settled. Some danger might have been expected from the N. York members but Hamilton has kept them with us.*

Benjamin Goodhue expressed a common opinion when he noted that "the Patomacke scheme is so absurd that very few expect Congress will ever go there — but continue in Philada."

William Maclay, who had complained that "these Yorkers are the vilest of people" and that he had never been in such an inhospitable place, now pronounced that New York's "Allurements are More than Ten to Two compared with Philada." As he departed the city, he reflected, "The Citizens of Philada. (such is the Strange infatuation of self-love) believe That ten Years is Eternity to them with respect to the residence, & that Congress Will in that Time be so enamoured of them As never to leave them."

THE CONGRESS LEAVES NEW YORK

On July 2, 1790, after the residence bill had passed the Senate and was about to be voted on in the House, Henry Wynkoop of Pennsylvania expressed his satisfaction: *Thus we have a prospect at length to put an end to this disagreable busyness, & upon Terms tho' not altogether so advantageous to Pennsylvania as might have been wished, yet the best possible to be procured, and such as must be considered a great Acquisition to the State, for the Financial Arangements once established there, it is improbable that their Removal to an Inland Situation will be convenient to Government; the credit of this Measure is due to our Senators. Mr. Morris, who is ridiculed, insulted & abused here, is entitled to the gratitude & Esteem of every man who regards the Interest of Pennsylvania.*

Although, in fact, Robert Morris played a lesser role than others in the compromise that moved the capital to Philadelphia and hence to the Potomac, angry New Yorkers labeled him as the villain in the piece. New Yorkers, Morris wrote to his wife, "lay all the blame of this measure on me, and abuse me most unmercifully both in the Public Prints private Conversations and even in the Streets. . . . However I dont mind all they can do if I carry the point. I will like a good Christian forgive them all."

On August 6 Wynkoop sent home "some of the caricatures sold about the streets, expressive of the Spleen of the Citizens on account of the Removal of Congress." He commented, "The Rabble here are very free in bawling out some one or other of the dirty expressions you will see in the Labels, when they perceive a Pennsylvania Delegate passing the Streets."

"The prints contain some angry pieces & several caricatures have been circulated ridiculing the principal advocates for the removal," DeWitt Clinton told his uncle the governor of New York on July 20. *The last that I have heard of is one that represents Robert Morris the great engine of the departure carrying federal hall on his back — Jay in one Pocket, Hamilton in the other and the members of Congress peeping their Heads out of the windows & asking where are we going to which Morris replies, "Where I please." Another represents some of the Congress as mere toys of Morris — Mr. Maddison for instance hanging at his watch fob. There is one in which Morris is carrying a ladder of promotion on his back to Philadelphia filled with the majority & dragging the minority after him. One of the former holds a purse of gold in his hand and says "This is what influences me" intimating that some of the members were bribed.*

What think ye of C-o-n-ss now

My Name is Robert Coffer," exclaims Robert Morris, with money bag in hand, as he carries behind him, on the ladder of preferment, the fourteen Senators who had voted for the residence bill. Dragged along by leading strings through their noses are the twelve members who voted against the measure. "Stick to it Bobby," cries one of the majority; "We are going at the rate of 6 Dollars pr. day," says another; "Money & preferment," adds a third; "This is what Influences me," states the man holding a money bag. Those in the minority declare, "It is bad to have a gouty Constitution"; and from another, "I am affraid Bobbys dance will not mend it." A third declares, "I hope the Philadelphians will not serve us as they once did." His companion answers, "So do I for I am tired of traviling." Came the question, "What will they move to prolong our next session"; and the reply, "the devil & bobby will have them do something." One man observes, "This looks like disinterested proceedings," and he is answered, "O yes we will be comeing the servants of the people." Another goes on, "The move has deprivd us of our fish & lobsters"; adds the last man, "Ay and Oysters too." These last remarks were directed at complaints, often made by New Englanders, that in Philadelphia "lobsters and other fish are scarce and high."

By "Y.Z. Sculp."; engraving, 1790. The Historical Society of Pennsylvania, Philadelphia

Robert Morris moving the capital from New York City to Philadelphia

There is a caricature print designed and it is said executing," Theodore Sedgwick wrote to his wife on July 4, 1790, *which is to represent Mr. Morris with the federal building on his shoulders, in one of his pockets Mr. Jay and in the other General Knox. In his right hand is Mr. Jefferson instead of a walking staff, in his fob Col. Hamilton & at the chain Madison hanging as a bauble. The Senators it should seem caused by the motion of the building are looking out of the windows and perceiving the cause they exclaim, "where are you going to carry us Robert?" He answers by a label "wherever I please." In the back ground are represented the members of the house of Representatives, with myself in front. These words are put into my mouth "Stop Robert you rascal and take my assumption with you." To which he answers, "I'll be da — nd if I do."*

The cartoon as described by Sedgwick has not come to light, but the extant rendition of Robert Morris with Federal Hall on his shoulder is in a similar vein. "Huzza for Philad:" shouts the member on the roof. "Too Rash to hold long," remarks a skeptical New Yorker. "D — d dirty Work," says his fellow. A third declares, "The Public pay for this." A clergyman exclaims, "If I get my Fee I will pray any where." A figure with back turned simply says, "I must Obey." To the left, the devil says, "Come along Bobby here's the Girls." A prostitute stands between a man holding a bag of coins, who says, "I am Purse bearer" and another, who says, "I hope his back will hold." The woman declares, "I will ease you both."

By an unidentified artist; hardwood engraving, 1790. American Antiquarian Society, Worcester, Massachusetts

Con-g-ss Embark'd on board the Ship Constitution
of America bound to Conogocheque by way of Philadelphia

Many commentators presumed that the capital would be fixed on the upper Potomac near the Conococheague Creek in the vicinity of Hagerstown, and before Washington determined on a tidewater site, the name "Conococheague" was synonymous with the Potomac residence.

"This way Bobby," calls out the devil, diverting the Congress away from the unencumbered course to the Potomac and directing it over the falls toward Philadelphia. Headed for a disastrous crash on the rocks, the ship is decorated not with an eagle, but with a goose. Pulled behind by its painter is a boat carrying the northern members of Congress: the helmsman— threatening disunion — calls out, "Cut the Painter as soon as you see the Ship in danger"; and the bowman, knife poised, replies, "Ay, Ay. I had best do it now, for I believe she is going to the devil." In a barbed reference to Washington's refusal to veto the residence bill on the grounds of unconstitutionality, another figure exclaims, "I wonder what could have induced the Controller [the President] to sign our Clearance." His fellow replies, "self gratification, I suppose for it cannot be any advantage to the owners" (that is, the citizens of America). Just outside of Philadelphia, three men are waiting in a rowboat, and one remarks, "If we can catch the cargo," by which he meant the Treasury, "never mind the Ship."

By an unidentified artist; etching, 1790. Division of Prints and Photographs, Library of Congress, Washington, D.C.

Congress Embark'd on board the Ship Constitution of America bound to Conogocheque by way of Philadelphia.

"This session has been marked with great dispatch of business"

The punctual attendance of the members of the Federal Legislature," the *Federal Gazette* reported on December 8, 1790, "by which both houses were enabled yesterday to proceed to business, is a circumstance worthy of notice."

Many of the members, Joshua Seney observed from Philadelphia, "have encountered difficulty, some great hazard, in coming to this place." Seney reported that four of the Massachusetts delegation—Tristram Dalton, Elbridge Gerry, George Partridge, and Jonathan Grout — had suffered an accident. "Their Stage Waggon was overturned near Brunswick, Mr. Partridge so much hurt as to disable him from proceeding further. Mr. Gerry considerably bruised and his Face skinned; Mr. Dalton and Mr. Grout less injured." Traveling from the other direction, Aedanus Burke of South Carolina underwent extreme distress "in a Vessel cast away in the Bay of Delaware." And from Georgia, James Jackson's "sufferings by violent and repeated Storms on the Coast have also been immense."

There were immediate grumblings about the difficulty in obtaining suitable lodgings in Philadelphia and the exorbitant price of everything. "The scarcity of good Houses to rent in this city has been productive of dreadful inconvenience to many families who were comfortably settled at New-York," said William Smith of South Carolina, who, along with his father-in-law, Ralph Izard, had transported an entourage to Philadelphia. "What a serious business it is to move the seat of government," said Smith with wry amusement. *No one anticipated the extreme embarrassment, trouble, difficulty & expence which it has induced & the innumerable quantity of little tradesmen which (like the followers of a Camp) have attached themselves to the Seat of Govt. & have removed hither: my Tayler, hattier . . . Mrs. Smith's & my brother's Hairdressers, in company with a flight of office hunters, speculators, merchants, shopkeepers, milliners, etc.* Smith concluded his report to a friend in South Carolina, "The Quakers wish us at the Devil, I need not tell you where I wish them."

William Maclay, who had no quarrel with the Quakers on ideological grounds, was nevertheless critical of the Quaker influence. "To tell the Truth I know no so unsocial a city as Philada. The Gloomy Severity of the Quakers has proscribed all fashionable dress and Amusement," Maclay wrote. "Denying themselves these enjoyments they as much As in them lies endeavour to deprive others of them Also; While at the same Time there are

View of the City of Philadelphia by Gilbert Fox (1776–circa 1806), after John Joseph Holland; hand-colored etching, Philadelphia, circa 1796. The I. N. Phelps Stokes Collection, The Miriam and Ira B. Wallach Division of Prints and Photographs, The New York Public Library, New York City; Astor, Lenox and Tilden Foundations

not in the World more scornful or insolent Characters than the Wealthy among them."

Theodore Sedgwick of Massachusetts found no cause to complain of Philadelphia's lack of sociability. "I have told you that I have been treated with great attention by the citizens," he wrote to his wife. "Every day almost I have an invitation to dine and spend the evening." Sedgwick went on, *I have been tonight at Mrs. Washington's rout, which was very crowded and which they called very brilliant. I saw assembled all the Beauties of Philadelphia. I staid about an hour and returned home satiated with the stupid formality of a great number of well dressed people assembled together for the unmeaning purpose of seeing and being seen.*

On Christmas Eve 1790, Abigail Adams attended Mrs. Washington's Friday-evening levee for the first time at Philadelphia. The circle was very brilliant, she reported to her daughter: "How could it be otherwise, when the

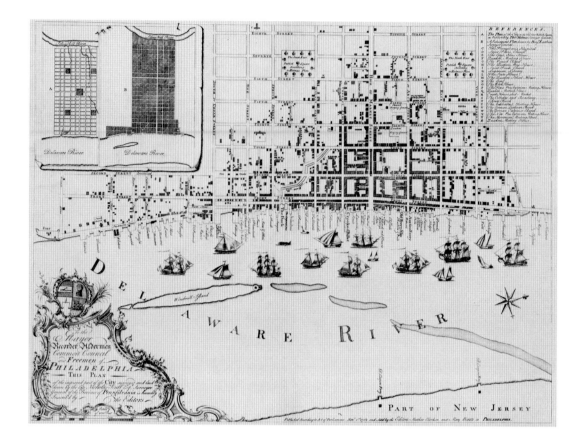

Plan of the city of Philadelphia by Nicholas Scull; engraving, 1762. The I. N. Phelps Stokes Collection, The Miriam and Ira B. Wallach Division of Prints and Photographs, The New York Public Library, New York City; Astor, Lenox and Tilden Foundations

dazzling Mrs. Bingham and her beautiful sisters were there." Mrs. Adams avouched, "Mrs. Bingham has certainly given laws to the ladies here, in fashion and elegance; their manners and appearance are superior to what I have seen."

The dazzling Mrs. Bingham was Anne (Nancy) Willing, who at sixteen had married William Bingham, Robert Morris's sometime trading partner. From 1783 to 1786 the Binghams lived in Europe, where the lovely Nancy had been admired even at the Court of St. James's. Upon their return to Philadelphia, the Binghams erected an enlarged version of the Duke of Manchester's London town house on a three-acre plot on the corner of Third and Spruce streets. Here Mrs. Bingham gave "brilliant balls, sumptous dinners and constant receptions."

Even William Maclay seems to have enjoyed himself when he dined at the Binghams'. They entertained, he wrote, "in a stile beyond every thing in this place, or perhaps in America," and, added Maclay in a rare burst of approbation, "There is a propriety a neatness a Cleanliness that adds to the Splendor of his costly furniture, and elegant Apartments." The following day Maclay was invited to "eat Pepper Pot" with the Morris family.

Congress met in the new County Court House, close by the State House where independence had been declared. Thomas Affleck, one of Philadelphia's leading cabinetmakers, had gone up to New York "to view the Federal Hall & take Drafts of all the Seats, Desks & other Furniture & Accommodations," in preparation for fitting out the Philadelphia meeting-place in the manner to which the Congress had grown accustomed. Boasted the *Pennsylvania Gazette*, "The exertions of our citizens to accommodate Congress in a decent and republican manner deserve the highest praise."

"The building in which we set is neat, elegant & convenient," Sedgwick informed his wife, "but partakes not of the splendid grandeur of federal stile in New York, yet I believe the citizens are determined to make efforts in the next season to outshine their rivals."

Sedgwick also reported that he had visited Charles Willson Peale's museum, where in addition to the "skins of beasts & birds, minerals, fossils, coins, shells, insects, moss & dirt," he viewed *a long gallery with nearly an hundred portraits of those characters who have made the most distinguished figure during the american revolution. Many of these men are now no more. The various affection with which my heart was expanded, as the likeness of departed heroes & statesmen brought to my remembrance the great events in the production of which they in the hands of providence were the instruments, cannot be described. I will say, however, till then I never so well knew the value of portraits.*

At Philadelphia, as it had been at New York, members of Congress resorted to the various local taverns to smoke their pipes, drink a bowl of punch, and discuss political strategy.

Philadelphia tobacconist's trade card, circa 1790. The Library Company of Philadelphia, Pennsylvania

The young architect Charles Bulfinch, visiting Philadelphia shortly after his tour of England and the Continent, pronounced William Bingham's town house to be *in a stile which would be esteemed splendid even in the most luxurious part of Europe. Elegance of construction, white marble staircase, valuable paintings, the richest furniture and the utmost magnificence of decoration makes it a palace in my opinion far too rich for any man in this country. We are told that his mode of living is fully equal to the appearance of his house.*

By Charles Bulfinch (1763–1844); pen, ink, and pencil on paper, circa 1789. Prints and Photographs Division, Library of Congress, Washington, D.C.

As requested by the Congress, the secretary of the treasury presented proposals for raising the additional revenues required because of the passing of the funding and assumption bill, and the hated subject of an excise tax on distilled spirits raised its ugly head.

Fisher Ames was among those who from the first had seen "the most evident necessity for drawing from that resource some part of the revenues." He acknowledged that "the southern people dread it, and say that the excise is an odious, unpopular tax, and will fall unequally on them. They are afraid for their whiskey."

Senator Paine Wingate of New Hampshire brushed aside southern protestations that an excise on whiskey would shift the great burden of taxes onto them with the assertion that "their Indian affairs, their western country and their other expenses of government will nearly absorb all their proportion of taxes."

Thomas Jefferson, among those captivated by Anne Willing Bingham (1764–1801) in France, had challenged her, after she had been back in America for a year, to tell him "truly and honestly whether you do not find the tranquil pleasures of America preferable to the empty bustle of Paris." She noted in her response, "I agree with you that many of the fashionable pursuits of the Parisian Ladies are rather frivolous," but she pointed out that French women "are more accomplished, and understand the Intercourse of society better than in any other Country. We are irresistibly pleased with them, because they possess the happy Art of making us pleased with ourselves." And so it was with Mrs. Bingham as she tried to approximate the French salon in the Philadelphia of the Washington administration.

John Adams, conversing with the lady at dinner, was pleased to find that he was able to carry on "something of a political conversation with her." Mrs. Bingham, he pronounced, had "more ideas on the subject . . . and a correcter judgement" than he had suspected.

By Gilbert Stuart (1755–1828); oil on canvas, 1797. Private collection

According to family tradition, this armchair (left) was part of the furnishings of the executive residence at Philadelphia and was later given by President Washington to Delaware Senator George Read. It reflects the French taste espoused by fashionable Philadelphians, among them the Robert Morrises and William Binghams.

Armchair; painted and gilded ash, Philadelphia, circa 1790. Historical Society of Delaware, Wilmington; gift of Marguerite de Carron Read

"I have presented the Drafts of the Federal hall for which I took at New York; to the Corporation of this City," Thomas Affleck wrote to Tench Coxe, who was Alexander Hamilton's deputy at the Treasury Department, "and mentioned to them your Friendly assistance in procuring me Liberty from the Mayor to take so minute a measurement of Each apartment and furniture with which they are much pleased." Writing on September 16, 1790, Affleck noted, "they have already pulled down all the Inside of the new Court house and are going on with great spirit to fit it up in the best and most Commodious manner and have Engaged me to make the Furniture nearly on the same plane with that at N York."

Thirty of the original chairs that Affleck made for Congress Hall are in the National Park Service Collection at Independence Hall.

Armchair (right) by Thomas Affleck (1740–1795); mahogany and white oak, Philadelphia, 1791–1793. Independence National Historical Park Collection, Philadelphia, Pennsylvania

Plan of the City Hall of Philadelphia as it may be laid out to contain 96 Chairs for the Representatives of the United States, or in Case of need by putting the Chairs nearer together 106 — as 2 f. are allowd for each Chair whereas 20 Inches is sufficient.

N.B. — A Chimney is proposed for each Corner & sufficient space is left to sit round them

A Passage 3½ f wide is left on the Sides & behind the Speakers Chair to communicate with the Offices in the Philosophical Hall by a Door thro the Middle of the Bow —

A Passage is left of 3 f between the Desks from the North Door to the Chair —

A Passage of 3 f. 3 In.t between each Row of Desks for the Members to sit & pass round each other without disturbance —

In preparation for the government's move to Philadelphia, the Philadelphia Common Council appointed a committee of three "to consider which of the public Buildings will be most proper for the reception and accommodation of Congress."

Draft of a plan for the accommodation of Congress, September 1790. Etting Collection, The Historical Society of Pennsylvania, Philadelphia

This watercolor shows Congress Hall, just to the west of the Philadelphia State House (temporarily without its bell tower, which had rotted away) where the Declaration of Independence had been signed. Moored on the Chestnut Street lawn of the State House from 1788 until 1792 was the thirty-three-foot federal ship *Union*. This elaborately crafted vessel was featured in the grand federal procession of July 4, 1788, which had celebrated the imminent ratification of the Constitution by the ninth state.

Statehouse and Congress Hall by James Peller Malcolm (1767–1815); watercolor, circa 1792. H. Richard Dietrich, Jr.

"A more exceptional mode of taxation could not be devised than the excise," avowed John Steele of North Carolina. "A direct or poll tax would not be so odious. Such was the aversion of the people to it that they would prefer almost any alternative."

But James Madison, who well realized that further taxation was an implicit part of the Compromise of 1790, argued, "Considering the aversion to direct taxes & that the imports are already loaded, I see nothing else that can be done."

The only advantage that the excise had over the poll tax, snorted William Maclay, was "That You may refrain from using your mouth in drinking liquor. With some people this is as impossible as to do without an head." It irritated Maclay to find that Hamilton was sitting with the committee on the excise. "Nothing is done without him."

On February 11, 1791, the secretary came in with three new clauses to the proposed excise bill, and the most obnoxious to Maclay was the establishment of districts for collecting the revenue without regard for state boundaries. Maclay was well-nigh apoplectic when Rufus King declared that "he wanted the United States divided into a number of Districts independent of any of the State Boundaries."

Public opinion was roused. A petition circulating in Philadelphia reminded the Congress "that excise laws . . . have long been held in detestation by the good people of America." Had not the aversion to the British excise taxes bought about the war for independence?

But supporters of an excise offered a rebuttal in the press: "There exists some difference in bearing a burden imposed by a government in which we had no participation, and in paying a tax laid by our immediate representatives, and for the support of a government of our own choice."

Then came the argument that an excise on distilled spirits "will bear unequally." And the answer was given: *This will probably be the case. It is not every citizen of these States who thinks distilled spirits necessary to his happiness;—the burden will be confined to those who chuse to indulge in guzzling a beverage that is strong but not strengthening,—that maddens the brain and weakens the body. If it is a desideratum that every citizen should pay an equal share of each tax, they all must be laid upon bread, water, fire, etc. because these articles are and must remain in universal use.*

The College of Physicians of the City of Philadelphia weighed in with a memorial entreating the Congress "to impose such heavy duties upon all distilled spirits as shall be effectual to restrain their intemperate use in our country."

James Jackson of Georgia answered the College of Physicians with "a long vehement harrange" on the floor of the House. The press reported that Jackson *in the course of his Phillipic, shrewdly insinuates, that some of the members of the college are concerned in breweries and cyder-presses, with the juices of which the college and people of Pennsylvania may get drunk as often as they please, while the poor inhabitants of Georgia, having neither apples nor barley to make beer or cyder, cannot drink a bowl of grog or toddy, without paying such a nefarious d—ble excise, as will oblige them to go to bed sober almost every night in the week.* The correspondent, who signed himself "A Friend to the College," went on, *General James Jackson tells us, that his constituents claim a right to get drunk, that they have been long in the habit of getting drunk, and that they will get drunk in defiance of a dozen colleges, or all the excise duties which Congress might be weak or wicked enough to impose.*

Southerners were not the only ones upset by the excise bill. The distillers of Philadelphia declared that the tax was so excessive that "the Business must end in this Country, and our foreign Neighbours be enrich'd by our distress." They concluded, "The Dutys too high and the revenue would be much benefitted by reducing it one half."

The distillers of Providence petitioned the Rhode Island delegation to use their exertions "to avert a precipitate Passage of the Bill, which we again assure you is Pregnant with Consequences the most alarming Detrimental and even ruinous to the Northern Interests." They pointed out that the proposed excise was exorbitant and higher than the proposed rates on imported spirits. *If an adequate Drawback is not granted on all Spirits Exported to foreign Markets, the Importation of Molasses which now employs the most of our Navigation and procures an advantageous Sale for our Fish, must be reduced to a very small Quantity, of Course our Vessels will be useless Ship Building Discouraged the fishery in a great Measure fail, and in Time the Injuries which will result to every Description of People are too numerous to be specified and we Conceive too obvious to escape your attention.*

Joseph Stanton of Rhode Island and his colleague Theodore Foster declared that, although they approved of the general principles of the excise bill, "we Should have liked it Better, if the Duty had been Lower On Our Own Manufactured Spirits, & higher on Imported."

When the time came for the Senate decision on the excise bill, William Maclay perceived that many of the members wished to avoid a recorded vote. Gleefully he demanded the yeas and nays. "I . . . called them sharply and enough rose, and I had the pleasure of giving my decided negative against what I consider the Box of Pandora with regard to happiness of America."

Maclay declared that he "was perhaps never more vexed. . . . The Excise bill is passed and a pretty business it is." He foresaw, correctly as it turned out, that western Pennsylvania — where there were said to be some three thousand small distilleries — would soon be in an uproar over the tax on whiskey. *The Ministry fore see opposition and are preparing to resist it by a band, nay an host of Revenue Officers. It is put in the power of the President to make as many Districts, appoint as many General Surveyors & as many Inspectors of Surveys as he pleases, and thus multiply force to bear all down before him. War and bloodshed is the most likely consequence of all this.* Huffed Maclay, "Congress may go home. Mr. Hamilton is all powerful and fails in nothing which he attempts."

"After a most strenuous opposition, and much time spent in debate," John Steele of North Carolina wrote on January 27, 1791, the excise bill "passed the House of Representatives this day by a large majority; Ayes 35, Nays 21. Thus you see my Friend, that assuming, funding and excising have taken root in America. How these foreign plants will flourish in free soils, time must determine."

Representative Alexander White of northwestern Virginia, whose vote had been crucial to passage of the funding bill, rationalized that he had done the right thing in voting for the excise. It "being a new Mode of Taxation and bearing an unpopular name," he explained to his constituents, "I wished to wait, but on the most attentive considerations of all the objects of Taxation within the power of Congress, I could not select any to substitute which in my opinion would be so productive, and bear so lightly on the People." Passage of

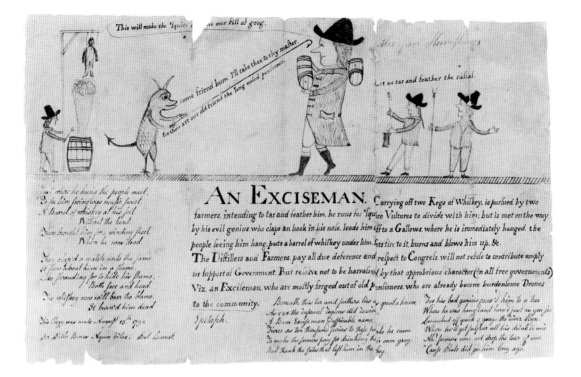

William Maclay's dire prediction that the excise would engender indignant opposition was swiftly borne out. "The Distillers and Farmers pay all due deference and respect to Congress, will not refuse to contribute amply for Support of Government," it was explained in this depiction of the hanging of an exciseman. "But resolve not to be harrassed by that opprobrious character (in all free governments) Viz. an Exciseman, who are mostly forged out of old Pensioners, who are already become burdensome Drones to the community."

"An Exciseman" by an unidentified artist; caricature, August 13, 1792. Atwater-Kent Museum, History Museum of Philadelphia, Pennsylvania

the excise was attended with the pleasing circumstance, White concluded, "that no New Money will be required while we remain in peace."

Before December was out, Alexander Hamilton presented the final section of his financial plan, which called for the creation of a national bank. Modeled after the Bank of England, one-fifth of its ten-million-dollar capitalization would be subscribed by the government and the remainder by private individuals.

Banks, the agencies for commercial interests, in their nature aroused the suspicions of agrarians like William Maclay, who constantly fretted that a few individuals might profit at the expense of the many. "Considered As an Aristocratic engine I have no great predilection for Banks," Maclay wrote as soon as he learned of Hamilton's proposal. "They may be considered in some Measure as operating like a Tax in favor of the Rich against the poor, Tending to the Accumulating in a few hands, And Under this View may be regarded As opposed to republicanism."

The bank bill was reported on January 3, 1791, and Maclay noted, "It is totally in Vain to oppose this bill." As the bank came under debate on January 17, Maclay derided, "And now such a Scene of confused Speeches followed as I have seldom heard before. Every One affected to understand the Subject, and undervalue the Capacities of those Who differed from himself." Maclay went on, "I am now more fully convinced than ever I have been of the propriety of Opening our doors. I am confident some Gentlemen would have been ashamed to have seen their Speeches of this day, reflected in A News paper of tomorrow."

On January 20 the bank bill was agreed to by the Senate, and William Maclay recorded on that day that he had voted against the measure to limit its

Philadelphia commercial interests, it was feared by southerners, would take advantage of the twenty-year bank charter to so fix the city as the center of financial activity that the bargain to move the capital to the Potomac in 1800 would not be kept.

A Merchant's Counting House in Philadelphia by Alexander Lawson (1773–1846); engraving, circa 1800; published by T. Dobson, Philadelphia. The Library Company of Philadelphia, Pennsylvania

charter to ten years after conversing "on the Subject with every Money'd Man I could find, and they uniformly declared that they would not subscribe on so short a period, and the Consequence would be that they would all join in supporting the old banks and bearing down the national One."

Pierce Butler was among the unhappy southerners who wrote home sourly, "A National Bank is establishing on strong Aristocratick Principles." William Few of Georgia, although admitting the "convenience and utility" of the bank, declared, "I consider it in its present form as a Dangerous combination of the monied interests of the United States and a monopoly of extensive advantages that are local and will operate partially."

Senator James Gunn of Georgia minced no words in his report to Governor Edward Telfair. "The great object of the Bank Bill is to *consolidate* the *monied* Interest of America and Strengthen; in an astonishing degree, the Executive department of the General Government; and an excise was necessary to discharge the Interest on the *assumed* debt."

Upon the bill's third reading, Madison suddenly proclaimed that the creation of a national bank had not been within the original intent of the framers, but he was challenged by John Vining of Delaware, who pointed out that no fewer than eleven members of the House had also been delegates to the Grand Convention.

Abigail Adams commented to her uncle, Cotton Tufts: *You will learn by the publick papers that Mr Madison is come forward with all his powers, in opposition to the Bank it is difficult for the world in general to discern why a wise man or rather why so learned a man can take up such opinions as he does.*

Fisher Ames insisted that if Congress was denied the right to govern by implied powers, "a great part of our two years labor is lost . . . for we have scarcely made a law in which we have not exercised our discretion with regard to the true intent of the Constitution." He went on to say that "not exercising the powers we have may be as pernicious as usurping those we have not."

What made Hamilton's bank particularly alarming to the southerners was the provision calling for a twenty-year charter for the bank, which would continue Philadelphia as the financial center for ten years beyond the date when the seat of government was to have removed to the Potomac. Philadelphia, Fisher Ames acknowledged, "will become the great centre of the revenue and banking operations of the nation. So many interests will be centered here, that it is feared that, ten years hence, Congress will be found fast anchored and immovable."

Benjamin Huntington of Connecticut summed up the reasons for the opposition to the bank. *The Ostensible Objections are first that the Constitution will not Warrant the Measure. 2dly That it is not a Necessary Measure[.] They admit it to be a Measure of Great Utility but that the Government may be Administered without it — But there is a Snide Suspicion that the Real objection is that the Establishment of a National Bank in Philadelphia will have a tendency to fix the Seat of Government in or*

Near this Place & that the Potomack Plan will be in Danger of a Defeat.

Benjamin Bourn of Rhode Island observed that the members south of Virginia were nearly to a man opposed to the bank bill. *Mr. Maddison spoke yesterday an hour & an half on the Subject. He Combats it both on the ground of unconstitutionality and inexpedience. But I am persuaded we should not have heard anything of either, did not the Gentlemen from the Southward View the measure, as adverse to the removal of Congress, ten years hence, to the Powtomack.*

Madison delivered another long speech on February 8 but swayed no minds. The House, by a vote of 39 to 20, concurred with the Senate. Jonathan Grout, the Antifederalist from the "Shaysite" part of Massachusetts, was the only member north of Maryland to cast a vote in the negative. Only five southerners voted in favor of the bank—Joshua Seney and William Smith of Maryland, William Loughton Smith of South Carolina, and North Carolinians John Sevier and John Steele.

Should the President disapprove the bank bill, Theodore Sedgwick wrote on February 18, "it will be a very unfortunate event; though I believe there will be found a sufficient number to pass the bill against his *veto.*"

As the President pondered whether or not he should sign the bill, Madison continued to insist that a strict construction of the Constitution was in order, and that by no means could a national bank be deemed legal.

Madison's opinion was challenged by Alexander Hamilton, who, at the President's request, penned a masterful defense, declaring that since the bank was necessary and proper to carry out the funding and assumption laws, Congress had the implied power to create it. Traditionally, Hamilton's brilliant essay has been credited with persuading Washington to sign the bill, but Congress proved adept at applying its own pressure. A supplemental residence bill — including, at Washington's personal request, Alexandria within the ten-mile square — was held up until the bank bill was signed.

Near the end of the session, Virginia's Senators — Richard Henry Lee and James Monroe — on instructions from their legislature moved a resolution that the doors of the Senate chamber should be opened. Maclay recorded that *Elsworth said they amounted to no more than a Wish, and ought to be no further regarded. Izard said no legislature had any right to instruct at all, any more than the Electors had a right to instruct the President of the United States. Mr. Morris followed, said Senators owed their existence to the Constitution; the legislatures were only the Machines to chuse them, and was more violently opposed to Instruction than any of them. We were Senators for the United States and had nothing to do with One State more than another. Mr. Morris spoke with more Violence than Usual.* The vote was taken, and the Senate declined to open its doors to the public. It would not do so until 1794.

There was general satisfaction as the Congress came to its close. "We leave unfinished the Post Office, the Militia and the Mint," Alexander White of Virginia detailed, "but on a basis of what we have done, and the manner it has

The President of the United States and M:rs Washington, request the Pleasure of

Company to Dine, on _____ next, at ____ o'Clock.

_____ 179

An answer is requested.

William Maclay considered that dining with the President was something he must submit to "as a part of my duty as a Senator." He detailed the menu on one such occasion as "Fish roasted & boiled meats, Gammon Fowls &ca." followed by the dessert course of "Apple pies puddings &ca. then iced creams Jellies &ca. then Water Melons Musk Melons apples peaches nuts." Maclay declared, "it was the most solemn dinner ever I eat at, not a health drank scarce a Word said untill the Cloath was taken away."

That bids to dinner had their political implication Maclay had no doubt. When the bank bill was under consideration, Maclay, who for some time had been neglected by the President, received an invitation to dine. He observed that President Washington treated him with "Marked Attention," helping him to dessert and "soon after asked me to drink a Glass of Wine withe him."

Engraved invitation from the President of the United States and Mrs. Washington. Division of Political History, National Museum of American History, Smithsonian Institution, Washington, D.C.

been done in the course of two years—I think we may return to our Countries without a Blush."

A few days after adjournment, Abigail Adams noted, "This session has been marked with great dispatch of business, much good humour, & tho varying in sentiment upon some very important subjects those subjects have been ably discussed, and much light thrown upon them, and finally carried by large majorities."

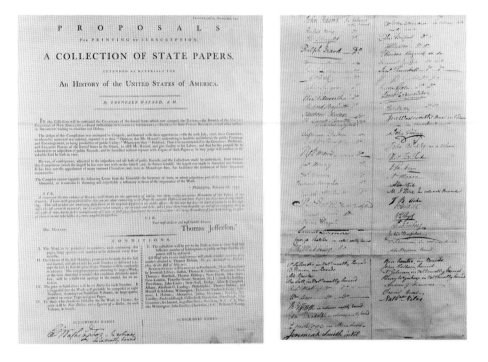

Fifty-five members of the First Federal Congress were among the subscribers to Ebenezer Hazard's proposal of February 24, 1791, for the printing of the important manuscripts and public records of America's history.

The Historical Society of Pennsylvania, Philadelphia

The *Gazette of the United States* summed up on March 2, "Perhaps no body of men has ever attended more punctually at the daily hours of meeting, or continued more closely occupied during the sitting. The whole number has generally voted." The newspaper concluded, "A great deal has been done, and truth seems to authorize us to say, that no very dangerous mistakes have been committed in the two years."

The accomplishments of the First Federal Congress were saluted in the Philadelphia *Federal Gazette*:

It snatched from impending ruin,
PUBLIC CREDIT:
"RAISED the FUNDS;"
EXTENDED COMMERCE,
& ESTABLISHED
A REVENUE,
Without imposing excessive burthens on
The People.
It invariably watched over
and protected

The Rights of the individual States,
and of the Citizens.
And though th' historic page may scan
Some errors,
"On the whole,
We are warranted in this wish —
May its successor equal it"
In firmness, Integrity, Patriotism,
attention to Business,
And Public Confidence.

At the Constitutional Convention, the distribution of seats in the first House of Representatives was agreed to only with the understanding that corrections would be made when a true count of the populace could be ascertained. The bill for enumerating the inhabitants of the United States originally stated "that every male or female, of 21 years of age, shall be obliged to render a true account of the number of persons, etc. in their families." Samuel Livermore of New Hampshire, however, moved that the word *female* be struck out, "that it would be sometimes indelicate in a marshal to ask a young lady how old she was, or too make too strict enquiry." The amendment was agreed to; the bill passed the House on February 8, 1790, and the Senate on February 18. The law provided that the census was to begin on the first Monday in August 1790 and be closed six months later.

Creamware pitcher with transfer design showing the population of the United States as enumerated in the first census. Liverpool or Staffordshire, circa 1790–1810. S. Robert Teitelman

"It is a silly Opinion of mine,
but I cannot get rid of it,
That every Man like a labelled bottle,
has his Contents,
marked in his visage."

William Maclay, May 2, 1789

PART THREE

PORTRAITS

OF THE

MEMBERS

JOHN ADAMS
1735–1826
President of the Senate

John Adams, the Vice-President-elect, whose sole duty according to the Constitution was to preside over the Senate, took the oath of office as president of that body on April 21, 1789. "A trust of the greatest magnitude is committed to this Legislature," Adams told the Senate in his initial address, "and the eyes of the world are upon you." Adams candidly admitted, "Not wholly without experience in public assemblies, I have been more accustomed to take a share in their debates, than to preside in their deliberations."

"My office requires rather severe duty," the Vice-President complained to his eldest son, "and it is a kind of duty which, if I do not flatter myself too much, is not quite adapted to my character—I mean it is too inactive and mechanical." The temptation to join in the debate was almost more than his nature could bear. "It sometimes happens that I . . . think I could throw a little light on the subject."

Adams could not keep silent as the debate on titles for the Chief Executive raged. When Oliver Ellsworth enumerated "how common the appellation of President was," Adams volunteered that "there were Presidents of Fire Companies & of a Cricket Club." On May 9, as the report of the committee on titles came to a vote, William Maclay recorded, "Up now got the [Vice-]President and for 40 minutes did he harrangue Us from the Chair." Sneered Maclay, "dignities distinctions Titles, &ca., Are his Hobby Horses and the Creature must ride." As Adams presided over the Senate, sword properly affixed, some members called him "His Rotundity" or "His Superfluous Excellency" and whispered that he ought to get his wig dressed.

Why should "Men of greatest Fortune, Talent, Birth, or Virtue," pondered Adams, "live at uncomfortable Lodgings, instead of their own houses: alone, instead of in the Society of their Families and Friends: at a great distance from their Estates and Business. Professions, Faculties, Property, Families, all going to ruin at home." What allurement had government service to offer? "If the People would give Titles or Marks of distinction, this would go a great way. — The Title of Right Honourable would raise the Senate and make it an object of ambition."

Fresh from nearly a decade of association with the courts of Europe,

John Adams by John Singleton Copley (1748–1815); oil on canvas, 1783. Harvard University Portrait Collection, Cambridge, Massachusetts; bequest of Ward Nicholas Boylston, 1828

Adams was adamant that the new republic must be dignified and respectable. Symbols and pageantry, he thought, were crucial to the good order of society. "If government cannot be had nor laws obeyed without some parade, as I fully believe, we must have some parade or no laws." Declared the Vice-President, "To talk of a Government without all Etiquette is to betray a total Inattention to human life and manners. Can Subordination be preserved in the Smallest Society, without distinctions?" But he sighed in exasperation, "A Man must take so many pains to carry little points that seem of no importance that he is despised for a fool by many and not thought very wise by any."

The Vice-President's agitation in favor of titles, Thomas Jefferson reflected to James Madison, was proof of Benjamin Franklin's characterization of John Adams as "always an honest man often a great one but sometimes absolutely mad."

The Vice-President grumbled, "My country has in its wisdom contrived for me the most insignificant office that ever the invention of man contrived or his imagination conceived." Nonetheless, Adams had the opportunity to cast the deciding vote on a number of important issues, including the determination that the President should have the right to remove appointed officials without the consent of the Senate.

This portrait of John Adams, large as life, was executed by John Singleton Copley in London shortly after Adams had signed the definitive treaty of peace with England. Adams paid the Boston-bred artist the substantial sum of one hundred guineas for the aristocratic depiction, which the sitter later referred to as "this Piece of Vanity." In 1793 Adams declined to have the image used as the frontispiece of the new edition of his *Defence of the Constitutions of the United States*. He confessed that "I should be much mortified to see such a Bijou affixed to these Republican Volumes."

FREDERICK AUGUSTUS
CONRAD MUHLENBERG
1750–1801

Representative from Pennsylvania, Speaker of the House of Representatives

My friends here," Frederick Muhlenberg wrote to Dr. Benjamin Rush, as he waited for the House of Representatives to gather a quorum, "who indeed entertain a much better Opinion of my Abilities than I deserve think of me as a Candidate for the Speakers Chair." Muhlenberg was unnerved by the prospect. *Never did I dread a Business more, & I feel the want of Abilities & knowledge to such a Degree that the Thought of it makes me tremble & yet on the other Hand to refuse in toto what would in some Measure do honour to those who have honoured me with their Confidence & a Seat in the Legislature would in my opinion be a Crime which I hope never to be guilty of.* Therefore, he was determined "if chosen to exert the utmost of my Abilities to meet the Expectations of my Friends."

Frederick's brother Peter, who was also a Representative from Pennsylvania, reported to Rush on April 4, 1789, that "Fred. A. Muhlenberg was chosen Speaker haveing 23 Votes out of 30."

"The blood of the grandchildren of our grandchildren," proclaimed a correspondent in the German language *Philadelphische Correspondenz,* "will proudly well up in their hearts when they will read in the histories of America that the first Speaker of the House of Representatives of the United States of America under the new Constitution was a German, born of German parents in Pennsylvania."

Muhlenberg's election to the speakership, however, was not so much a tribute to the largest minority group in federal America, as it was to other considerations. Some suspected that the choice of Muhlenberg was an effort to deflect Pennsylvania framer James Wilson's chances for appointment as Chief Justice, while others looked upon the decision as a bribe to Pennsylvania for the continuance of the Congress at New York. In any case, Muhlenberg, despite his protestations of inadequacy, was a well-tried parliamentarian, having been Speaker of the Pennsylvania Assembly, as well as presiding officer at his state's ratifying convention.

Twenty years earlier, Muhlenberg's father, who intended that his son follow in the family tradition of great Lutheran divines, had written that Frederick "has by nature an honest heart, some experience of God's grace, a tolerably clear head, a sound stomach and moderate bodily vigor. He can endure hardships . . . he has a fine, clear penetrating voice." These qualities had served Frederick Muhlenberg equally well when, shortly after the beginning of the Revolution, he abandoned the ministry for a career in politics, and they would stand him in good stead as Speaker of the House of Representatives.

It was intended that the speakership, modeled after that of the British House of Commons, should be an office of high honor. The rules adopted by the House of Representatives provided that "when the House adjourns, the members shall keep their seats until the Speaker shall go forth; and then the members shall follow."

The salary was twice that of other Congressmen, twelve dollars a day, but entailed an expectation that the dignity of the office would be upheld with a certain amount of hospitality. "I sincerely confess that I would rather have had a less Sum," Muhlenberg confided to Dr. Rush, "& not be under the Necessity of keeping up that Form & parade which is now in some Measure expected & which I ever had a natural Aversion to." Later William Maclay would note in his journal that Muhlenberg was very busy in giving oyster suppers.

A reporter for the *Columbian Magazine*, observing Muhlenberg as he presided over the last session of the First Congress in Philadelphia, wrote that the Speaker "by his portly person and handsome rotundity, literally filled the chair. His rubicund complexion and oval face, hair full powdered, tambored satin vest of ample dimensions, dark blue coat with gilt buttons, and a sonorous voice . . . all corresponding in appearance and sound with his magnificent name."

We know, however, that Muhlenberg's portrait by Joseph Wright — whose mother, the celebrated wax modeler Patience Wright, had arranged for his art study in Europe — was painted in New York just three weeks before the Congress adjourned the second session. Visible on one of the bills awaiting his signature are the words "5 Act to regulate the," which has been determined to be "An Act to regulate Trade and intercourse with the Indian Tribes," a bill signed by the Speaker on July 20, 1790. His wide chair—"to hold two, I suppose," Vice-President Adams remarked — was one of a pair ordered in 1789 for the presiding officers of the House and Senate, and it is extant in New York City Hall.

Muhlenberg remained in Congress until 1796, when his deciding vote allowing for the implementation of the explosively unpopular Jay Treaty brought an end to his political career.

Frederick Augustus Conrad Muhlenberg by Joseph Wright (1756–1793); oil on canvas, 1790. National Portrait Gallery, Smithsonian Institution, Washington, D.C.

FISHER AMES
1758–1808
Representative from Massachusetts

If James Madison could be said to have had a rival for celebrity in the House of Representatives, that man would be Fisher Ames. Ames, as dazzling an orator as Madison was understated, was a favorite among those who flocked to the visitors' gallery.

"Mr. Ames, who, though a very young man, is *second* only to the great Madison," noted a correspondent from New York in a letter published in the Boston *Herald of Freedom*. "In oratorical powers he perhaps exceeds him."

In private correspondence, Ames reveals a charming levity that contrasted sharply with Madison's gravity. "A representative," Ames jested to a friend, "is a kind of wife to the public — and ought to be submissive as well as faithful."

But when it came to the great question of public credit, Ames could be as pompous as the next man. William Maclay, describing the debate in the House of Representatives on Madison's proposal for a discrimination between original and subsequent security holders, recorded that *Ames, delivered, a long String of studied Sentences — But he did not use a single Argument, which seemed to leave an impression. He had public faith public Credit, Honor & above all Justice, as often over as an Indian would the great Spirit, and if possible with less meaning and to as little purpose.*

It exasperated Ames to have the all-important matter of assumption unresolved while the debate over the place of residence preoccupied the members of Congress. "I care little where Congress may sit," he wrote from Federal Hall on June 11, 1790. *I would not find fault with Fort Pitt, if we could assume the debts, and proceed in peace and quietness. But this despicable grog-shop contest, whether the taverns of New York or Philadelphia shall get the custom of Congress, keeps us in discord, and covers us all with disgrace.*

Throughout the next decade Fisher Ames, a staunch guardian of public order and property rights, was the Federalist champion in the House of Representatives. When Gilbert Stuart came to paint his likeness, the ailing but still-youthful-looking Ames was at the close of his life, and the portrait served as the frontispiece for the posthumous publication of "The Dangers of American Liberty," in which Ames warned against the excesses of democracy.

Fisher Ames by Gilbert Stuart (1755–1828); oil on panel, circa 1807. National Portrait Gallery, Smithsonian Institution, Washington, D.C.; gift of George Cabot Lodge

ABRAHAM BALDWIN
1754–1807
Representative from Georgia

Transplanted Connecticut native Abraham Baldwin was characterized by his Georgia colleague James Jackson as "one of the most obliging Men on Earth." Baldwin's strain of Yankee humor was apparent when he observed that he favored a single head for the Treasury rather than a board of three, since "boards are little better than shingles in such work."

Baldwin was no shirker. At the Grand Convention he was the most faithful and active member of the Georgia delegation. In the First Federal Congress he served on thirty-nine different committees and was chairman of sixteen of them.

As a Representative of a state dependent upon foreign imports, Baldwin was concerned that the rates on the impost were being set too high. After the Senate bill was returned to the House, Baldwin wrote, *In my opinion, their amendments are according to the present fashionable use of the word, for the worse. They have lowered the duties one third on rum, wine and such like bulky articles of general consumption, the proper subjects of revenue; and have raised one third on all articles for the protection of American manufactures & commerce.* He fretted, "These protections and commercial regulations will surely lead us a wild dance."

Before the First Congress had concluded, Baldwin was clearly increasingly out of step with Alexander Hamilton and attuned to the principles of Madison and Jefferson. For four terms in the House and two in the Senate he would be a dedicated Republican.

Robert Fulton, a protégé of Baldwin's brother-in-law, the poet and diplomat Joel Barlow, executed the only known life portrait of Baldwin when the two were together in Washington. The portrait was engraved to accompany Baldwin's biography in *The National Portrait Gallery of Distinguished Americans,* published by James B. Longacre and James Herring in 1839. Wrote Barlow in summarizing Baldwin's life, "He may have wanted ambition to make himself brilliant, but he never wanted industry to render himself useful."

Abraham Baldwin by Robert Fulton (1765–1815); pencil on paper, not dated. National Portrait Gallery, Smithsonian Institution, Washington, D.C.

RICHARD BASSETT
1745–1815
Senator from Delaware

Richard Bassett had been adopted by a relative — a wealthy lawyer — and brought up on a Maryland plantation called Bohemia Manor, but his political enemies taunted him for his origins as the son of a tavern-keeper who had deserted his wife. "Being bred Up in low life," declared one detractor — in recalling that Bassett, as a captain of a cavalry company, had sought to protect some Tories from a Dover mob—he "is capable of the most Odious Viliany." Bassett was derided as "a Mere Mushroom Started up from the filth of a Stable . . . and Still possesses all the evil & desperate qualities of low life."

These characterizations of Bassett, reflective of the often-raucous nature of local Delaware politics, are in marked contrast to the description of Bassett given by William Pierce of Georgia, who met Bassett at the Constitutional Convention. Pierce found the Delaware delegate to be a "Gentlemanly Man" and described him as "a religious enthusiast, lately turned Methodist, and serves his Country because it is the will of the people that he should do so. He is a Man of plain sense, and has modesty enough to hold his Tongue."

At the Grand Convention, James Madison recorded Bassett as saying nary a word, and at the First Federal Congress he usually seemed disposed to look to fellow Senator George Read for leadership. He fretted to his absent colleague that if assumption was adopted, *Poor little Delaware will have saddled upon her between two and three hundred thousand dollars more than her former supposed quota. This will never do; but how to help it is the question. Do come forward and lend us your aid. I feel my own weakness upon subjects of this kind in a very eminent degree, and therefore want your aid.* On March 1, 1790, he pleaded, "For God's sake, come along; I cannot stay here much longer without you."

William Maclay regarded Bassett with scorn, particularly when he reneged on his repeated assertions that the Susquehanna was the only proper place for the residence. "Basset got up and recanted, said he had not understood the Question; this is usual with him." Maclay reflected, "There is really such a thing as Worrying weak or indifferent Men into a Vote." On the assumption issue, however, Bassett stuck to his guns and voted against the bill, even though Read — whom William Maclay called "the flexible *Reed*" — went the other way.

Richard Bassett by Charles Balthazar Julien Févret de Saint-Mémin (1770–1852); black and white chalk on paper, 1802. The Baltimore Museum of Art, Maryland; bequest of Ellen Howard Bayard (BMA1939.181)

At the close of his term, Bassett left the Senate to become chief justice of Delaware. Six years later he was elected governor. In 1801 Bassett was one of the aborted "midnight judges" appointed by John Adams during the last hours of his administration.

Bassett's portrait was executed by the French emigré artist Charles Balthazar Julien Févret de Saint-Mémin, shortly after Bassett retired from office to spend the last dozen years of his life entertaining his friends and promoting his religion.

EGBERT BENSON
1746–1833
Representative from New York

Egbert Benson, in recollections dictated shortly before his death, declared, "I am the surviving member of the first Provincial Congress of the state," which had assembled in April 1775. Benson went on, *I am the survivor of the first Revolutionary Legislators of the State. It met in September 1777. I am the survivor of the commissioners appointed to settle the controversy between us* [New York] *& Massachusetts relative to their claim to the territory of the Western portion of the state and between us & Vermont relative to their claim to be independent of us.* The old man continued, "I have served as Attorney general & as one of the Judges of the Supreme Court of the state, and as chief Judges of the second district of the United States under the Judiciary act." Not a word does he mention about his service in the Congress of the United States.

Benson had been a delegate to the Annapolis convention in 1786 and might have been sent to the Philadelphia convention, had the Federalists been successful in their attempts to expand the New York delegation.

Closely associated with Alexander Hamilton on both national and local questions, Benson was a strong advocate of the secretary of the treasury's financial program. Benson, who had a reputation for extensive legal knowledge, served on some thirty-eight committees and presented reports from eleven of them.

Benson never married. At the time of the First Federal Congress, General Philip Schuyler claimed that Benson and the widowed John Laurance were

Egbert Benson by Gilbert Stuart (1755–1828); oil on canvas, circa 1800. New York State Office of Parks, Recreation, and Historic Preservation; John Jay Homestead State Historic Site, Katonah, New York

rivals for one of Jeremiah Wadsworth's daughters. Benson, pronounced Schuyler, "is too grave when with a woman."

After two terms in Congress, Benson became justice of the Supreme Court of New York. His loyalty to the Federalist cause was recognized when John Adams appointed him a federal judge in the closing hours of his administration, a position aborted by the Jeffersonians. Thereafter Benson retired to private life. In 1804 he was one of the founders and the first president of the New-York Historical Society.

The portrait of Egbert Benson, painted by Gilbert Stuart, was originally owned by John Jay. Benson and Jay were at King's College together, and Benson noted in his memoir that he and Jay were "as close for sixty five years as between brothers."

Benson, remembered one of his contemporaries, *was of medium height, of compact frame, with light eyes and complexion. He possessed a calm, equable temperament, although quick and energetic in his movements; was cheerful in manner and fluent in conversation, abounding in anecdote. He was an antiquarian; colloquial in his manner as a speaker; brief and sententious, bordering on obscurity in his style of writing, and possessed a mind stored with classical, legal and historic knowledge.*

ELIAS BOUDINOT
1740–1821
Representative from New Jersey

After wartime service as commissary general of prisoners and his two terms in the Confederation Congress, Elias Boudinot declared that he was tired of public life and retired to his law practice in Elizabethtown, New Jersey. But Boudinot's son-in-law, Pennsylvania Attorney General William Bradford, wrote that he was not surprised that Boudinot had agreed to enter the elections for the House of Representatives. "There are occasions where a person appears to be so particularly called on that it seems like an indifference to public opinion to refuse," Bradford opined to Boudinot. "The objects of discussion will be so important in the first Congress, that it seems to me, a man's industry, & knowledge cannot in the course of the present Century, have the same oppertunity of being serviceable."

Elias Boudinot by Charles Willson Peale (1741–1827); oil on canvas, 1782. Independence National Historical Park Collection, Philadelphia, Pennsylvania

"If I could possibly get clear of my present appointment consistant with duty & in an honorable Manner," Elias Boudinot wrote to his wife Hannah Stockton (1736–1808) as he took his seat in Congress, "I would most certainly fly to the Arms of my beloved wife & spend the rest of my Days with her in Retirement."

By Charles Willson Peale (1741–1827); oil on canvas, 1784. The Art Museum, Princeton University; gift of Mr. and Mrs. Landon K. Thorne for the Boudinot Collection

Boudinot, no doubt because of his experience as president of the Confederation Congress, expected that he might be a likely candidate for the speakership. But after Frederick Muhlenberg was chosen, Boudinot wrote to his wife, *I feel myself very happy that I am clear of it. I am sensible the honor is great, but then the Confinement is what I could never have submitted to without having you in the City. This would have obliged us to remove our Family and run to a very large Expense without any Certainty of an Adequate Provision & if made, there would always have been a Jealousy among narrow Minds if supported with Dignity. It would also have brought you as well as myself into an amazing Scene of dissipation, which even you could not have wholly avoided. I believe I should not have refused it had it been offered, on account of the Interests of the State, but I am much better pleased without it, and consider it as a kind Providence towards us.*

Boudinot would prove to be a conspicuous figure in the new Congress, a member of many committees, and a ready debater. Arguing against the permanent residence along the Susquehanna, Boudinot particularly annoyed William Maclay when he was "so hardy as to deny that the Susquehannah affords any navigation at all." Snorted Maclay, "It would really be of Service to him if he could be made to blush."

"From a young man," Dr. Benjamin Rush remarked of Boudinot in 1808, "he was noted for his jocular and hyperbolical conversation. In Congress at New York, an improbable story (Mr. Clymer informs me) was called a 'Boudinot.'"

To his wife, Boudinot described the congressional routine: *I am up at 7 o'Clock or a little after; spend an half hour in my Room—dress & Breakfast by half past 8—in Committee at 9—from thence immediately to the House—adjourn at 3 o'Clock— In Committee ag[ain] at 6—return at 8—and write till 12 at Night. This has been my Course for some Time, except when I dine out, which to me is harder Service.*

Had I my charming wife to repay me, by her tenderness when the business of the day was done, it would add an invaluable pleasure to all my Engagements—but it cannot be for the Present, and therefore I will regale myself (tho at a Midnight hour) with scribbling to her.

Boudinot—the only member of the New Jersey delegation to win reelection — served three terms in the House of Representatives and was director of the United States Mint from 1795 until 1806.

Elias Boudinot was among the first of those asked to sit for Charles Willson's Peale's collection of portraits depicting eminent American patriots.

BENJAMIN BOURN
1755–1808
Representative from Rhode Island

Benjamin Bourn arrived at Philadelphia shortly after the third session of the Congress had commenced and took his seat on December 17, 1790, as the final member of the First Federal Congress.

The Harvard-educated Providence lawyer came with a letter from Rhode Island Federalist Jeremiah Olney introducing him to Philip Schuyler, Alexander Hamilton, and Henry Knox as "a Gentleman whose Principles and Conduct have ever been uniformly Federal; whose amiable Disposition and fair Deportment in Life have gained him; not only the Confidence of his fellow Citizens, but the Friendship and Esteem of the first Characters in the State."

Soon after his arrival, the House was engaged in discussion of a militia bill, and Bourn, who had a large a Quaker constituency, believed that "None should be required to Train but such as may be willing to fight." He declared, "I have always been taught to bear a Sacred regard to the rights of Private Judgment and of Conscience and shall always oppose every measure tending to violate them." The matter of exceptions he thought should be left to the state legislatures. "You may be assured that I shall use my endeavours in the formation of a Militia Law to prevent the Introduction of any Clause which shall infringe on the Liberty of Conscience," he wrote to the prominent Quaker Moses Brown, "& in these my endeavours I shall derive additional satisfaction in reflecting that while I am discharging my duty I shall at the same time conform to The declared sense of the State I represent and manifest my Friendship for a Society which I sincerely regard & respect." The militia bill was one of the matters left in abeyance when the First Congress adjourned.

Bourn served through the first four Congresses and in 1801 was named judge of the United States District Court for the District of Rhode Island.

This silhouette, which descended in his family, is the only known portrait of Benjamin Bourn.

Benjamin Bourn by an unidentified artist; reverse painted silhouette, not dated. Mary Thurber Clark

JOHN BROWN
1757–1837
Representative from Virginia

John Brown, sent to the Confederation Congress by Virginia in 1787, was disappointed in his inability to effect statehood for Kentucky — in part because of the reluctance of the New England states to add to the southern scale, but more definitively because the nine states necessary to take action could not be gathered.

The egocentric James Wilkinson characterized Brown as "of respectable talents but timid, with small political experience and little knowledge of the world." Moving to Kentucky from the Shenandoah Valley of Virginia around 1786, Brown was active in the cause of Kentucky independence.

The appointment of his friend Thomas Jefferson as secretary of state removed Brown's fears that the government might fritter away control of Mississippi in return for a commercial treaty with Spain. "I am now fully convinced that we [have] nothing to fear on that score from the present [Govern]ment at least during the administration of the present President."

When he stood for reelection in 1790, Brown was challenged by James M. Marshall, the younger brother of John Marshall, who openly charged — to little effect — that Brown had been in conspiracy with the Spanish minister Don Diego de Gardoqui to attach Kentucky to Louisiana. "The opposition to Mr. Brown scarcely merited attention," Madison heard from a Kentucky friend. "He possesses the confidence of most of the people in the District."

During the third session of the Congress, Brown had the satisfaction of overseeing passage of the bill admitting Kentucky to statehood.

In 1792 Brown resigned from the House of Representatives to represent the new state in the Senate. It was during this tenure that his portrait was drawn by James Sharples, an English artist who had come to America in 1794.

John Brown by James Sharples (circa 1751–1811); pastel on paper, circa 1795–1801. The National Society of The Colonial Dames of America in The Commonwealth of Kentucky

AEDANUS BURKE

1743–1802

Representative from South Carolina

Instituting extensive honours and privileges of an Hereditary Order," Aedanus Burke proclaimed in his 1783 pamphlet denouncing the Society of the Cincinnati, "is a daring usurpation on the sovereignty of the republic, a dangerous insult to the rights and liberties of the people, and a fatal stab to that principle of equality, which form the basis of our government." Burke's "Considerations on the Order of the Cincinnati" had brought him a measure of fame, and the French abolitionist Jacques Pierre Brissot de Warville pointed him out as the man "who so forcefully demonstrated the fatal consequences of the inequality which that order would introduce among the citizens of the United States. This same man defended the much more revolting inequality established between whites and Negroes." Burke, Brissot noted, "nearly always employed invective."

Burke was known for his irascible temper as well as for his Irish wit. William Loughton Smith, the polished man of the world, wrote with some astonishment that Burke "is become very pleasant—a great Speaker, and often entertains us with humorous strokes of fancy." Burke won further praise from Smith when he came around in support of assumption. His colleague, Smith pronounced, "has behaved exceedingly well hitherto in this business: he has taken a decided part & come forward manfully." But, as Burke continued his fiery orations, Smith acknowledged, "Burke has been warmly with us but his mode of speaking & his roughness only excite Laughter."

Thomas Fitzsimons observed of the Irish-born Burke, "My countryman Burke is oftener heard than attended to and never less than when he expresses himself by illiberal reflections."

In the debates on the assumption of the state debts, Burke, detailed William Smith of Maryland on April 4, 1790, "took occasion to Shew the great Services rendered by the Militia of that State *in fighting the battles of the United States,* as an argument Why their Debts ought to be paid out of the gen[era]l funds." Thereupon Burke suddenly brought up Alexander Hamilton's oration of the previous Fourth of July, and charged that Hamilton, in extolling General Nathanael Greene, had referred to the militia as "the mere mimicry of Soldiers." The observation, Burke declared, *was like a Dagger in my breast, but it was impossible for me to notice it at the time; I was called an antifederalist, the people of this city were all federalists, Mr. Hamilton was the Hero of the day & the*

Aedanus Burke by an unidentified artist; oil on canvas, not dated. Hibernian Society of Charleston, South Carolina

favorite of the people & had I hurt a hair of his head, I am sure I should have been dragged thru the Kennels of New York & pitched headlong into the East River: But now I have an opportunity in as public a manner of retorting the lie *which he gave to the character of the Militias.* Burke was called to order and sat down. "After sometime he again rose, & told the Speaker, he was perfectly cool, *never more so in his life.*" Went on Smith, "but Supposing Col. Hamilton in the Gallery (which was filled with Ladies) he faced around to that quarter, & called out aloud, that he threw the lie in Col. Hamiltons face."

A duel was averted when Alexander Hamilton made haste to explain that he meant no reflections "on the militia in general or that of South Carolina in particular," and Burke in turn apologized for calling the secretary a liar.

William Maclay observed, soon after the Congress had moved to Philadelphia, that Burke in New York had *railed so tremendously against the Quakers and against Philada. and indeed all Pennsylvania for having Quakers. But behold a wonder. Now he rails against Slavery, extols Quakers, and blazes against the Attentions shewed to General Washington, which he calls Idolatry; and That a Party wish as much to make him a King as ever the Flatterers of Cromwell wished to raise him to that dignity.*

Burke, who had been a judge on the state circuit court since 1778, declined to become a candidate for reelection, since the South Carolina legislature had passed a law prohibiting a state judge from undertaking duties that would cause him to be absent from the state.

LAMBERT CADWALADER
1743–1823
Representative from New Jersey

A member of a prominent Quaker family, Lambert Cadwalader had been born at Newark and educated at the College of Philadelphia. Prior to the Revolution he had engaged with his brother John in the importing business at Philadelphia. Early in the war he was captain of the Philadelphia company and, as colonel of the Fourth Pennsylvania Battalion, was taken prisoner at the fall of Fort Washington.

After his resignation from the army in 1779, Cadwalader settled in New

Lambert Cadwalader by Charles Willson Peale (1741–1827); oil on canvas, 1772. Philadelphia Museum of Art, Pennsylvania; The Cadwalader Collection: purchased with funds contributed by the Pew Memorial Trust and gift of the Cadwalader Family

Jersey, where he had an estate outside of Trenton, which he called Greenwood. From 1785 until 1787 he represented New Jersey at the Confederation Congress.

During his term at the First Congress, Cadwalader had a hand in the copyright and patents bill and participated in the setting up of the Treasury and War departments. He was not reelected to the Second Congress but was returned to the Third.

Charles Willson Peale shows Cadwalader at the age of twenty-nine. The portrait was commissioned by Cadwalader's brother to be hung — alongside those of their parents — in the parlor of John Cadwalader's new house on Second Street. The carved and gilded frame, ordered from the shop of James Reynolds, is an indication of the rococo decoration of the magnificently furnished Cadwalader establishment. Lambert Cadwalader rests his hand on the carved rail of a chair that was undoubtedly among the pieces his brother ordered from Philadelphia's finest craftsmen.

Interestingly, Lambert Cadwalader, whose family had such a taste for grandeur, had himself a humorous disdain for titles and trappings. "There have been much Altercation in all Companies relative to the Title to be given to the President," Cadwalader related in May 1789. "The Lovers of Fringe & Embroidery, have, however, been defeated, and a Taste for Simplicity has prevailed over adulation." Cadwalader reflected, *The great Man at the Helm has too dignified a Mind to have been affected with the most pompous appillations — but we may not be so fortunate in the Person who may come after him. There was a good deal of Meaning in the Speech made by the honest Scotsman who accompanied King James 1st. from Scotland to London, he said that "so much Flattery was enough to spoil a gude King." And to say the Truth we have few Heads among us that would prove steady enough to walk the Path of common Sense, with so many Honors playing round them.*

As to Cadwalader himself, a contemporary recorded, *To the good breeding, courtesy and elegance of the gentleman he united the advantage of early education and the acquisition of an enlarged and cultivated understanding, regulated by classical taste and improved by habits of general reading. Few were so happily gifted with the power of pleasing and the disposition to be pleased; few have enjoyed in an equal share the friendship, respect, and affection of all around him.*

CHARLES CARROLL OF CARROLLTON
1737–1832
Senator from Maryland

W e have one Roman Catholic Senator from Maryland," wrote Paine Wingate of New Hampshire, meeting Charles Carroll for the first time at the First Federal Congress, "who is a very worthy sensible man. He is said to be the richest man in America, worth half a million sterling, but is as plain in his dress and manners, and as easy of access, as any man whatsoever."

Carroll incurred William Maclay's commendation when he spoke up against titles for the President and answered Ralph Izard's pontificating on parliamentary ceremonies by saying "he thought it of no consequence how it was in Great Britain; they were no rule to us." The Marylander soon fell out of Maclay's favor, however, because he did not object to Richard Henry Lee's motion that following the oath of office the Congress should accompany the President to a religious service at St. Paul's Chapel. The joint committee had rejected the motion, and Carroll, related Maclay, "tho' he had been the first to speak against it, Yet was silent on the Vote; this proves him not the Man of firmness which I once thought him." But Carroll was back in Maclay's good graces when he voted for a five-dollar-a-day compensation for members of Congress instead of the six recommended by the Senate committee.

Dutifully, Charles Carroll moved Baltimore as the seat of federal residence but thought the matter well settled with the choice of the Potomac. "I am confident, if the seat of Govt. of the US is placed on the Potomack the States will be unified." He told his daughter, "Keep this letter by you, and when these great events shall happen, shew it to your children; they and the descendants of my fellow citizens will perhaps then applaud the foresight wh[ich] contributed to frame such solid advantages to Maryland at the expence of loosing popularity."

Political popularity Charles Carroll certainly did lose. A letter in the *Maryland Gazette* of July 30, 1790, which bitterly deplored that all chance of bringing Congress to Baltimore-town had been lost, pointed out that Carroll's term would soon expire, and thereupon "our Assembly men ought to be instructed to vote for no one as his successor, whom they could suppose capable of confeiting the interest of a corner of the state in preference to that of the majority of the people." The writer concluded, "It is really hard such a man as Mr. Carroll should be our enemy, when most of us were so extremely desirous of putting him into the Senate."

Despite the criticism, Carroll was reelected in 1791, but he resigned from the Second Congress in November 1792 because the Maryland legislature

made it impossible for him to continue his concurrent service in the state Senate.

Rembrandt Peale, who in 1815 established a "Baltimore Museum and Gallery of Fine Arts" in imitation of his father's Philadelphia museum, very likely intended this portrait of Carroll to hang among his assemblage of distinguished Americans.

The citizens of Baltimore, in a bid to have their city become the capital of the nation, directed a letter to Congressman William Smith on June 20, 1790, in which they informed him that a "Square of 500 feet, on each Side, at the head of Markett Streett. Situate on an eminence, that commands one of the most delightful prospects in Maryld or perhaps in the U. S." would be given to the Congress. "The Area, thereof, will be fully Sufficient to erect thereon, the Federal building" as well as *the Presidents House, the Hotels, of each State, & the officers of government. The water is excellent, the air pure, & Situation healthy. A number of good dwelling houses to be had for the immediate accomodation, of Public Officers. And it is unnecessary to add, that the Boarding houses, are as good as any in America, & Sufficient, fully, to accomodate Congress, to their Satisfaction. It is further to be Observed, that Baltimore, is the only commercial Town, of Consequence, in the Union, that has been offered to Congress. And among the few, of dificult access, to an enemy.*

View of Baltimore by an unidentified artist, after Francis Guy; watercolor on paper, circa 1798. Maryland Historical Society, Baltimore

Charles Carroll of Carrollton by Rembrandt Peale (1778–1860); oil on canvas, circa 1816–1819. The Baltimore Museum of Art, Maryland; bequest of Ellen Howard Bayard (BMA 1939.180)

DANIEL CARROLL

1730–1796

Representative from Maryland

Daniel Carroll, who had spent six years in Europe being educated at the Jesuit college of St. Omer in France, was wary of foreign entanglements. He said, in the debate on the establishment of the Department of Foreign Affairs, that he hoped "a time would come when the United States would be disengaged from the necessity of supporting such a Secretary . . . he wished some security against being drawn into the vortex of European politics."

Although Carroll's family fortune originated in Prince Georges County, where his father sold European and East Indian goods from his store on the Patuxent River, Carroll had moved to Montgomery County after his wife's death in 1763. There he maintained a plantation near his mother's large establishment at Rock Creek. During the debate on the residence he noted that he lived near the Potomac, "which he could observe from his door."

Carroll voted against the assumption bill on June 2, 1790, but when the final vote was taken on July 26, he was one of those whose change of mind allowed for passage of the bill. His vote in favor of the residence on the Potomac brought down upon him a barrage of criticism. One who signed himself "A Marylander" proclaimed in the Baltimore newspaper, "It is absolutely necessary, that every exertion should be made next October, to turn out Messrs D. Carroll, Contee, Gale, and Stone." He went on, *I do not wish our four members to be turned out from motives of revenge, now it is impracticable to repair the mischief they have done us, but solely to show our members hereafter, that they are not to run counter to the interest of a majority of the state with impunity.* In the ensuing election Carroll was defeated, soundly trounced in the city of Baltimore, where he received but 7 votes compared with the 5,510 cast for his opponent.

So anxious was the President to provide for his friend and loyal supporter that Carroll—on January 21, 1791—was named as one of the three commissioners who would survey the permanent seat of government. Since the Constitution forbade the holding of two public offices at one time, Carroll was unable to act in this capacity until the expiration of his congressional term in March.

Carroll was portrayed by the English artist John Wollaston at about the

Daniel Carroll by John Wollaston (active 1742–1775); oil on canvas, circa 1753–1754. Maryland Historical Society, Baltimore; gift of Dr. Clapham Pennington

time of his marriage to Elizabeth Carroll of Duddington, whose fortune further increased the substantial business and landholdings that Carroll inherited from his father and received by transfer from his brother, the Reverend John Carroll.

GEORGE CLYMER
1739–1813
Representative from Pennsylvania

George Clymer had not, in the course of a political career that stretched back to the days of pre-Revolutionary ferment, learned to be a patient man. At the very beginning of the first session of the Congress William Maclay characterized his colleague as "peevish and fretting at every thing."

"Disgust and disappointment have found their way to my breast," Clymer wrote in June 1789, as protracted debate on the impost ensued. "We have pedlars in politicks north and south and molasses is the rock on which all the N[ew] E[ngland] patriotism is to split."

Clymer himself, however, was tireless in support of tariffs high enough for the protection of Pennsylvania's industries. He was forced to concede defeat in the matter of cotton manufacture, "which was thought in too early infancy to ask sacrifices," but he was "in great hopes than in a short time this manufacture will be in a capacity to claim protection." Once the impost was passed, he wrote with satisfaction, "I could have wished that a more decided preference would have been generally given to American Manufactures, but you will observe nevertheless that in what has been done Pennsylvania will receive considerable advantages."

After Clymer heard from Dr. Benjamin Rush that the Pennsylvania delegation was being criticized for instigating increased salaries and wages voted by the Congress, he replied with asperity, "This will have no effect on me nor do I care should it be preclaimed on the house-top that I will never suffer myself in any public duty or trust or honor to be controlled by the rage ignorance or folly of any of my constituents."

Under pressure from both sides on the question of assumption, Clymer

George Clymer by an unidentified artist, after Charles Willson Peale; oil on canvas, circa 1807–1810. National Portrait Gallery, Smithsonian Institution, Washington, D.C.; gift of W. B. Shubrick Clymer

complained at the end of April 1790 that "the petulant pertinacious wrangling and disingenuity and sophistry of that month is not to be matched since the days of the Council of Trent." He finally declared that he would vote for the assumption, "for confirming the Government & for National Purposes," even though Pennsylvania would have to pay two-and-a-quarter million "more than she ought to pay."

Commented John Armstrong, "Clymer is supposed deep because he refuses to be fathomed." In characteristic trenchant fashion Armstrong went on, "But were his talents and knowledge better and more unequivocal than they are, they would go for nothing, obscured, and embarrassed by his monkish shyness off the floor, and his most wretched of all contemptible figures upon it."

Clymer did not seek reelection, and by the time he posed for Charles Willson Peale in 1807, he had forsaken public life to devote himself to the improvement of agriculture and to the presidency of the Pennsylvania Academy of the Fine Arts. Cooled now were the violent political animosities that had been engendered by Pennsylvania's radical constitution, and far in the past was the Assembly election of 1779 when the conservative Clymer lost his seat, ironically, to Charles Willson Peale.

TRISTRAM DALTON
1738–1817
Senator from Massachusetts

H aving for near forty years enjoyed so much health as not to have been obliged to keep my bed one day," Tristram Dalton — on the verge of setting out for Congress — was confined for three weeks because of "an ulcer tooth — and a fractured Jaw, occasioned by the Extraction of it."

As soon as he was able, Dalton, accompanied by his wife and servants in livery, traveled to New York in his coach. Dalton had "a relish for gay and foolish extravagance," reported Samuel Breck in his *Recollections*. "A large house was taken and a course of fashionable life adopted."

Dalton was determined to do his best for his constituents. "The impost bill will come up tomorrow, when every exertion shall be made by me to place

Tristram Dalton attributed to Joseph Blackburn (active in America 1754–1763); oil on canvas, circa 1758. Private collection

molasses on a better footing," he advised his brother-in-law. "The Southern gentlemen tell me they are sick of the word. Pennsylvania is against us and no state is particularly interested in the business except Massachusetts. Brother Strong and myself have a hard and unequal battle." He closed, "No difficulty, however, shall deter me from performing what I esteem to be my duty — having discharged that I rely on the candor and good will of my fellow citizens."

He felt a special responsibility for the interests of his Newburyport neighbors. "Everything that can affect shipbuilding I shall watch with a jealous Eye—This manufacture appearing to me to deserve every encouragement upon *National* principles and the attachment I feel for my Native Town adds force to my inclinations to protect a Business which is of so much Consequence."

Despite his diligence, Dalton, who drew the two-year senatorial term, was denied reelection in 1790. When the Massachusetts legislature balloted, he was last in a field of four candidates, having received only 6 votes out of 123 cast. Dalton "must be greatly chagrined," wrote Theodore Sedgwick, "for there certainly is no more reason to leave him out than there was originally to choose him." Sedgwick was informed that "no exceptions it is said were made to his political character or conduct," other than his vote for congressional salaries at six dollars a day rather than five.

So loath was Dalton to quit the scene of government that he suggested to New York Senator Rufus King that if Samuel Osgood resigned as postmaster general when the capital was moved to Philadelphia, the duties of that office "would be as agreeable to my disposition as any I could obtain." He was willing to quit his seat early if necessary. "I should suppose I might rely upon the Senates consenting if the President should think proper to nominate me."

Dalton failed to secure this appointment, but, undaunted, he moved his family to Philadelphia, where he took "at a great rent" a house by the Conestoga Tavern. In June 1792 Dalton was named cashier of the United States Mint.

This portrait shows Dalton as a young man of about twenty, near the time he was a classmate of John Adams at Harvard or perhaps three years after graduation, when he married Ruth, the daughter of "King" Hooper of Marblehead. Dalton, it was said in his obituary, "was tall and finely formed and added to his personal beauty the most graceful and polished manners."

OLIVER ELLSWORTH
1745–1807
Senator from Connecticut

Oliver Ellsworth, one of the most active members of the Senate, served on twenty-two committees during the first session of Congress and thirty-six in the second. His was the chief hand in the drafting of the judiciary bill. "Mr. Elsworth who was principally concerned in

Oliver Ellsworth (1745–1807), who played a major role in the drafting of the judiciary bill—shown with his wife Abigail at home in Connecticut—proudly displays a copy of the Constitution that he had labored to draft, ratify, and amplify.
  By Ralph Earl (1751–1801); oil on canvas, 1792. Wadsworth Atheneum, Hartford, Connecticut; gift of Ellsworth heirs

253

drawing the Bill," explained William Loughton Smith, "is a Judge of the State of Connecticut of much reputation for legal knowledge: he is a man of remarkable clearness of reasoning & generally esteemed a person of abilities."

Snorted William Maclay, tired of hearing Ellsworth expound, "This Vile Bill is a child of his, and he defends it with the Care of a parent, even with wrath and anger. He kindled as he always does When it was medled with."

The Senator from Connecticut spoke often and at length, causing William Maclay to dub him "Endless Elsworth." Few members of Congress annoyed William Maclay more than did Ellsworth, "the most conceited Man in the World." Never satisfied with other people's resolutions, Maclay sarcastically observed, "Elsworth, according to his custom drew another one."

In the debate on the penal law, Maclay recorded, "Elsworth had a String of Amendments. For a While he was listened to, but he wraught himself so deep in his niceties and distinctions as to be absolutely incomprehensible. He fairly tired the Senate and was laughed at." When Ellsworth drew up and brought in a bill "respecting Consuls & Vice Consuls," Maclay declared, "of Course he hung like a Cat to Every particle of it."

According to Maclay, Ellsworth made "a most elaborate Speech" supporting the President's exclusive power of removal, saying *"It is Sacrilege to touch an Hair of his head, and we may as well lay the President's head on a block and strike it off, with one blow."* Ellsworth "had sore Eyes and a green silk over them. On pronouncing the last of the Two Sentences, he paused put his hand kerchief to his face and either shed tears or affected to do so." Ellsworth asked, "Did we *ever quarrel* with the power of the Crown of Great Britain?"

It was with the greatest of pleasure that Ellsworth reported to his wife on June 7, 1790, that "Rhode Island is at length brought into the Union." He exulted, "The Constitution is now adopted by all the States, and I have much satisfaction & perhaps some vanity in seeing at length a great work finished for which I have long labored incessantly."

Ellsworth resigned from the Senate in 1796 to become Chief Justice of the United States, but four years later he retired and was appointed by John Adams as a peace commissioner to France.

In 1834 the Congress commissioned Hezekiah Augur, a Connecticut-born self-taught sculptor, to portray Oliver Ellsworth for the Capitol's collection of marble busts of the Chief Justices of the United States.

Oliver Ellsworth by Hezekiah Augur (1791–1858); marble, 1837. United States Senate Collection, Washington, D.C.

WILLIAM FEW
1748–1828
Senator from Georgia

William Few had grown up on the North Carolina frontier and was twenty-eight when he settled in Georgia. No sooner had he arrived than he was elected to the state constitutional convention in 1776 and, in the Assembly elections that followed, was chosen to represent up-country Richmond County. In 1780 he was elected to the first of his four terms in the old Congress. Following his wartime activities as a militia colonel, Few related in his autobiographical notes, he decided to commence the practice of law, "although I had never spent one hour in the office of an attorney to prepare for the business, nor did I know anything of the practice, but I well understood the general principles of law, and I had acquired a tolerable proficiency in public speaking."

One of Few's major concerns as a Representative from Georgia at the First Federal Congress was the protection of his state's frontiers from hostile Indians. When the President decided to send a three-member commission to negotiate a treaty with the Creek Nation, Few asked to go along. "The State has been long insulted, and the tranquility of the Inhabitants interrupted by those perfidious Savage tribes," said Few. "It is high time that something decisive should be done." Few sailed for Georgia in September, but since the half-breed Indian chief Alexander McGillivray refused to deal with the commission, nothing was accomplished. Ultimately McGillivray came to New York, but the treaty, which was signed in August 1790, displeased Georgia, and Few voted against its ratification.

By the third session of Congress, Few feared that the "principles and genius" of the Constitution that he had helped to frame were in danger of violation. "Already we begin to perceive the collision of the Government of the United States with that of the individual States," he wrote to Governor Edward Telfair. "I am sorry to observe that there are to be found too many public characters that wish to augment and extend the power of the former over the ruins of the latter." Those who aimed toward consolidation, Few wrote, "cover themselves [with] what is termed the sweeping clause," contending that the federal government possesses "all powers that they may think necessary to exercise for the general interest and safety." Few reflected, "It is true there is no line [that] can be drawn—that will ascertain precisely the powers of the National Government. The great law of necessity will

William Few by John Ramage (1748–1802); watercolor on ivory, circa 1790. The Manney Collection

sometimes extend it — occasionally with propriety; but the lesser pretence of expediency is too often found operating in the same direction."

Few, who drew the four-year term in the Senate, retired at its close to his plantation in Columbia County. Chagrined, however, when the Georgia legislature failed to appoint him to a vacancy in the United States Senate, he moved permanently to New York in 1799 and was thus relieved of "the scorching climate of Georgia, under all the accumulating evils of fevers and negro slavery, those enemies to humane felicity." He purchased a little farm on Greenwich Lane, was elected to the New York Assembly, and was later a United States district judge.

The miniature of William Few, painted by John Ramage, was likely intended for the lady he had recently wed.

CATHARINE NICHOLSON FEW

born circa 1764

Lady of the Senator from Georgia

Forty-year-old William Few married, in June 1788, Catharine Nicholson, the second daughter of Commodore James Nicholson, who had been senior officer in the Continental navy. In April 1789 Nicholson was in command of the decorated barge that transported President-elect Washington from New Jersey to New York.

Three of Catharine Few's sisters made alliances with members of Congress: Frances married Joshua Seney of Maryland in 1790; Hannah in 1793 wed Albert Gallatin—Thomas Jefferson's future secretary of the treasury — who was elected to the Fourth Congress; and Maria became the wife of John Montgomery, who represented Maryland in the Tenth, Eleventh, and Twelfth Congresses.

As a schoolgirl in Bordentown, New Jersey, Kitty Nicholson had been a favorite of Thomas Paine, and in reply to her letter announcing her marriage, the author of *Common Sense* wrote from London, "I request my fair correspondent to present me to her partner, and to say, for me, that he has obtained one of the highest Prizes on the wheel." In a long and very personal letter, Paine noted, *When I see my female friends drop off by matrimony I am sensible of something that affects me like a loss in spite of all the appearance of joy: I cannot help*

Catharine Nicholson Few by John Ramage (1748–1802); watercolor on ivory, 1787. The Manney Collection

mixing the sincere compliment of regret with that of congratulation. It appears as if I had outlived or lost a friend. He went on, *But the sentiment your letter contains has prevented these dull Ideas from mixing with the congratulations I present you, and is so congenial with the enlarged opinion I have always formed of you, that at the time I read your letter with pleasure, I read it with pride because it convinces me that I have some judgment in that most difficult science—a Lady's mind.* Paine told his "female literary correspondent" that he had sent her letter to Edmund Burke's wife "as a specimen of the accomplishments of the American Ladies."

Mrs. Few's miniature records her appearance when she participated in the official entertainments of the "Republican Court." The artist, whose studio was at 25 William Street, was a neighbor of the Nicholsons and later of the Fews.

ELBRIDGE GERRY
1744–1814
Representative from Massachusetts

William Duer, who as a schoolboy often slipped into the gallery of the House of Representatives to watch the show, remembered Elbridge Gerry as "grave, garrulous, crotchety, and nervous." Although he was a tense man, afflicted with a nervous tic and an impediment in his speech, Gerry never held back from debate. One who had known him at the Constitutional Convention recalled that Gerry was "a man of sense, but a Grumbletonian, he was of service by objecting to every thing he did not propose."

On constant guard against a concentration of power, Gerry sought to have the Treasury in the hands of three men and the Senate given the authority to check the President's powers of removal. The judiciary Gerry dreaded "as an awful Tribunal. By its institution the Judges are completely independent, being secure in their salaries, & removable only by impeachment."

Even Abigail Adams, who would never forget Gerry's steadfastness in the days leading to independence, had doubts about her dear old friend. "There is not a member whose sentiment clash more with my Ideas of things than Mr. G[err]y," Mrs. Adams wrote shortly after her arrival at New York. "He

Elbridge Gerry by John Vanderlyn (1775–1852); pencil on paper, 1798. Harvard University Art Museums, Fogg Art Museum, Harvard University, Cambridge, Massachusetts; purchase from the Louise E. Bettens Fund

certainly does not comprehend the Great National System which must Render us respectable abroad & energetick at Home and will assuredly find himself lost amidst Rocks & sands."

Most of the Massachusetts delegation thought Gerry insufferable. "Gerry has as high notions of profusive grants as any person I ever knew," complained Benjamin Goodhue when congressional pay was under discussion. He "has manifested such an illiberal and ugly a disposition since he has been in Congress that I believe no man has fewer friends than Mr. Gerry." Gerry, related Goodhue, "was throughout the whole business as warm an advocate for those high grants as any member of the House and was exceedingly angry at our wishing to have the yeas and nays and was even so indelicate as to charge us of being influenced by views of popularity." Then, to everyone's astonishment, Gerry voted against the higher salaries because "the sums were so paltry."

Sighed Abigail Adams, "Mr. G what can I say, you see him always in the minority, you see him very frequently wrong and the poor man looks gastly. I believe he is worried, mortified and quite in the horrors."

To the surprise of many, Gerry emerged as one of the most zealous supporters of Alexander Hamilton's financial program. Usually the strictest of the strict in interpreting the Constitution, Gerry found no difficulty in accepting the implied powers that would allow for a national bank. He himself bought thirty shares. He declared assumption "important to the *preservation* of the States Governments—for if the debts should not be assumed by Congress, a clamour would be raised against the State governments for not doing justice."

On September 6, 1790, Abigail Adams wrote to Cotton Tufts about the coming elections in Massachusetts, where she feared "a rage for rotation" on the part of a few restless spirits. *If they change Mr. Gerry for Mr. anybody else, they will lose one of the firmest men they have, as independent a man, and as honest a one. In the first session his mind was irritated & he was hurt, his speeches were misrepresented, and his conduct misconstrued, but through the whole of the last session no man has exerted himself more for the honour and reputation of the Nation, nor more firmly guarded the constitution against innovation.* Gerry was safely reelected.

In 1797 John Adams appointed Gerry one of the three commissioners sent to seek an understanding with the French Directory. At Paris he posed for John Vanderlyn, the first American to study art in France.

After many futile attempts, Gerry in 1810 defeated Caleb Strong and became governor of Massachusetts. His term of office is best remembered by the redistricting bill, which brought the term "gerrymander" into the language. Gerry died in office, as Vice-President of the United States under James Madison, a position, ironically, that he had been against at the Constitutional Convention.

NICHOLAS GILMAN

1755–1814

Representative from New Hampshire

Nicholas Gilman thought that his New England colleagues were unreasonable in their desire to keep Congress at New York, "which subjected some of the southern members to travel of more than a thousand miles; and as it was the wish of many of them to meet in Philadelphia a safer & more suitable place than this; I always considered it unwise in the northern people to oppose it." He trusted, however, that the

New England's fundamental governmental unit, the town, is represented in this composite of several New Hampshire communities and was originally painted for a house in Exeter, the home territory of the prominent Gilman family and the base of Nicholas Gilman's political support.

Overmantel by an unidentified artist; oil on panel, circa 1800, from the Gardiner Gilman House, Exeter, New Hampshire. Amon Carter Museum, Fort Worth, Texas

move to the Potomac would not take place as scheduled.

"To the general Idea of assumption," Gilman declared, he "lent a favorable ear." In the end, however, he voted against the bill, as he explained to the president of New Hampshire, because "the plan proposed by the Senate contains so large a sum and the proportion to be assumed from each state [is] so manifestly unjust." When Gilman sought reelection, his political foes derided, "He changed his mind very suddenly, and he has not explained his motive to the world. Have we not the right to say, *this is mysterious conduct?*"

Further criticism was leveled at Gilman for not supporting all of the amendments recommended by the New Hampshire ratifying convention. An anti-Gilman piece published in the *Concord Herald* charged that Gilman was "also in favour of the President's having the power or removing the great officers of government, without the consent of the Senate. This is pretty generally looked upon as a stride towards arbitrary government, and much disliked in those part of the countries where the people are fond of *republicanism.*" Wrote the same critic, "It is said by his friends, that he has influence with the *President* — that he was formerly his *aide de camp* etc." But, concluded the writer, "We do not send men to represent us in Congress because they are, or have been, favourites; but because we suppose them to be firm *substantial men* and have an opinion of their own; and will not lose sight of the true interest of this state."

Gilman's friends came to his defense, however, quoting Chief Justice John Jay as saying that Gilman "was closely attach'd to the northern interests — and that by being particularly intimate with the southern gentlemen, to whom the politeness of his manner recommended him, he had a large share of influence with them."

Gilman remained in the House of Representatives for four terms, and his only recorded speech was a succinct appeal for a post office in his home district. "It is a vulgar error that a man's attendance and usefulness in Congress depend on the frequency and length of his speeches," declared a Gilman supporter. "The *vote* of some men has much more influence than the most *labor'd harrangues* of others."

Elected to the Senate as a Republican in 1805, Gilman died before the conclusion of his second term.

John Ramage, the Irish-trained miniaturist, shows Gilman as he appeared at the time of the First Congress.

Nicholas Gilman by John Ramage (1748–1802); watercolor on ivory, circa 1790. Mr. and Mrs. Eddy G. Nicholson

BENJAMIN GOODHUE
1748–1814
Representative from Massachusetts

Benjamin Goodhue arrived at New York and sniffed at those of his colleagues who had gone to the expense of bringing "their Families and keeping their Servants and carriages." The six-dollar-a-day compensation for members of Congress he regarded as "enormous and unreasonable."

Goodhue was one of those labeled by William Maclay as Hamilton's "gladiators." Assumption of the debts of the states Goodhue regarded as essential to the "future prospects of the Union and government," but for the record he declared that he was "not the holder of one farthing of securities either Continental or State." Madison's proposal for paying subsequent holders of continental securities less than the original holders Goodhue regarded as a breach of faith. "What reason have we to expect that in any future contest in which the United States may be engaged where necessity may compel them to issue promissory obligations to continue their exertions that those obligations will obtain the least degree of credit."

Funding and assumption, Goodhue wrote in July 1790, have "engrossed all my thoughts and exertions to accomplish, for without it, to me nothing appeared worth preserving."

"You Know I am apt to be gloomy, and have my fears," Goodhue wrote as he worried that the union would be torn apart by dissension over the residence. "Mr. Goodhue," wrote Fisher Ames in early June of 1790, "frowns all day long, and swears as much as a good Christian can about the perverseness of Congress." It was at almost at this precise moment that Goodhue's visage was captured by Joseph Wright. The portrait was completed by the time the second session of Congress adjourned on August 12. Goodhue carried his image home and inscribed on the back of the canvas: "Salem Sept, 13th 1790/this picture is acknowled,d/a strong Likeness/ B. Goodhue."

Goodhue remained in the House of Representatives until he resigned during the Fourth Congress, and he later served in the Senate. On the day following Goodhue's death, Salem's inimitable diarist, Judge William Bentley, assessed, "He was not of splendid talents, but he appeared of such firm habits as fixed the public favor."

Benjamin Goodhue by Joseph Wright (1756–1793); oil on canvas, 1790. Private collection

SAMUEL GRIFFIN
1746–1810
Representative from Virginia

S amuel Griffin did not fall into the common pattern of the reluctant candidate who sought election only after repeated appeals from his friends. Griffin, a member of a prominent Virginia family and the brother of Cyrus Griffin, the last president of the old Congress, decided to seek election from the Henrico district on his own initiative. An aide-de-camp to General Charles Lee during the Revolution, Colonel Griffin was a lawyer and had represented Williamsburg in the Virginia Assembly since 1786.

Griffin, a Federalist, vanquished two opponents. Miles King, however, a Hampton merchant and member of the Virginia legislature, explained to James Madison on March 3, 1789, *Mr. Griffin is the Representative from our District. You May think it odd I did not Vote for him as he and myself was both in favour of the Constitution, but Sir as a friend to my Country I Could not think him a proper Man. You know his Inattention to Business and being two fond of pleasure, I thought we ought to send Men of Example.* King concluded that he hoped "Mr Griffin will be More Attentive than he Was in Our Assembly." There is no indication that Griffin ever spoke on the floor of the House of Representatives.

It would appear, however, that Griffin's constituents were well enough satisfied with his conduct in office, for he was returned to the Second and Third Congresses. But by the end of this time, the sentiment in his district, which included the city of Richmond, was strongly in support of Madison's Republican policies, and Griffin, who smelled defeat, declined to stand for reelection.

Griffin's last years were spent in New York. There he was depicted in the domestic setting sometimes utilized by William Dunlap, who had studied painting with Benjamin West in London but was also active as a playwright and theatrical manager. Dunlap's play, *The Father; or, American Shandyism,* was presented at New York's John Street Theatre in September 1789.

Samuel Griffin attributed to William Dunlap (1766–1839); oil on canvas, circa 1806. National Gallery of Art, Washington, D.C.; gift of Edgar William and Bernice Chrysler Garbisch (1953.5.80)

THOMAS HARTLEY
1748–1800
Representative from Pennsylvania

Thomas Hartley, from York, Pennsylvania, was one of only thirteen Representatives ready to proceed to business on March 4, 1789. "As I have been punctual to appear at the Day," he noted, "I shall be put down for good scholar and so many have pleaded private Convenience."

The jovial Hartley William Maclay characterized as "the most extravagant Member of the Pennsylvania Delegation." That the man lacked prudence Maclay was sure, when he heard from Frederick Muhlenberg "that Hartley is very dependent in his circumstances, a mere Borrower and Discounter of Notes at the Philada. bank." Maclay was outraged when Hartley appeared dressed "fine as a lord," and declared him to be "more affected and disgusting than ever."

Maclay characterized his colleague as a "Strange peice of Pomposity," yet Hartley's private letters reveal him to be a man of few pretensions. As the business of the Congress got under way, Hartley confided, *So many local Interests & so many Prejudices to be reconciled we may readily suppose that Decions in Congress at least in her Infancy — cannot be very speedy. It is a great school for Improvement — I wish I may approach a great degree of Perfection myself. I shall at least study to understand my Duty and endeavour to practice it.*

In the midst of the debate on the President's sole right to remove appointees, Hartley seized the opportunity to write to his friends in Pennsylvania, since "my Mind has been made up for two Days," and "other Gentlemen are repeating what has been said over and over again." Before he closed, he advised that the matter had been resolved by a vote of 30 to 20. "This was a very cardinal Point — upon which the Happiness or Misery of this Country much depends. The responsibility of the President is much established. . . . He will have it in his Power to remove such improper Persons as soon as he discovers their unfitness."

Hartley's likeness, attributed to the noted miniaturist Edward Greene Malbone of Rhode Island, was likely executed in Philadelphia during his last term in the Congress. The portrait early entered the City of Philadelphia collection, as much because of Hartley's Revolutionary War exploits — particularly against the Indians in the Wyoming area of Pennsylvania — as for his political services.

Thomas Hartley attributed to Edward Greene Malbone (1777–1807); oil on ivory, circa 1798. Independence National Historical Park Collection, Philadelphia, Pennsylvania

RALPH IZARD

1742–1804

Senator from South Carolina

Ralph Izard, educated in England and well traveled throughout the Continent, looked with scorn upon republican plainness. He was dismayed that the Congress — in disregard of civilized custom — decided to present their address to "the President of the United States," leaving out "George Washington." He wrote in disgust to Edward Rutledge that the business was "a contemptible affectation of Roman Simplic[it]y, & which in my opinion bord[ers] very much on the vulgar."

The South Carolina nabob was warm in calling for respectable salaries for members of Congress. "Up now rose Izard," reported William Maclay, to protest "that members of the Senate went to boarding Houses lodged in holes and Corners, associated with improper Company, and conversed improperly, so as to lower their dignity and Character." Izard pointed out that at the Confederation Congress "the Delegates from South Carolina Used to have £600 sterg. per Year and could live like Gentlemen."

Mrs. Izard, who had been a DeLancey of New York, accompanied her husband to the Congress, and the family set up there in style. Ralph Izard, along with William Few, who had also married a New York wife, were the only two southern Senators to vote, on July 1, 1790, against the bill to leave New York for Philadelphia and move ten years hence to a permanent site on the Potomac.

When it came time to move to Philadelphia, Izard wrote ahead to say that he must have a coach house "large enough to hold my Coach, Post Chaise & one horse Chair." It would be inconvenient to have the coach house and stables at a distance, because "Servants always take advantage, & pretend to be there whenever they are wanted."

At the expiration of his six-year senatorial term, Ralph Izard retreated from the political arena. Long afterward, John Adams reflected that Izard "had a Warmth of Temper and sometimes a violence of Passions, that were very inconvenient to him and his Friends, and not a little dangerous to his Enemies."

Izard's portrait was painted sometime between 1764, when he returned to South Carolina to assume charge of his extensive landed inheritance, and 1771, when he went back to England to indulge his fondness for art, music, and literature. The image conveyed by Charles Town's resident artist,

Ralph Izard by Jeremiah Theus (1716–1774); oil on canvas, circa 1764–1771. Henry Ford Museum & Greenfield Village, Dearborn, Michigan

J.as Jackson.

Jeremiah Theus, gives credence to Izard's daughter's contention that her father refused to be presented at the Court of St. James's because he would never "bow the knee . . . to mortal man" and suggests the warmth of temper that Izard frequently displayed in Senate debate.

JAMES JACKSON
1757–1801
Representative from Georgia

James Jackson raged so loudly against the speculators in state certificates that he disturbed the Senate above, Fisher Ames related, "and to keep out the din, they put down their windows."

Jackson's celebrated temper was much in evidence when the Quaker memorial concerning the slave trade came before the House. "Is the whole morality of the United States confined to the quakers? Are they the only people whose feelings are to be consulted on this occasion?" he roared. "Is it to them we owe our present happiness? Was it they who formed the constitution? Did they, by their arms, or contributions, establish our independence?" asked Jackson, who had for six years commanded the Georgia Legionary Forces during the Revolution. "Why do these men set themselves up, in such a particular manner, against slavery? Do they understand the rights of mankind, and the disposition of Providence, better than others?"

Defeated by Anthony Wayne for a seat in the Second Congress, Jackson contested the election, and the place was declared vacant by the House. In 1793 Jackson was elected to the Senate and won fame when he resigned to return to Georgia to wage a successful campaign for repeal of the notorious "Yazoo" law, which virtually gave away thirty-five million acres of western lands to speculators.

Jackson's biography was included in *The National Portrait Gallery of Distinguished Americans*, published in 1835 by James Barton Longacre and James Herring. His portrait, drawn by Longacre after a profile executed by Charles Balthazar Julien Févret de Saint Mémin, was engraved by W. A. Wilmer for the third volume of the work.

James Jackson by W. A. Wilmer (died 1855), after James Barton Longacre, after Charles Balthazar Julien Févret de Saint-Mémin; stipple engraving, not dated. National Portrait Gallery, Smithsonian Institution, Washington, D.C.

WILLIAM SAMUEL JOHNSON
1727–1819
Senator from Connecticut

Shortly after he had signed the Constitution, William Samuel Johnson accepted the presidency of Columbia College and settled down in New York. There seemed to have been no questions raised about his eligibility to represent Connecticut in the United States Senate.

But a correspondent in a letter of March 31, 1790, published in the *Connecticut Journal,* pointed out that Johnson had been an inhabitant of the state of New York at the time of his election—a matter that the writer would not have brought up had the Senator not drawn the six-year term. The author went on to say, "I venerate the man, but if he remain in congress, let it be as a senator from New-York, and not for Connecticut." The article closed, "We cannot suppose that our interest will be so fairly represented by members from any other state, as by those from our own: Particularly by those from the State of New-York, whose interest in a commercial view is altogether repugnant to ours."

Some also thought that Johnson's preoccupation with the Senate inter-fered with his teaching responsibilities. Young John Randolph of Roanoke, who was then a student at the college, complained that Johnson "is so engross'd by the Business of the Senate that he can do no other Affairs. We all go in to the hall & take seats; every one reads a paragraph upon which he makes no observation either on the author or the manner of reading."

It was obvious to Johnson that the debts of the states should be assumed. Maclay reported that he "deny'd there was any such thing as a State Debt; they were all equally the debts of the United States."

After the excise was passed, Maclay hissed, "Doctor Johnson spoke with great Joy," declaring, "The Business is compleat. We have a Revenue that will support Government, and every necessary Measure of Government."

While the Congress sat in New York, Johnson asserted, he was able to "fulfill with ease" the duties of both Senator and college president, but he found it impossible to hold both offices in different cities. At the end of the third session he resigned, saying, "the state of my health, the situation of my affairs, & my time of Life render it very inconvenient for me longer to attend Congress." Persistent ill health forced his resignation from Columbia in 1800. He retired to Connecticut, took a second wife, and lived for nineteen more years.

William Samuel Johnson by Gilbert Stuart (1755–1828); oil on canvas, 1793. Private collection

Johnson's portrait by Gilbert Stuart shows him in the scarlet robe of an Oxford Doctor of Civil Law; it was painted in New York shortly after the artist's return to America, a time when he was at special pains to impress his countrymen with his genius.

RUFUS KING
1755–1827
Senator from New York

Rufus King's rise in the world of New York politics had been meteoric. A month after he had formally transferred his allegiance from Massachusetts, he was elected to the New York legislature, and ten days later that body had promoted him to the United States Senate. Noted Massachusetts Representative George Thatcher, writing from New York, "This State think they have made a considerable acquisition in him, & I think that Massachusetts has suffered a great Loss."

As a young lawyer in the Confederation Congress, King had achieved a reputation as an orator, and when he represented Massachusetts at the Constitutional Convention, William Pierce of Georgia took note of King's "sweet high toned voice," and added, "there is something peculiarly strong and rich in his expression, clear, and convincing in his arguments, rapid and irresistible at times in his eloquence." After King's election to the Senate one Federalist reflected, "Although from the character I have heard of Mr. King, I could rather have wished to see him in the House of Delegates, his eloquence being better adapted to a popular than a select branch."

Brissot de Warville, meeting King in 1788, observed that he "is reputed to be the most eloquent man in the United States. What impressed me most about him was his modesty; he seems completely unaware of his worth."

William Maclay, who scorned King as one of the secretary of the treasury's chief allies, characterized him as "plausible and florid." Snorted Maclay as King defended Hamilton's proposal for giving the President the power to form revenue districts without regard to state boundaries, "Like an Indian at the war Post he wrought himself into a passion, declared that *we had no right to pay any more attention to the State boundaries than to the boundaries of the Cham of Tartary.*"

Rufus King by John Trumbull (1756–1843); oil on canvas, circa 1801. Mr. and Mrs. Christopher W. Wood

King's failure to keep his Massachusetts friends from voting to abandon New York could not be helped, Alexander Hamilton explained to his friend, because nothing but Philadelphia as the permanent residence, or that place temporarily and the Potomac permanently, would insure the assumption.

Among the Federalists King was a luminary, and he would remain so throughout his career as a Senator, minister to Great Britain, and his party's last candidate for the presidency of the United States.

King, who had known John Trumbull since their days together at Harvard, commissioned portraits of himself and his wife at a time when the artist, after a seven-year stint as a diplomat and art dealer, stood in need of encouragement to resume his painting career. King was then minister to Great Britain.

MARY ALSOP KING
1769–1819
Lady of the Senator from New York

R ufus King's marriage in March of 1786 to sixteen-year-old Mary Alsop, daughter of a prominent New York merchant, seemed a happy omen to the nationalists. "I am pleased with these intermarriages," John Jay noted to John Adams. "They tend to assimilate the States, and to promote one of the first wishes of my heart, viz., to see the people of America become one nation in every respect." The union had further political consequences when his wife's attachment to her aged father — of whom she was an only child—proved to be a powerful inducement for King to forsake his native Massachusetts and settle at New York.

Mrs. King was pregnant with her first child during the summer of 1787, and King returned to New York from the Constitutional Convention to stay at her side until she was brought to bed. To the great relief of the Massachusetts Federalists, she gave birth to a fine son on January 3, just in time for her husband to hurry on to the ratifying convention at Boston. Fourteen months later her second son was born. In mid-May of 1790, as her husband concerned himself with heading off schemes to remove the capital from New York, she added a little daughter to her flock. By the fall, Mrs. King was active once more in the social circles of the administration, attending Mrs. Washington's receptions, dining at the President's, and sharing his box at the

Mary Alsop King by John Trumbull (1756–1843); oil on panel, circa 1801. Mr. and Mrs. Christopher W. Wood

theater, but soon she would be confined with yet another son.

Her portrait by John Trumbull, painted when she was a year or so past thirty, does not belie the description of Mary King given in 1788 by George Thatcher as "the best looking woman I have seen since I have been in this city." The future Congressman from Massachusetts added, "She is a good hearted woman, and, I think, possesses all that Benevolence and kind, friendly disposition, that never fail to find respectable admirers."

JOHN LANGDON
1741–1819
Senator from New Hampshire

"Tho' fully Sensible, that my Abilities, are by no means equal to the important Business," John Langdon reflected to Benjamin Rush on March 21, 1789, "I am clear in opinion, that it was the *Duty* of every Gentleman, who has the Confidence of the people, (let his Situation as to private business; be what they may) to come forward at this all important moment." And so, at the expense of his "Domestick peace and happiness," Langdon had accepted the appointment to the Senate. To make his situation more agreeable, he brought his wife and daughter to New York with him.

The assumption was a difficult issue for Langdon, because New Hampshire had a small war debt, and the legislature declared Hamilton's proposal to be "objectionable and disgusting" to the citizens of the state. It was contended that New Hampshire had contributed one twenty-eighth part of the wartime expenses, but the sum proposed to be assumed of the debts of the states was less than one-seventieth part of the whole. Langdon, asked by a constituent if New Hampshire would not be "paying seven or eight hundred thousand dollars of the debt of some other state," replied, "It is a *great national* measure. New Hampshire does not contribute her proportion of the public revenue."

William Maclay recorded on April 27, 1790, "Langdon who lodges nearly opposite called to me from a Window. I went over and had a long discourse with him on the Subject of removing Congress. He wants to make the Assumption of State Debts the Condition of it." Langdon, went on Maclay,

John Langdon attributed to Edward Savage (1761–1817); oil on canvas, circa 1790. Society for the Preservation of New England Antiquities, Boston, Massachusetts; bequest of John Elwyn Stone, 1975

"avowed in the most unequivocal Manner, That *Consolidation* of the different Governments was his Object in the Matter; That perhaps it was against the Interest of his State in particular &ca."

Langdon did support Alexander Hamilton on funding and assumption as well as the national bank, but by 1794 his dislike of England and friendly regard for France caused him to leave the Federalists and support the party of Jefferson and Madison. Langdon retired from the Senate in 1801 and, as the spearhead of the Republican party in New Hampshire, resumed the governorship in 1805.

His portrait, which hangs today in the elegant mansion he erected at Portsmouth in 1783, has been attributed to Edward Savage, the artist who in 1789 numbered among his sitters the President of the United States.

JOHN LAURANCE
1750–1810
Representative from New York

Alexander Hamilton, who managed John Laurance's campaign for the New York City seat in the House of Representatives, dismissed his candidate's deficiency in mercantile knowledge with the observation that *it was supposed that a man of information, accustomed to political enquiry could easily supply that deficiency, by consulting such of his constituents as were capable of advising him on the subject; and the known disposition of Mr. Lawrence left no reason to doubt that he would always take care to avail himself of this resource.* Laurance, who had a reputation for legal learning, had served in the Confederation Congress and had been a state Senator since 1788.

The English-born Laurance readily undertook the obligation to the city's commercial interest, denouncing James Madison's proposal to give lower tonnage duties to America's ally, France, as detrimental to New York's heavy trade with Great Britain. Laurance's prominence in debate excited a denunciation from a writer to the *Pennsylvania Gazette,* who expressed "the most alarming apprehensions at the zeal and steadiness [with] which a certain eloquent member of the House of Representatives, from the *city of New York* opposes every measure which affected the trade or dignity of the merchants and parliament of Great Britain."

John Laurance by John Trumbull (1756–1843); oil on panel, 1792. The New-York Historical Society; gift of George C. McWhorter and John L. McWhorter

That Laurance was held in respect by his colleagues is attested to by his appointment to a multitude of committees, among them those dealing with appropriations, bankruptcy, duties on distilled spirits, duties on teas, Indian trade, lighthouses, naturalization, revenue laws, salaries, seat of government, sinking fund, and Vermont statehood.

A dependable Federalist, Laurance remained in the House until 1793, at which time President Washington — to whom he had been a wartime aide — appointed him a federal judge. Subsequently he returned to fill the Senate seat relinquished by Rufus King.

Laurance was among the members of Congress who posed at Philadelphia for a miniature portrait in preparation for John Trumbull's unrealized depiction of the inauguration of the first President of the United States.

RICHARD BLAND LEE
1761–1827
Representative from Virginia

I went up to the Election of a Representative to Congress for this district," noted George Washington in his diary on February 2, 1789. "Voted for Ricd Bland Lee Esqr." The twenty-eight-year-old Loudoun County planter, a cousin of Richard Henry Lee, was from the solidly Federalist branch of the family.

"Mr. Richard Bland Lee gained very great applause as a member in the house of Deligates last Session of assembly," Robert Carter of Nomini Hall testified, "in the part he took with the Feaderalists and it is expected that he will be Chosen a representative of the new Congress. His Abilities fall to the Lot of few men." By December of 1790, however, Carter, apparently annoyed by some of Lee's political positions, abruptly terminated the Congressman's courtship of his daughter, Sarah.

Antifederalists in Virginia denounced Lee for failing to support all of the amendments recommended by the Virginia ratifying convention. "Mr. Lee voted against even taking up the consideration of the Virginia amendments; and when some of the most important of them, were brought forward, he voted against their adoption," charged George Mason's son, Stevens Thom-

Richard Bland Lee by an unidentified artist; watercolor on ivory, circa 1785–1800. Joseph and Margaret Muscarelle Museum of Art, The College of William and Mary in Virginia

son Mason. "It must be admitted, even by his admirers, that he is a man devoid of truth and honor."

Lee had been as alarmed as the next Virginian when he heard rumors that Hamilton planned to call for the consolidation of state and national debts. "I conceive [it] impracticable at this time," he noted, and thought that it "would I fear put weapons in the hands of the adversaries of the government which might be tend very much to its injury." Initially Lee voted against the assumption, but then he cast a vote that allowed for its passage.

By bargaining away his vote on the assumption in return for the permanent residence on the Potomac, Lee recognized that he had put his political career in jeopardy. He had no doubt, however, that his action had been proper. "The success of this measure," he wrote privately, "cannot fail to add vastly to the prosperity of my constituents." Moreover, he rationalized, the assumption "is so calculated to conciliate the most populous & wealthy portion of the United States, that I have no doubt it should be agreed to."

In a broadside of August 21, 1790, addressed to the voters, Lee proclaimed that he had "the conscious satisfaction of having served my country with zeal and fidelity, and not without effect—particularly on some recent and important occasions. I have been grossly censured and misrepresented, and am determined to stand or fall by an appeal to the free and independent voices of my constituents." Lee was reelected for two more terms.

Lee's miniature, which descended in his family, is now owned by the College of William and Mary, where his education had been interrupted by the advance of the British in late 1780.

RICHARD HENRY LEE
1732–1794
Senator from Virginia

Revolutionary firebrand Richard Henry Lee, who had moved in 1776 that "these United Colonies are, and of right ought to be, free and independent States," came to the first Senate of the United States determined to force amendments to a Constitution that he regarded as threatening to hard-won liberties. Senator William Maclay characterized

Richard Henry Lee by Charles Willson Peale (1741–1827); oil on canvas, circa 1795–1805. National Portrait Gallery, Smithsonian Institution, Washington, D.C.; gift of Duncan Lee and his son, Gavin Dunbar Lee

During the tariff debate, Richard Henry Lee, whose constituents were heavily dependent upon importations, gave opposition, charged William Maclay, "to every Article especially the protecting duties he declares openly against the Principle of them." Lee spoke for an hour and a quarter against taxing twine "because the Virginians, had hitherto imported their nets from Britain." Said an exasperated Maclay, "It was in Vain Lee was told he could be supplied with all the Nets Virginia wanted from any part of New England."

The Plantation by an unidentified artist; oil on panel, not dated. The Metropolitan Museum of Art, New York City; gift of Edgar William and Bernice Chrysler Garbisch, 1963 (63.210.3)

him then as "the man who gave independence (in one sense) to America. A man of a clear head and great experience in public business; certainly ambitious and vainglorious, but his passions seek gratification in serving the public."

James Madison was shocked when Lee proved to be second only to John Adams in favor of presidential titles. He was further appalled that Lee was "for admitting Britain to an equality with the most favored nation."

Outflanked when James Madison early brought the matter of amendments to the floor, Lee wrote sulkily, "How they will terminate I cannot say—But my wishes are stronger than my expectations." The old revolutionary grumbled, *It is too much the fashion now to look at the rights of the People, as a Miser inspects a Security, to find out a flaw—What with design in some, and fear of Anarchy in others, it is very clear, I think, that a government very different from a free one will take place eer many years are passed.*

Lee reported to Patrick Henry on September 14 that the twelve amendments agreed to by the Congress fell far short of the recommendations made by the Virginia ratifying convention. "You may be assured that nothing on my part was left undone to prevent this, and every possible effort was used to give success to all the amendments proposed by our country. We might as well have attempted to move Mount Atlas upon our shoulders." However, he conceded, "The great points of free election, jury trial in criminal cases, and the unlimited rights of taxation, and standing armies, remain as they were." Lee concluded, "The most essential danger from the present system arises, in my opinion, from its tendency to a consolidated government, instead of a union of Confederated States."

In June 1790, as debate on funding and assumption waxed furious in the Senate, Lee told Henry, "It is impossible, for me to describe the scene here, and shall I content myself with saying, that every thing met with in my former life is mere trifling, compared with this, and you know that I have been in very stormy legislative scenes." He predicted, "A vast monied interest is to be created, that will forever be warring against the landed interest, to the destruction of the latter." The evil of funding the debts of the United States, Lee expounded, would be increased tenfold by the assumption of the state debts. "By possessing the general government, with the sole cause, and consequently, with the whole power of taxation," the state legislatures would be converted "into mere corporations."

Lee resigned from the Senate in October 1792 and retired to his plantation, Chantilly, in Westmoreland County. After his death, his family asked Charles Willson Peale for a replica of the portrait that the artist had painted for his gallery of heroes when Lee was president of the old Congress. This portrait was presented to the National Portrait Gallery by Lee descendants in 1974.

SAMUEL LIVERMORE
1732–1803
Representative from New Hampshire

Samuel Livermore was the lone member among the New Hampshire delegation in the House of Representatives to consistently vote against assumption, a position popular with New Hampshire voters. He was rewarded with a resounding vote of confidence in the 1790 election.

A correspondent pointed out in the *New Hampshire Gazette* that Livermore's fellow Representatives, Abiel Foster and Nicholas Gilman, were in disagreement with him on almost every question. "If Mr. *Livermore* voted on one side, the other two were almost sure to vote on the other." The article, which appeared on November 27, 1790, went on to note that Livermore had carried every single town in the state except Exeter, the home of Gilman — "from this circumstance it may fairly be presumed that his conduct has been generally approbated."

Another article, signed "Philo Patrie," expressed similar sentiments and noted that the division between Livermore and his colleagues "has arisen to a degree of personal animosity, that prevents all friendly intercourse, and the good of the public is thus in danger of being sacrificed to their mutual dislike."

A card signed "A Countryman" declared that Livermore's election proved that the people were "satisfied with his doings in Congress," and it would be better to provide him with two new colleagues "as probably they will better agree in opinion, and the wishes of the people of this state will be better attended to than heretofore. Perhaps there may be more questions about *Assumption*."

Abiel Foster, who had supported assumption, was not reelected, but Nicholas Gilman, who had finally come around to voting for the measure, was returned. Livermore, at the close of his second term in Congress, was promoted to the Senate.

Livermore, summed up his senatorial successor, William Plumer, *rose, and continued in office, by the force of talents, and the reputation of integrity, and not by the mildness of his temper, or the amenity of his manners. He was a man of strong intellectual powers, of great shrewdness — possessed much wit, and had a vein for severe satire.* Plumer declared that Livermore "reasoned and studied much — he drew from himself more than from books — indeed he was not a great reader — not being fond of books." He was a man who "loved wine, ardent spirits,

Samuel Livermore by John Trumbull (1756–1843); oil on panel, 1792. The Currier Gallery of Art, Manchester, New Hampshire; Museum purchase

and a good table, but was not intemperate."

John Trumbull asked Livermore to pose for his portrait so that his visage might be incorporated into the artist's contemplated—but never executed—depiction of the inauguration of the first President of the United States.

JAMES MADISON
1751–1836
Representative from Virginia

I confess I have always attributed to you," John Page wrote to James Madison after ratification of the Constitution had been assured, "the Glory of laying the Foundation of this great Fabric of government, of supporting the Plan of it in Convention & of animating all the States to cooperate in the great Work." Thus it was in the First Federal Congress, with Madison the commanding figure in getting the "new Machine into operation."

Madison was influential, not only in the House of Representatives but also as an adviser to the President. It was at his suggestion that Washington abandoned the seventy-page inaugural address drawn up for him by his secretary, David Humphreys, in favor of a brief statement devoid of specific proposals other than a request that Congress consider amendments to the Constitution.

In his capacity as a legislator, Madison drafted the House's message to the

The use of snuff, a fashionable indulgence of eighteenth-century gentlemen, was much in evidence at the First Federal Congress.

Silver snuff box owned by James Madison. Mabel Brady Garvan Collection, Yale University Art Gallery, New Haven, Connecticut

James Madison by James Sharples (circa 1751–1811); pastel on paper, 1796–1797. Independence National Historical Park Collection, Philadelphia, Pennsylvania

President of the United States; then, in his role as Washington's confidant, he drafted a response to his own rhetoric as well as the President's reply to the Senate address.

Madison introduced the first revenue bill, played a major role in organizing the executive departments, and singlehandedly arranged and engineered the passage of the Bill of Rights. During the first session of the Congress, Madison suffered defeat only in his efforts to secure a favorable treatment for French commerce. But by the second session of the Congress, he was surpassed in influence by Alexander Hamilton, and by the third session was in decided conflict with the administration.

Fisher Ames described Madison as "a studious man, devoted to public business, and a thorough master of almost every public question that can arise, or he will spare no pains to become so." Went on Ames, "He speaks low, his person is little and ordinary." Ames, who found the Virginian to be no kindred spirit, noted that "Madison is cool and has an air of reflection, which is not very distant from gravity and self-sufficiency. In speaking he never relaxes into pleasantry." Ames conceded, "I think him a good man and an able man, but he has rather too much theory, and wants that discretion which men of business commonly have." Thomas Hartley of Pennsylvania was of the same opinion, saying that Madison "is certainly an extraordinary Man — and when he comes to have a sufficient knowledge of practical Life — there will be few beyond him."

James Sharples shows Madison near the close of the Washington administration, when he was the leader of the Republican opposition in the House of Representatives. Madison's countenance, noted Brissot de Warville, "was that of a person conscious of his talents and of his duties."

JAMES MONROE
1758–1831
Senator from Virginia

After James Monroe was defeated by James Madison for a seat in the House of Representatives, he told Thomas Jefferson, "As I had no private object to gratify so a failure has given me no private concern." In March 1790 Monroe's name was mentioned to fill the vacancy

James Monroe by John Vanderlyn (1775–1852); oil on canvas, 1816. National Portrait Gallery, Smithsonian Institution, Washington, D.C.

caused by the death of William Grayson, but he was superseded by one vote in the executive council, with the interim appointment going to John Walker, an Albemarle County planter. At the October meeting of the Assembly, however, Walker was dropped and Monroe elected in his stead.

Monroe wrote to Jefferson that the commission "will contribute greatly to my own & the gratification of Mrs. M. as it will place us both with & nearer our friends." The Monroes arrived at Philadelphia on December 17, and Mrs. Monroe and her daughter lingered only long enough to have the child inoculated against smallpox before going on to visit her family, the Kortrights, at New York. James Monroe joined James Madison and Thomas Jefferson at the boardinghouse kept by Mrs. Mary House and her daughter Eliza Trist, which for a decade had been "home away from home" for the Virginians.

Monroe took his seat eleven days into the third session of the Congress and readily joined the southern contingent in resistance to a national bank. He stood also against the excise tax.

In accordance with his instructions from the Virginia legislature, Monroe moved—but to no avail—that the doors of the Senate be open to the public.

Monroe was reelected in 1791 and served in the Senate until 1794, when he was appointed minister to France. At the time this portrait was painted by John Vanderlyn, the French-trained protégé of Aaron Burr, Monroe was about to become the last of the Virginia dynasty to succeed to the presidency.

ROBERT MORRIS
1734–1806
Senator from Pennsylvania

Few people were ambivalent about Robert Morris. Those who admired him thought him second only to Washington in bringing about the independence of the country; those who hated him called him a monopolizer, a profiteer, a self-interested manipulator, and worse.

Born in Liverpool, England, Morris had come to America at thirteen and, with the death of his father two years later, was left to make his own way in the world. His business success had come by taking risks. "Miss Fortune is fickle

Robert Morris by Charles Willson Peale (1741–1827); oil on canvas, circa 1782. New Orleans Museum of Art, Louisiana; Museum purchase through Art Acquisition Fund Drive

The Committee appointed to provide a House for the Residence of the President of the United States Report —

That no House was to be found in the City that would accommodate the President & his Family without Additions or Alterations, that the House of Robert Morris Esquire approached the nearest of any to what was desired & was capable of being rendered sufficiently commodious at the least Expence — Wherefore the Committee applied to him & he politely agreed to give it for two Years upon the following Conditions —

That the Committee would procure him the House then in the Tenure of General Stewart under a Lease for about three Years —

That the Corporation would advance to him a Sum of Money sufficient to pay for Work & Materials necessary to complete the Additions & Alterations pointed out by the President for his Accommodation, & make such Repairs to the said House, as he should think necessary of which he would keep an exact Account

That all such Additions & Alterations & Repairs as should be permanently useful & Ornamental to the Building should be charged to the said Robert Morris & allowed out of the Rent to be hereafter agreed on, & all those that should be temporary or merely

"My having given up my house to accommodate the President," Robert Morris declared, "I consider . . . amongst the sacrifices I have made, both of interest and convenience, and I think there is no other man for whom I would have done it."

"Report of the Comm[itt]ee of Aug. 9th. & 23 for the Accommodation of the President." The Historical Society of Pennsylvania, Philadelphia

and coy," he wrote. "Therefore if you court her you must not only be bold, adventurous, and attentive to her humours, but persevering in your endeavours to win her."

Morris, assessed William Pierce, his fellow delegate at the Constitutional Convention, "has an understanding equal to any public object, and possesses an energy of mind that few Men can boast of. Although he is not learned, yet he is as great as those who are."

At the Congress, Morris, an easy man of tolerant disposition, suffered the tediousness of the proceedings with good humor. "We go on but slowly in the business of organizing the new Government," he wrote on July 9, 1789. *There are a great many to speak in the Public Debates and they seem fond of exercising their rights, but for my part I have so often seen good Consequences arise from Public debate and discussions that I am not amongst the number of those who complain of the delay occasioned thereby.*

As superintendent of finance during the near-bankrupt days of the Confederation, Morris had substituted his personal credit for that which the country had lost. No member of the First Congress had a keener appreciation for the necessity of Alexander Hamilton's financial program.

In the portrait that Morris commissioned from Charles Willson Peale, there appears a monumental structure that surely must symbolize the Bank of North America, which Morris instigated in 1781 "to obtain the Money of Individuals for the benefit of the Union and thereby bind these individuals more strongly to the general cause by the ties of private interest."

Morris served out his six-year Senate term but declined renomination. In 1798 his tottering structure of speculations collapsed, and he was confined in debtors' prison until 1801.

MARY WHITE MORRIS
1749–1827
Lady of the Senator from Pennsylvania

Robert Morris's lady was a fashionable woman, but never a great beauty. The most that one French visitor could say by way of description was that she had "an agreeable expression." Married to the already-successful merchant in 1769, before she was twenty, Molly ultimately became the mother of five sons and two daughters. "I am indeed very sensible that our existence on earth is very necessary to each others happiness," her husband wrote to her in 1788, "for the departure of either

would leave the other in a very uncomfortable position being too far advanced in Life & too large a Family to admit of any reparation of the loss by new connection."

Martha Washington, on her way to join the President in New York, was put up by Molly at Philadelphia and then accompanied by her to the seat of government. When Mrs. Washington held her first levee, Mrs. Morris stood to her right during the entire time. It should be pointed out, however, that the Vice-President's lady had not yet arrived. Abigail Adams would later note, "My station is always at the right hand of Mrs. W.; through want of knowing what is right I find it sometimes occupied, but on such an occasion the President never fails of seeing that it is relinquished for me."

On June 11, 1789, William Maclay dined with the Morrises and recorded in his diary, "Mrs. Morris talked a good deal after dinner. She did it gracefully enough, This being a gayer place and she being considered as at least the 2d female Character at Court. As to taste etiquette &ca. she is certainly the first."

When the government removed to Philadelphia, the Morrises obligingly gave up their dwelling on High Street—"the best single house in the city"—as a residence for the President. They themselves moved just around the corner, and Washington paid Mrs. Morris the highest of all compliments when he declared her to be "a notable lady in family arrangement."

Charles Willson Peale posed Mrs. Robert Morris, wife of the man reputed to be the richest in the country, in an elaborate formal garden that one would assume to be imaginary. Nonetheless, Abigail Adams, writing in 1791 from Bush Hill, the house that the Vice-President had taken just outside of Philadelphia — remarked that she had "a beautiful grove behind the house, through which there is a spacious gravel walk, guarded by a number of marble statues, whose genealogy I have not yet studied." First among the row of sculptured busts shown in the background of Mrs. Morris's portrait is that of General George Washington, whom the Morrises revered as a public figure and cultivated as a private friend.

Mary White Morris by Charles Willson Peale (1741–1827); oil on canvas, circa 1782. Independence National Historical Park Collection, Philadelphia, Pennsylvania

JOHN PAGE
1744–1808
Representative from Virginia

One of the most amiable and convivial members of the First Congress was John Page, who had been like a brother to Thomas Jefferson since their days together at the College of William and Mary. Inheritor of Rosewell, one of the grandest of all the Tidewater plantations, Page presided over a vast—albeit unprofitable—tobacco plantation and was the owner of some 160 slaves. His great interest in life was astronomy, but he confessed that he was too sociable to shut himself off for serious study.

Page and his friend Thomas Tudor Tucker of South Carolina relieved the tedium of sitting through debates by penning verses to be sent to their friends. "This rhyme-making does not interrupt our Attention to Business," Page noted to his correspondent, "for I arose between my 1st and 2nd stanza & rep[orted for the] committee." On another occasion, Page noted that his verse was composed "whilst Mr. Smith was Justifying slavery & abusing the Quakers." And in response to Thomas Tudor Tucker's poetic query aimed at John Adams, "In gravity clad, He has nought in his Head, But Visions of Nobles & Kings," Page immediately shot back:

> *I'll tell in a Trice—*
> *'Tis Old Daddy Vice*
> *Who carries of Pride an Ass-load;*
> *Who turns up his Nose,*
> *Wherever he goes*
> *With Vanity swell'd like a Toad.*

A widower with twelve children, Page declared during his first months in New York, *I never was less disposed to marry than now. Business & Dissipation & a great Variety of fine Figures divert the Attention from fixing on one Object—but I am sure whenever I venture from this Place I shall be again miserable. . . . In short I have seen no one yet who would suit me. The rich Widows are ugly & old & the rich Maids too young.* Less than a year later—in March of 1790—Page married Margaret Lowther, whom Jefferson described as "a maiden lady of about 30. a great poetess."

As the congressional elections approached, James Madison received an urgent message that Francis Corbin, who had offered for Congress in 1788, was making "uncommon exertions" to unseat Page. "These aided by strong

John Page by Charles Willson Peale (1741–1827); oil on canvas, circa 1790. Independence National Historical Park Collection, Philadelphia, Pennsylvania

grogg & roasted piggs have had their weight, & if Mr. Page does not hurry in I realy believe that he will be left out." Page returned to Gloucester County and was safely reelected. He did not, however, travel to Philadelphia for the third session of Congress because of his anxiety over his wife's impending motherhood. Page continued in the Congress until 1797, when he left the national legislature to resume service in the Virginia House of Delegates. At the time of his death, he was governor of the state.

Among Page's many friends was Charles Willson Peale, who asked the legislator to pose for a portrait for his gallery of distinguished Americans. "Very often looking at the portrait, I venerate the firm and friendly character of my departed friend," Peale wrote to Page's widow. "I wish I could have been favored with another setting to have made it a more finished picture. However, the likeness is striking, and posterity will admire the man when looking on the worthies of the Revolution."

JOSIAH PARKER
1751–1810
Representative from Virginia

Colonel Josiah Parker had fought with Washington at Trenton, Princeton, and Brandywine but resigned from the army over some pique in 1778. Elected to the Virginia House of Delegates in 1780, he was afterward appointed naval officer at Portsmouth, Virginia. He came to the First Federal Congress as an Antifederalist but was not perceived to be violent in his sentiments.

Back in Virginia in July of 1789, however, Parker was frank in his disapproval of the President's levees and dinners. "In short," Edmund Randolph reported to James Madison, Parker "represents every thing, as marching with furious rapidity, toward monarchy; as far as manners can work such an effect."

At the time the impost was under consideration, Parker proposed that a tax of ten dollars be placed on each slave brought into the country. The Virginian failed in his purpose but was heralded for his efforts in the Rhode Island press as "the first gentleman who, to his immortal honor, introduced a motion in

Josiah Parker by John Ramage (1748–1802); watercolor on ivory, circa 1789. National Museum of American Art, Smithsonian Institution, Washington, D.C.; Catherine Walden Myer Fund

Congress to discourage the 'disgraceful slave trade.'"

It was rumored in 1790 that "a quondam Parson will probably supply the place of Parker," but Parker survived the election and remained in Congress until 1801, when he retired to his family seat, Macclesfield, in Isle of Wight County.

John Ramage, an Irish-trained miniaturist who enjoyed a wide New York clientele—including the President of the United States, whom he also painted in military dress—executed Colonel Parker's portrait at the time he was at the First Congress.

GEORGE PARTRIDGE
1740–1828
Representative from Massachusetts

George Partridge, who represented the Cape Cod district of Massachusetts, was surprised to find one of his constituents calling upon him in New York in September 1789. Samuel Davis, the young visitor, recorded that Partridge "told me I was the first person he had ever seen from his district. Engage to breakfast with him to-morrow."

Partridge was sensitive to public opinion. "I perceive that the pay of us Reps makes much Speculation in our Country," he wrote to a supporter, "but I do not see it yet in the newspapers & hope I may not for tho' it is not a matter very important in itself, yet it may prove an Occasion of much reproach & real discredit to our Government." He noted that all of the Massachusetts delegation, except for Elbridge Gerry, thought that five dollars a day was "much too high, and here I think our constituents will agree with us."

Passage of an excise bill and the bill for the assumption of the state debts Partridge regarded as "important objects and from my heart I wish they were effected." But despite his reputation for "firmness, sobriety, good sense and sound Judgment," Partridge was defeated when he ran for reelection.

Following his graduation from Harvard, Partridge had taught school for about ten years, and in his will he bequeathed $10,000 to provide an academy "in my native town for a higher degree of instruction in mathematics, geography, history, languages and other branches of good learning than the common schools supply." Partridge Academy was opened in 1844. Further-

George Partridge by Rufus Hathaway (1770–1822); oil on canvas, 1793. Private collection

more, Partridge, who had also studied for the ministry, left $2,000 to Harvard University "for the promoting [of] theological education," and $10,000 to the Partridge Ministerial Fund of the First Church of Duxbury. His philanthropy had been made possible by investment in government securities, and the original bequests were made "in the six per-cent stock of the United States."

Partridge was painted at the age of fifty-three by Dr. Rufus Hathaway, a remarkable self-taught artist who worked in southeastern Massachusetts.

WILLIAM PATERSON
1745–1806
Senator from New Jersey

G ay life has never been my Wish," William Paterson protested soon after he took his seat in the first Senate. "My Disposition is naturally pensive, and in general I had much rather take a solitary Walk in a Grove, or among Tombs than mingle in the Festivity and Pleasure of a Ball." Nonetheless, his letters to his wife, who had been left behind in New Jersey, indicate a ready acceptance of many invitations to dine abroad.

To Mrs. Paterson, who found herself "low spirited" since his departure, her husband replied that he had *left home with much regrets; my absence is not a thing of choice; it is incidental to my station, the duties of which it is incumbent on me to discharge. I am fond, passionately fond of the still, quiet scenes of private and domestick life. I hate noise and bustle; they are not congenial with my soul—Remember that I am in the path of duty.*

Paterson, framer of the Constitution, prominent lawyer of long legislative experience, and former attorney general of New Jersey, was chosen to serve on the committee to draw up the judiciary bill, and he played an active role in its formation.

To William Maclay's disappointment, Paterson voted to give the President the power to remove appointments without the consent of the Senate. "Of All the Members of our House," wrote Maclay, "the Conduct of Patterson surprizes me most. He has been characterized to me as a Staunch Revolution Man & Genuine Whig. Yet he has in every republican Question deserted and in some instances betrayed Us."

William Paterson attributed to James Sharples (circa 1751–1811); pastel on paper, circa 1798. The Supreme Court of the United States, Washington, D.C.

By the second session Maclay pointed to Paterson and Rufus King of New York as flagrant members of Alexander Hamilton's "gladiatorial band." Paterson, Maclay described as "more taciturn and lurking in his Manner, and Yet when he speaks, commits himself hastily. A *Summum Jus* Man."

To Paterson, upholder of the sanctity of contracts and a spokesman for stability, order, and property, the passage of the funding and assumption bill was a cause for national optimism. "The next Session will *complete the System of Finance,* and I hope give Stability and Efficacy to the Government, and shape its future progress and operations," he wrote to his wife. *Much remains to be done; new Sources of Revenue are to be opened and applied to the support of national Credit, and the honorable Fulfillment of Contracts. We are laying the Foundations of a great Empire; the Prospect widens and brightens as we proceed; and to every enlarged Mind must give the highest Pleasure.*

Despite the elocution, Paterson was restive. "He talks of resigning," William Maclay noted in March 1790, "and I suppose we will hear of his being a Judge, or something better than a Senator." After Governor William Livingston's death in July, there was immediate talk of Paterson as his successor, and he resigned on November 23, 1790, to accept that office.

Paterson's portrait shows him as associate justice of the Supreme Court, to which he was appointed by President Washington in 1793.

GEORGE READ
1733–1798
Senator from Delaware

Despite entreaties from Charles Thomson, secretary to the old Congress, that his presence was needed to enable the new Congress to proceed to business, George Read did not take his seat until April 13, 1789. "I came to this place in ill health," Read wrote in June, "and continued so for some time."

Read, the leader of the Delaware conservative faction—the so-called "aristocratic party"—arrived in time to take part in the wrangling over whether it was proper for a republican Senate to thank the President for "his most gracious speech," the traditional response to an address from the King.

George Read by Robert Edge Pine (circa 1720s–1788); oil on canvas, begun 1784. National Portrait Gallery, Smithsonian Institution, Washington, D.C.; gift of W. B. Shubrick Clymer

"Up now rose Mr. Read," related William Maclay, who "saw no reason to object to it, because the British Speeches were stiled *most gracious*. If we chose to object to Words because they had been used in the same sense in Britain, we should soon be at a loss to do Business."

On the motion that would give the Senate a voice in the removal of appointments, Maclay reported that Read "was swinging on his legs for an Hour. He had to talk a great deal before he could bring himself, to declare against the Motion." At the Constitutional Convention, Read had been so much in favor of a strong executive that he proposed to give the President the power of an absolute veto.

Maclay called Read "a Man of Obstructed Elocution" and found him "excessively tedious." William Pierce, a Georgia delegate to the Grand Convention, gave a like description, writing that Read's "legal abilities are said to be very great, but his powers of Oratory are fatiguing and tiresome to the last degree; — his voice is feeble, and his articulation so bad that few can have the patience to attend him."

Read was derided by one of his enemies as a lawyer who "was esteemed a plodding rather than a sprightly genius," and who at the beginning of his career had "acquired an obsequious and courtly form of manners."

A Senator of the two-year first class, Read was reelected for a second term. He resigned in 1793 to become chief justice of Delaware.

George Read's portrait, commissioned when he was in the Confederation Congress, was thought by his family "to have an expression of sternness not his." Others, however, saw in the depiction by Robert Edge Pine the fastidiousness, dignity, and a certain austerity that Read's contemporaries mentioned as characteristic of the man.

PHILIP SCHUYLER
1733–1804
Senator from New York

After the secretary of the treasury had presented his detailed and intricate financial report to the Congress, the French minister, Louis-Guillaume Otto, reported to his government, "Mr. Hamilton had employed a clever mathematician to calculate all the risks of the annuities and

Philip Schuyler by John Trumbull (1756–1843); oil on mahogany, 1792. The New-York Historical Society

of the plan he proposes." The clever mathematician was his father-in-law, General Philip Schuyler.

"General Schuyler possessed the highest order of talents, but without varied scholastic attainments," remembered Elkanah Watson, who was an Albany neighbor of the Senator. "He was a profound mathematician, and held a powerful pen; his industry was unexampled; his business habits were accurate and systematic." In his memoir, Watson recalled Schuyler as "eminently refined in his sentiments, and elegant in his address." William Maclay viewed him quite differently: "This wretch is emaciated in person slovenly in dress, and rather aukward in address." Maclay, classifying Schuyler as among the worst of the speculators, derided, "Nor is it possible to assign to his appearance, any other passion property or affection but the love of Money, and the concomitant Character of a Miser." Sputtered Maclay, "Schyler is the

Bookplate engraved with the Schuyler family coat of arms. New York State Office of Parks, Recreation, and Historic Preservation; Schuyler Mansion State Historic Site, Albany, New York

supple Jack of his Son in law Hamilton."

Certainly Senator Schuyler was ardent in support of the financial program put forward by the secretary of the treasury. During the assumption debate, Maclay affirmed that so agitated was Schuyler by the opposition that his hair stood "on end as if the Indians had fired at him."

Defeated in his efforts to keep the residence at New York, Schuyler complained bitterly that if the wrongheaded members of the New York delegation — William Floyd, Jeremiah Van Rensselaer, and John Hathorn— had voted in favor of assumption, New York would have retained the government for many years.

Schuyler drew the short term, and the Antifederalist Clintonians, combined with the disgruntled Livingstons, succeeded in replacing him with Aaron Burr. "I confess I would rather continue," Schuyler wrote from Philadelphia on January 15, 1791, "but if it is the will OF MY MASTERS AT NEW YORK, that I SHOULD RETIRE (FROM CONGRESS) TO PLANT CABBAGES, I shall acquiesce WITH CHRISTIAN RESIGNATION TO THEIR DISPOSAL."

Six years later Schuyler prevailed over Burr, but chronic gout forced him into permanent retirement in 1798.

At Philadelphia General Schuyler posed for two small portraits by John Trumbull so that his image might be incorporated into historical paintings the artist was then contemplating. Schuyler, in civilian dress, appears in the *Surrender of General Burgoyne*, although he was not in fact present upon that occasion. The painting here belonged to his daughter, Elizabeth Hamilton.

THEODORE SEDGWICK
1746–1813
Representative from Massachusetts

When Theodore Sedgwick, finally elected to Congress by eleven votes, departed to take his seat, a close associate cautioned, "You know some people think you are rather sudden. . . . I would therefore advise you . . . not to speak much in Congress — and never but on great questions;—let the little folks do the little Business." But, from his arrival in New York on June 15, 1789, when he was just in time to speak out in support of the President's sole right to remove appointments — "Is there [to be] no way suddenly to seize the worthless wretch, and hurl him from the pinnacle of power?" — Sedgwick did not draw back from the thick of things.

Conspicuous among Hamilton's "gladiators," Sedgwick was fervent in

This walking stick was carried by Theodore Sedgwick and inscribed with his name, as well as those of his sons Robert and Charles, his grandson William E., and his great-grandson Robert.

Stockbridge Library Association, Massachusetts

support of the secretary's entire financial program, but for this Representative from Massachusetts nothing was more vital than the federal assumption of the wartime debts of the states. Should assumption not be agreed to, he confided to his wife, he would consider himself justified to defeat, if he could, "any funding system at all, because if justice should not be the basis of the administration of this government I believe it cannot prosper."

From New York Sedgwick protested to his wife that political life was not the *most agreeable to my inclination, but is most painful and disagreeable. You, my love will know the progress of inducements which brought me here, and I have the vanity to believe my feeble aid in the important business in which I am engaged will not be altogether without effect. My children are dear to my heart and I love the companion of my life as I love my own soul. From your own tender sensibility you will then judge my pain in the separation. To deny my compliance, with the earnest solicitations of my friends, was impossible, and it was equally so not to wish them success after the vile and wicked arts which were used to defeat my election.*

It fell to Sedgwick, as Speaker of the House of Representatives during the Sixth Congress, to announce the election of Thomas Jefferson as President of the United States. "I declare," said Sedgwick privately, "I consider Jefferson the greatest rascal and traitor in the United States." Shortly after this, the unrelenting Federalist retired from the national scene, and it was in Boston, where Sedgwick served as justice of the Supreme Judicial Court of Massachusetts, that Gilbert Stuart painted his portrait.

Theodore Sedgwick by Gilbert Stuart (1735–1828); oil on canvas, circa 1808. Courtesy, Museum of Fine Arts, Boston; bequest of Charles Sedgwick Rackemann (33.508)

PAMELA DWIGHT SEDGWICK
1753–1807

Lady of the Representative from Massachusetts

Mrs. Theodore Sedgwick, pregnant with her ninth child, was left at Stockbridge with her seven children while her husband went off to attend to the affairs of the nation.

Her letters to her husband reveal the loneliness of separation, but also an acute appreciation of the problems of the Congress. "I am grieved I am mortified my dearest Mr Sedgwick," she wrote to him on July 8, 1790, *that those who have the reputation for wisdom Should not act wisely — It must be a matter of surprise I think to almost every Person in the United States that Congress should make the matter of their Temporary Residence a Subject of so much consequence at this time — The lovers of Good Government have with a pleasing Partiality Looked up to Those Fathers of the People and called them Gods have anticipated everything Great and Noble from their conduct — Alas they are but Men and Subject to all those Passions that Debace and Render Humane Nature contemptible; do I write Treason — I hear you say yes and that I am medling with a Subject I am Totally Ignorant of — Be it so then to my Lord & Master do I submit all my opinions on Politicks — to be corrected amended and if he should please wholly expunged — but you will Suffer me to be a little Angry with Congress for so long detaining my Husband from my Arms.*

Pamela Sedgwick is shown here with her youngest daughter Catharine — the future novelist — who was born on December 28, 1789. While her husband was at Philadelphia, where he succeeded Caleb Strong in the Senate, Mrs. Sedgwick saw the opportunity of complying with his request that she have a family picture painted. An itinerant artist, Joseph Steward, "whose Character as a good Painter I have often heard," she told her husband, "is now come into the County." Originally she had hoped to include all the children but that proved to be too expensive. She concluded to sit together with Catharine but reflected sadly, "I feel very sorry that a part should be taken without the whole." Shown in the background is the Sedgwick home in Stockbridge.

Steward, a Dartmouth-educated minister, turned to painting in about 1793, when ill health forced him to give up preaching.

Pamela Dwight Sedgwick by Joseph Steward (1753–1822); oil on canvas, 1795. Private collection

JOHN SEVIER
1745–1815
Representative from North Carolina

Indian fighter and land speculator, the intrepid John Sevier was a self-made man of the frontier. Born in the Shenandoah Valley of Virginia, he crossed the Alleghenies before the Revolution and rose to leadership on the strength of his personality and the daring of his military exploits. When in 1785 the citizens in the back counties, retaliating against North Carolina's cession of her western lands to the general government, formed the state of Franklin, Sevier was elected governor. The cession act was soon repealed, but the state of Franklin, although refused recognition by the Confederation Congress and torn by dissension, resisted reconciliation with North Carolina.

In July of 1788, North Carolina's new governor, Samuel Johnston, ordered

Gold-mounted sword presented to John Sevier by the state of North Carolina, in recognition of his valor at the Battle of King's Mountain, October 7, 1780.
Tennessee State Museum, Nashville

John Sevier by Charles Willson Peale (1741–1827); oil on canvas, circa 1790–1792.
Tennessee State Museum, Tennessee Historical Society Collection, Nashville

PHILADELPHIA, 10th January, 1791.

DEAR SIR,

THE news of this place is not very material. Many things are before Congress, but not much finished—A land office bill is before the house, and 30 cents per acre is proposed to be the price of our Federal lands. An excise bill is also on the carpet, for imposing duties on distilled spirits, stills, &c. though this, I hope, will not reach us. The news from Europe is, that Britain and Spain continue indefatigably their preparations for war; and it is thought, by many, that blows will inevitably follow. I am of opinion, should the excise bill be passed, we shall derive great benefits from it; (proviso) we can keep clear ourselves, as it would have a direct tendency to encourage emigration into our country, and enable us to sell the production of our own distilleries, lower than our neighbours.

General Harmer's expedition is much reprobated by many here, and it is generally believed, that the Northern Indians will be very troublesome the ensuing summer. A very cold winter here, which in a great measure prevents the sending of letters; but shall do myself the honor of communicating to you, every thing of importance that occurs, on every suitable opportunity. Kentucky is to be admitted a member of the union in June, 1792.

I have the honor to be, Sir,
with sentiments of esteem,
and much regard, your
most obedient and humble servant,

JOHN SEVIER.

During the final session of the First Congress, John Sevier, who represented the far western district of North Carolina, reported to his constituents in a printed communication. His is the earliest circular letter thus far located.

Circular letter to John Sevier's constituents, January 10, 1791. Tennessee State Library and Archives, Nashville

John Sevier's arrest for high treason. By this time the Franklin movement was in a state of collapse, and Sevier was never tried. While he was still under indictment, his neighbors elected him to represent them in the North Carolina Senate. As he took his seat in November 1789, a motion was made and passed unanimously to withdraw the charges against him and restore him to the rights of citizenship. The day following, the legislature commissioned him brigadier general in command of the military beyond the mountains.

Sevier's early chroniclers claim that he was so much the idol of the frontier people that when he ran for Congress no one dared contest him. Sevier's popularity is without dispute, but he also had some formidable enemies.

At the federal Congress, Sevier, in concert with North Carolina sentiment, opposed assumption and the excise. He was, however, one of the few southerners to favor the national bank.

In 1796 Sevier became the first governor of Tennessee, and that state has chosen him as one of their two citizens to be honored with a statue in the United States Capitol.

Charles Willson Peale shows Sevier as a lieutenant general in the North Carolina militia, a position he held from 1788 to 1790, and the portrait most likely was executed while the general was in Congress at Philadelphia. It was presented to the Tennessee Historical Society in 1891 by the surviving children of Sevier's eldest son.

ROGER SHERMAN
1721–1793
Representative from Connecticut

Sixty-eight-year-old Roger Sherman, who had been in politics since 1749, was among the most experienced members of the House of Representatives and certainly one of the most picturesque. William Duer, the son of Alexander Hamilton's assistant at the Treasury, recalled watching Sherman from the House gallery and detailed, "In spite of his gaunt and ungainly figure, his awkward gestures and nasal drone, he never rose to speak without receiving that best of all marks of approbation—silent attention."

In the debate on the impost bill, as arguments raged over what the public would think about this or that particular tax or rate, Sherman rose to say, in his New England way, "When gentlemen have recourse to public opinion to support their arguments, they generally find means to accommodate it to their own."

"I do not suppose the constitution to be perfect," Sherman said, in brushing aside calls for amendments, "I do not expect any perfection, on this side of the grave, in the works of man; but my opinion is, that we are not, at present, in circumstances to make it better." He could not suppose that any nine states could be persuaded to accept any alterations that the Congress might propose.

But when Sherman saw that Madison was determined to press the matter, he persuaded him to change his mind about incorporating amendments into the body of the document. "We ought not to interweave our propositions in the work itself, because it will be destructive of the whole fabric."

Richard Henry Lee wrote indignantly to Samuel Adams that Sherman, "our old Republican friend opposed a motion for introducing into a bill of rights, an idea that the Military should be subordinate to the Civil power — His reason, as stated, was *that it would make the people insolent!*'"

In 1791 Sherman was appointed to take the place of William Samuel Johnson, who had resigned as Senator at the end of the First Congress.

The only known life portrait of Sherman, painted by Ralph Earl when Sherman was in the Continental Congress, has been adopted and copied over the years by many artists. This well-executed version by the nineteenth-century Connecticut artist Nathaniel Jocelyn follows the Earl portrait in all particulars except for the substitution of an up-to-date Empire chair in place of the Windsor piece in the original.

Roger Sherman by Nathaniel Jocelyn (1796–1881); oil on canvas, 1854. New Haven Colony Historical Society; gift of Robert and Mary Lou Sutter, 1986

WILLIAM SMITH
1728–1814
Representative from Maryland

William Smith, the victorious Federalist candidate from Baltimore, was described in the *Maryland Journal* as "a Man of great commercial Knowledge, of known integrity, and possessed of a Character and independent Fortune which place him above Temptation."

Smith began his sittings with Charles Willson Peale on October 10, 1788, the very day on which he was given a dinner by the merchants of Baltimore in celebration of his election to Congress just four days before. Smith is posed with his two-year-old grandson, Robert Smith Williams. The child's father, General Otho Holland Williams, had commissioned the portrait, and although the painting was executed in Baltimore, the setting portrayed is the general's country estate, Eutaw, named after the battle in South Carolina at which Williams had distinguished himself. The books on the table have been identified as James Beattie's *Essay on Truth*, a volume of John Milton's poetry, James Thomason's *Seasons,* and a work entitled *Gardening.* Added to the scene of rural domesticity is an imposing classical structure intended to symbolize Smith's new responsibilities at the federal Congress.

Politically akin to his son-in-law, Smith regularly kept Williams apprised of the proceedings of the Congress. "Some Warm gentlemen," he reported on March 18, 1790, "have declared if they cannot have the assumption business to their Satisfaction they will be opposed to all funding Systems. And I am of opinion *That* Measure is yet Doubtfull." He added, "The house has been employed *foolishly,* all this week on the quaker's memorial."

By early April Smith was restless. "We proceed so slowly in business that it is truly distressing to be detained here so long & do so little good."

Smith moved that the Congress adjourn to Baltimore as a temporary residence but, as he explained to Williams at the end of May 1790, "unfortunately for poor Baltimore, the Representatives from Maryland were divided, George Gale, Daniel Carroll and Benjamin Countee for Philadelphia, the other three Joshua Seney, William Smith, Michael Jenifer Stone for Baltimore and so the question was lost."

At the end of his first term in Congress, Smith, who had not been a candidate for reelection, was appointed the first auditor of the Treasury by President Washington.

William Smith by Charles Willson Peale (1741–1827); oil on canvas, 1788. Virginia Museum of Fine Arts, Richmond; gift of the Robert G. Cabell III and Maude Morgan Cabell Foundation and the Glasgow Fund

WILLIAM LOUGHTON SMITH
1758–1812
Representative from South Carolina

Willliam Smith of South Carolina — he adopted his mother's maiden name of Loughton in 1804 — was the South's ultimate Federalist. So completely did "the honourable gentleman from South Carolina" make the case for a national judiciary that both Fisher Ames and Theodore Sedgwick declared that there was no need for them to add anything more.

Smith, vexed by James Madison's determination to take up amendments to the Constitution before the judiciary was established, reminded the House that "While we remain in this state, not a single part of the revenue system can operate; no breach of your laws can be punished; illicit trade cannot be prevented."

No group annoyed Smith more than the Quakers, whose memorials concerning the slave trade he took to be a direct threat against South Carolina and Georgia, the two southern states still dependent upon importation to augment their labor supply. Smith lashed out against "the intemperate & bigoted zeal of a class of men who seemed to take pleasure in accusing us of infamous & inhuman proceedings & who were pursuing with eager steps the ruin & destruction of our happiness & property." He added in a private letter that he was *much hurt at seeing the members of the Southern States dragged like Criminals to the Bar of the House to answer for crimes adjudged against them by the Quakers & others (whose applications were too warmly supported by some of the members from those States in which the Quakers have electioneering influence).* Smith admitted that he had entered into the debate with asperity, but trusted he would stand justified. "It was a mortifying thing, I assure you; to see an attempt made to deprive us of our property so soon after we had established a govern[men]t for the express purpose of protecting it."

Alexander Hamilton's financial program had Smith's energetic support. "I do not see how the Government can get along without it," Smith wrote as the opposition to assumption raged, "& I am persuaded that it will be impossible to have any funding System of which the State debts shall not make a part. To sacrifice the State creditors would be such a violent act of injustice as would convulse the Union & defeat the national revenue."

So confident was Smith of reelection that during the congressional recess he accompanied Washington to Rhode Island and then went on to tour New

William Loughton Smith by Gilbert Stuart (1755–1828); oil on canvas, circa 1795. The Gibbes Art Gallery, Carolina Art Association, Charleston, South Carolina

England, rather than return to South Carolina.

After the election Smith wrote to Edward Rutledge, "I Sincerely rejoice at finding myself almost the unanimous choice of a District which I truly believe contains more enlightened & Judicious men than any election district in the United States." He went on, "My being unopposed manifests a belief in those who were likely to be my competition that I had acquired the confidence of my Constituents & that an opposition would be ineffectual, & is therefore a pleasing circumstance." Smith remained in Congress until 1797, when he resigned to become minister to Portugal. At the time Gilbert Stuart arrived at Philadelphia to record the visages of federal America, William Loughton Smith was among those who commissioned a portrait.

JOHN STEELE
1764–1815
Representative from North Carolina

John Steele, who had turned twenty-five in November 1789, was the youngest member of the First Federal Congress. It is tempting to attribute his political precocity in part to his mother, an enterprising widow who supported her family by keeping a popular tavern, a place of inevitable exposure to the clamor of politics.

Steele took his seat just in time to join with his North Carolina colleagues in opposing assumption "spiritedly in all its stages." The passage of the bill, he noted afterward, "proved what can be effected by perseverance. In a good cause it is usually styled a virtue, but in this instance it deserves the appellation of obstinacy."

Forced to deny rumors circulating in his district that he had deliberately kept his constituents in ignorance of the funding and assumption bill because he himself was a speculator, Steele declared in the press "that I have not directly or indirectly been concerned in the purchase of certificates, and I defy the tongue of malice itself to make it appear that I have on any occasion deserted or neglected the interest of my constituents." He further explained that he had sent a letter, together with twenty or thirty newspapers detailing the funding bill, to a friend so that the information might be published in North Carolina. The packet, however, was never received, the intended

John Steele by James Peale (1749–1831); watercolor on ivory, 1797. The Newark Museum, New Jersey; purchase, Louis Bamberger Fund, 1965

recipient surmised, because it had "fallen into the hands of some person interested in keeping from the press the information contained therein." This was a common occurrence in North Carolina. Writing from New York in May 1790, Steele observed, "I am now writing you a letter which it is very doubtful whether it will ever reach you or not — The distance is so great, the people so inquisitive for news, that it is very common practice to break up letters by the way."

There was no post in the interior of North Carolina, and one of Steele's principal aims was to effect a continental post road through Fayetteville so that he could get timely and reliable information to his constituents. The bill for establishing the post office and post road, however, although passed in the House, was amended by the Senate on the ground of the great expense involved, and final agreement was not reached until the Second Congress.

President Washington appointed John Steele as comptroller of the Treasury in 1796. It was during his tenure in this office that James Peale, the younger brother of Charles Willson Peale and one of the most accomplished of American miniature painters, executed his portrait.

CALEB STRONG
1745–1819
Senator from Massachusetts

At sunrise on February 25, 1789, a great procession of sleighs gathered at the door of Caleb Strong's Northampton home, ready to accompany the new Senator twenty miles south to Springfield on the first leg of his journey to New York. From that city, after a five-week wait for the Senate to be formed, Strong wrote with irritation, "I assure you that my patience is almost exhausted. I have not been used to Idleness & am unwilling at this Distance from home to learn the Habit — the Gentlemen who occasion this Delay unless they can plead ill health must I think be inexcuseable."

Although Strong had left the Federal Convention before the Constitution was signed, he played a major role at the Massachusetts ratifying convention. The eminent legal authority Theophilus Parsons was reported to have told him at the time, "Strong, you can do more with that honest face of yours than I can with all my legal knowledge." Strong was delegated to reassure

Caleb Strong by Gilbert Stuart (1755–1828); oil on panel, 1813. Frederick S. Moseley III

334

The inscription on Caleb Strong's snuff box—
"The Honour of Massachusetts"—perhaps indicates
that the box was used to promote his election.
   Historic Deerfield, Inc., Deerfield, Massachusetts

Caleb Strong's sword. Northampton Historical Society,
Massachusetts

Governor John Hancock that he was doing the right thing by supporting the Constitution and that the amendments Hancock had been persuaded to introduce would, no doubt, be adopted by the new government.

Federalist to the core, Strong gave undeviating support to the administration and was easily recognized by William Maclay as one of Hamilton's "Senatorial Gladiators."

Strong's greatest distinction at the First Federal Congress was his service on the committee that drew up the judiciary bill. Wrote Fisher Ames on July 8, 1789, "Mr. Strong, Mr. Ellsworth and Mr. Paterson in particular, have their full share of the merit." In addition, Strong was a member of some forty other committees and was chairman of the committee that reported out the bank bill.

Strong drew a four-year term and was reelected in 1793 but resigned in 1796 to resume his private law practice. But so popular was Strong that the people would not let him keep out of office, and in 1800 he was back in politics as the Federalist candidate for governor. Eleven times he was elected and only once defeated. The Boston newspapers attributed Strong's popularity to his "Gentleness of manners, dignified deportment, uncommon abilities, unshaken patriotism, republican federalism, manly firmness, and strict morality."

Gilbert Stuart has portrayed Caleb Strong in the twilight of his long and successful political career.

THOMAS SUMTER
1734–1832
Representative from South Carolina

Thomas Sumter did not arrive at the Congress until May 25, 1789, but the combative Antifederalist hurried into the debate on amendments to the Constitution. He particularly wanted to make sure that "No soldier shall be quartered in any house without the consent of the owner." He also favored a provision to limit the power of Congress to impose direct taxes.

In his longest speech of the first session, Sumter expressed his opposition to the judiciary bill, maintaining that although Congress was given the power in the Constitution to adopt a federal court system, the country was in no condition to bear the expense. There were courts enough as it was. "The people of America do not require the iron hand of power to keep them within due bounds; they are sufficiently enlightened to know and pursue their own

good." A system of federal courts would be hostile to the liberties of the people "and dangerous in the extreme."

When Congress resolved to take a recess at the end of September, Sumter was indignant. "Our conduct in adjourning for so short a time, and leaving so much business unfinished, can never be approved by the people. Gentlemen talk of their private concerns; I do not think any member has made a greater proportional sacrifice than I have."

During the second session of Congress, Sumter was out of step with South Carolina's desire that the wartime debts of the state should be assumed. Sumter, charged William Loughton Smith, "is really more a Delegate from Virginia than our State." Smith related, "I employed all my rhetoric with Sumpter to change his vote," pointing out that Sumter had acknowledged that the measure was advantageous to South Carolina and that, *as he found other States opposing it from local motives, he was justified in supporting it from similar motives — that he would not be charged with inconsistency in now voting it, because he might alledge that he found his opposition ineffectual & that he thought it his duty to concur with the majority.* Smith concluded, "to the great astonishment of both parties, he said Aye when he was expected to say no."

Sumter did not arrive at Philadelphia for the third session of Congress until February 15, 1791. Smith commented sardonically to Edward Rutledge that Sumter came "just as the Session terminated, merely, (it is here said) to get travelling wages here and home, amounting to near 500 Dollars (including pay for 14 days attendance) which he pockets for a few days attendance — this is a new stroke of cunning!"

Portrayed in his military character, Sumter is believed to have been painted by Charles Willson's Peale's son Rembrandt after his election to the Fifth Congress in 1797. Accusations that he had been associated with Thomas Fitzsimons in speculation in government paper had cost him his seat in 1793.

Thomas Sumter attributed to Rembrandt Peale (1778–1860); oil on canvas, circa 1795–1797. Independence National Historical Park Collection, Philadelphia, Pennsylvania

JONATHAN TRUMBULL
1740–1809
Representative from Connecticut

As soon as the Connecticut election results became known, George Washington had written to Jonathan Trumbull, who had been his wartime aide, that he was "not a little pleased with observing that your name stood so high in the nomination of Representatives to Congress," and went on to declare, "Much will depend upon having disinterested and respectable characters in both Houses."

When the House of Representatives chose their Speaker, Henry Wynkoop of Pennsylvania related, "The competitor of Mr. Mughlenberg was Col. Trumbul from Connecticut, a gentleman well known for his singular Merrit & Repectabillity." James Madison reported to Washington that Trumbull "had a respectable vote." Trumbull was chosen to preside over the committee of the whole House during the period from May 19 to July 10, 1789.

A diligent member of the Congress, Trumbull served on many committees, including those dealing with rules, titles, oaths, duties on distilled spirits and teas, the settling of the accounts of the states.

At the Second Congress, Trumbull, ever an administration stalwart, defeated Frederick Muhlenberg for Speaker and served in that role for one term. He remained in the House of Representatives until 1795, when he was elected to the Senate. From 1797 until his death he was governor of Connecticut.

The domestic portrait, showing Jonathan Trumbull together with his wife, Eunice Backus, and eight-year-old daughter Faith at home in Lebanon, Connecticut, was executed by the Congressman's brother John in 1777. Faith, the artist's favorite niece, was in Philadelphia with her father during the third session of the Congress and would later marry Jeremiah Wadsworth's son, Daniel.

John Trumbull, who had returned to America from Europe in November 1789, accompanied his brother Jonathan and Jeremiah Wadsworth when they went to New York for the second session of the Congress. There, and subsequently in Philadelphia, he secured subscriptions from the President, Vice-President, seventeen Senators, and twenty-seven Representatives for the first two engravings of his Revolutionary War series — *The Death of General Warren* and *The Death of General Montgomery*.

Mr. and Mrs. Jonathan Trumbull and their daughter Faith by John Trumbull (1756–1843); oil on canvas, 1777. Yale University Art Gallery, New Haven, Connecticut; gift of Miss Henrietta Hubbard

THOMAS TUDOR TUCKER
1745–1828
Representative from South Carolina

Antifederalist Thomas Tudor Tucker had no great expectations for the success of the new government. In September 1789, when the House of Representatives resolved that the President should recommend a day of thanksgiving and prayer, Dr. Tucker declared sourly that citizens "may not be inclined to return thanks for a Constitution until they have experienced that it promotes their safety and happiness. We do not yet know but they may have reason to be dissatisfied with the effects it has already produced." In any case this was no business for the federal government; the states "know best what reason their constituents have to be pleased with the establishment of this Constitution."

There was no pretense of congeniality between Tucker and fellow Representative William Loughton Smith. Smith's father-in-law, Senator Ralph Izard, had kept Tucker out of the South Carolina Assembly in 1786 by making him "the Subject of a public Harangue." In consequence the hot-tempered Tucker challenged Izard to a duel and received another affront by way of a shot through his left thigh. But Tucker took a measure of revenge when he defeated an Izard cousin in an election to fill an Assembly vacancy.

The old irritations were heightened in New York as Tucker exasperated Smith and Izard by holding out against assumption of state debts until pressured to do by instructions from the South Carolina legislature. "He says he will vote for it now," observed Smith sarcastically, "but, tho' in the course of the debate much has been said respecting So. Car. & her enormous debt, he has not opened his mouth." Tucker had been in the old Congress in 1787 and 1788, and Smith thought him especially derelict, since "from his being so long in Congress, he is better able than any of us to explain the matter—the whole burden has fallen on myself & [Aedanus] Burke."

Tucker, dissatisfied with the amendments brought forward by James Madison's committee, proposed a multitude of changes, including the stipulation that no person be eligible to serve in the House for more than six years out of any eight, and that the President be forbidden to hold office for more than eight years in any term of twelve years. He also tried to restrict the powers of the Congress to levy direct taxes.

On August 8, 1790, as the residence bill was under debate, Smith recorded,

Thomas Tudor Tucker by Charles Balthazar Julien Févret de Saint-Mémin (1770–1852); black and white chalk on paper, 1807. Cynthia (Beverley Tucker Kimbrough) Barlowe

Tucker seemed sunk in an indifference proceeding from ill-humor — he was dissatisfied with every thing (as he generally is) — he hated the Assumption, but was obliged to vote for it — he didn't like the residence bill much better; he disliked the government itself, & was not therefore sorry to see it become contemptible — he accordingly took no part, but allowed things to take their own course.

Tucker was reelected to the Second Congress and in 1801 was appointed United States treasurer by President Thomas Jefferson.

From the image of Tucker taken with an automatic tracing device used by the French emigré artist Charles Balthazar Julien Févret de Saint-Mémin, one might conclude that displeasure was Tucker's characteristic expression. According to family tradition, at the time the British invaded Washington in 1812, Tucker sent the portrait to his brother St. George at Williamsburg, and during the passage on a small boat, the picture was stained by water.

JEREMIAH WADSWORTH
1743–1804
Representative from Connecticut

Jeremiah Wadsworth had a hand in many enterprises, among them the Hartford Woolen Manufactory, which he had helped to found in 1788. He arrived at New York early in March to promote the wearing of domestic textiles by officials of the new government.

Beginning as a sailor aboard one of his uncle's ships, Wadsworth moved on to command his own vessel and soon was one of the most successful merchants in the West Indies trade. Appointed Continental commissary general in 1777, Wadsworth, testified Washington, was "indefatigable in his exertions to provide for the army." Later, in partnership with Alexander Hamilton's brother-in-law John Church, Wadsworth engaged to supply the French forces in America.

Ever on the lookout for investment opportunities, Wadsworth was one of the largest shareholders in the Bank of North America, and his investments in domestic manufactories ranged from linen to rum.

In his *New Travels in the United States of America, 1788*, the French journalist Jacques Pierre Brissot de Warville reported on his visit to Hartford: *It is the home of one of the most respected men in the United States, Colonel Wadsworth. He*

Jeremiah Wadsworth by John Trumbull (1756–1843); oil on canvas, 1784. Wadsworth Atheneum, Hartford, Connecticut; gift of Mr. Faneuil Adams

enjoys a considerable fortune, which he owes entirely to his own labors and industry. He is perfectly versed in the arts of agriculture, in animal husbandry, and in the East India trade. During the last war he rendered the greatest services to the American and French armies, and he is generally liked and respected and has many fine qualities and virtues, the greatest of which is a singular modesty. His manner is frank, his countenance open, and his speech simple. You cannot help liking him as soon as you meet him, and you like him even more when you come to know him well.

Jeremiah Wadsworth likely acquired this monumental punch bowl (right) very near the outset of the American trade with China, since in about 1786 he ordered Hartford cabinetmaker Samuel Kneeland to encase it in an inlaid box. It is tempting to suppose that the Congressman might have carried it with him to New York to indulge his friends in a convivial bowl of punch. Most certainly the splendid object would have been put to use when President Washington—after the close of the first session of the Congress—traveled north to cement relations with New England and dined with Wadsworth at Hartford.

Chinese export porcelain punch bowl, circa 1780, and punch bowl case made by Samuel Kneeland of Connecticut, 1786. The Connecticut Historical Society, Hartford

Jeremiah Wadsworth, who arrived at the Congress with an elegant wardrobe purchased in France during his 1784 business trip, must have been a resplendent figure at the President's Tuesday- and Friday-afternoon levees and at Mrs. Washington's Friday-evening receptions.

Silk waistcoat worn by Jeremiah Wadsworth, embellished with metallic embroidery. The Connecticut Historical Society, Hartford

347

No member of Congress was more enthusiastically in support of Alexander Hamilton's financial program than was Jeremiah Wadsworth, and his natural proclivity toward speculation caused him to be much criticized by his colleagues. William Maclay charged in January 1790 that "Wadsworth has sent off Two small Vessels for the Southern States, on the Errand of buying up certificates." And Theodore Sedgwick wrote to his wife on March 22, "Wadsworth . . . has thought it more for his interest to speculate than to attend his duty in Congress, and is gone home."

Wadsworth's constituents were apparently not bothered by his making a good thing out of policies that most of them regarded as beneficial to the country, and he won reelection to the Second and Third Congresses. Thereafter he retired to devote himself to the arts and scientific agriculture.

In 1783 Wadsworth and his son Daniel traveled to Europe to settle his commissary accounts with the French government. On a visit to England he commissioned a portrait—which shows him as a father and as a merchant—from his Connecticut friend John Trumbull. The young artist, who had but recently resumed his studies with Benjamin West, reported to his brother Jonathan, "I have receiv'd from Wadsworth . . . the first fruits of my profession—W. gave me for the little picture which you will see. fifteen Guineas."

HUGH WILLIAMSON
1735–1819
Representative from North Carolina

H ugh Williamson, a physician by education, a scientist of international reputation, and an erstwhile merchant, had been one of the most conscientious members ever to serve in the old Congress, hardly missing a session from the time he took his seat on July 19, 1782, to the end of his term on December 24, 1784. Elected once more to the Congress in 1786, he had returned to New York after the close of the Constitutional Convention and was in attendance there for months beyond October 10, 1788, the last day in which the dying Congress had a quorum.

A bachelor until the age of fifty-four, Williamson in January 1789 was married to Maria Apthorp, the daughter of a wealthy New York merchant.

Hugh Williamson by John Trumbull (1756–1843); oil on canvas, circa 1805. William H. Swan and Carolyn Swan Parlato, on loan to the National Portrait Gallery, Smithsonian Institution, Washington, D.C.

She was described to James Madison as "a beautiful girl, about twenty-two. She appears much pleased with her bargain — may she never repent." Alas, shortly after the birth of her second child, in October 1790, Mrs. Williamson died.

On March 19, 1790, Williamson was the first of the North Carolinians to take his seat in the House of Representatives. Alexander Hamilton's financial plan was under consideration, and Williamson, although an adherent of Hamilton as the author of the *Federalist Papers,* now begged to differ with him on the question of assumption, since North Carolina had determined upon paying its own debts in its depreciated paper money.

Williamson's speeches against Hamilton's program — which were lauded in the press — availed him little when he returned to make his report before an angry North Carolina legislature. "Success in politics as well as war alone can gain esteem with the populace," one witness observed, "& Dr. Williamson could not receive a whiff of incence for his excellent opposition to the funding law, & they looked as angrily at him as if he had been its advocate." Williamson nonetheless was reelected.

Requested by the Italian sculptor Giuseppe Ceracchi to pose for his bust in 1791, Williamson refused, saying he believed "that posterity will not be solicitous to know what were the features of his face." But after Williamson retired from politics to devote himself to his many literary and scientific pursuits, he commissioned John Trumbull to paint his portrait.

HENRY WYNKOOP
1737–1816
Representative from Pennsylvania

On the day set for the opening of the Congress, Henry Wynkoop was in New York and took a room with William Maclay. The six-foot-four Bucks County farmer was jovially christened "His Highness of the Lower House," while Maclay, just one inch shorter, was dubbed "Your Highness of the Senate."

As the members of Congress began to grapple with more substantive issues, however, Maclay was harsh in the assessment of his fellow Pennsylvanian. *It would not be easy to find a more Useless member. He never speaks never acts in*

Henry Wynkoop by Rembrandt Peale (1778–1869); oil on canvas, circa 1816. Northampton Township Historical Society, Bucks County, Pennsylvania

Congress, but implicitly follows the Two City Members [Philadelphians George Clymer and Thomas Fitzsimons]. *He does not seem formed to act alone even in the most Triffling affair. Well for him is it that he is not a Woman & handsome, or every fellow would debauch him.*

Particularly was William Maclay disgusted when Wynkoop, under pressure from to vote for assumption, on April 1, 1790, took his wife and proceeded home to Pennsylvania. Snorted Maclay, "He has not firmness of mind to refuse them his Vote. But he has done What equally offends them, & subjects himself to Ridicule. He has abandoned the Whole Business, & deserted the Cause of his Country at a time When an honest Vote, is inestimable." By April 21, however, Wynkoop was back in New York and spoke out — this time in consort with Maclay — to oppose a standing army.

Maclay persisted in trying to persuade Wynkoop to vote against assumption. Wrote an exasperated Maclay, "But if I had talked to a mute Camel, or addressed myself to a dead Horse, my speech would have had the same effect; And Yet he seemed to have neither Opinion nor System of his own." A few days later Maclay wrote, "I never saw a Man take so much pains *not* to see a Subject."

In a letter of April 22, 1790, to his son-in-law, Wynkoop reveals the turmoil in his mind. "I must confess for my part no Proposition hitherto before Congress has so much embarrassed my mind, it is like Sylla & Charybdis, Dangers on every Side, & how the Ship will yet with perfect Safety be piloted into Port, Time will discover." On the final vote, taken on July 24, Wynkoop voted for the assumption bill.

The districts drawn for the congressional elections in 1791 pitted Wynkoop against his old friend Frederick Augustus Muhlenberg, and Wynkoop could not prevail against the popular German.

Rembrandt Peale has portrayed Wynkoop in his retirement, holding a book lettered "Agricult[ure]," reflecting his lifetime absorption in husbanding his large Bucks County acreage. William Maclay was speaking not altogether with irony when he noted, "The way in Which this good Man, can best serve his country is in superintending his farm."

Figures sketched by shorthand reporter Thomas Lloyd during debates in the House of Representatives.

Manuscript Division, Library of Congress, Washington, D.C.

NOTES ON SOURCES

References are given in full in the bibliography.

Part One: The Congress is Chosen

Prologue: "The fundamental defect," Alexander Hamilton to James Duane, September 3, 1780, in Harold C. Syrett and Jacob E. Cooke, eds., *Hamilton Papers*, vol. 2, p. 401. "There is no measure," Hugh Williamson to James Iredell, February 17, 1783, in Edmund C. Burnett, ed., *Letters of Members of the Continental Congress*, vol. 7, p. 46. "I know there is a Delicacy," Robert Morris to John Hanson, February 11, 1782, in E. James Ferguson and John Catanzariti, eds., *Robert Morris Papers*, vol. 4, p. 209. "If there be not," quoted in John Sanderson's *Biography of the Signers to the Declaration of Independence*, vol. 2, p. 421. "The Senate of NY," William Samuel Johnson to Jeremiah Wadsworth, March 26, 1785, Burnett, *Letters of the Continental Congress*, vol. 8, p. 74. "Who authorized them," quoted in Hugh Blair Grigsby, *History of the Virginia Federal Convention of 1788*, p. 82. "Their names then ought not have been distinguished," in Thomas Lloyd's *Congressional Register*, vol. 2, p. 196. "Pagans, deists, and Mahometans," in Cecilia M. Kenyon, "Men of Little Faith: The Anti-Federalists on the Nature of Representative Government," *William and Mary Quarterly* (hereafter *WMQ*), 3d ser. 12, p. 17. "They have reserved," Richard Henry Lee to Samuel Adams, October 27, 1787, in John P. Kaminski and Gaspare J. Saladino, eds., *The Documentary History of the Ratification of the Constitution*, vol. 13, p. 485. "Many a sleepless night," quoted in *Dictionary of American Biography*, q.v. Samuel Osgood. "I consider the first Congress," Samuel Osgood to Elbridge Gerry, quoted in Robert A. Rutland's *James Madison, the Founding Father*, p. 40.

Delaware: For elections see Merrill Jensen *et al.*, eds., *Documentary History of the First Federal Elections* (hereafter *FFE*), vol. 2, pp. 61–98.

Pennsylvania: For commentary on the election of Senators see *FFE*, vol. 1, pp. 193–296. Dr. Benjamin Rush's comments on at-large elections are on p. 302. George Thacher's comments are on p. 294. Tench Coxe to James Madison is on p. 296. Commentary on the elections to the House of Representatives is on pp. 328–40. Benjamin Rush to Coxe is on p. 385. Coxe to Timothy Pickering is on p. 371.

New Jersey: For elections see *FFE*, vol. 3. The letter from William Bradford, Jr., to Elias Boudinot is on p. 45. Abraham Clark's letter to the *New Jersey Journal* is on pp. 119–20. The letter to Jonathan Dayton is on p. 90.

Georgia: For elections see *FFE*, vol. 2, pp. 477–80.

Connecticut: For elections see *FFE*, vol. 2, pp. 45–46. Gouverneur Morris's letter to Jeremiah Wadsworth is quoted in Alden Hatch's *Wadsworths of the Genesee*, p. 31.

Massachusetts: For elections see *FFE*, vol. 1.

Maryland: For elections see *FFE*, vol. 2. On John Henry's reluctance to go into public life see p. 157. For the writer to the *Maryland Gazette* see pp. 162–63. For "A Marylander" see pp. 165–66. For the writer to the *Maryland Journal* see p. 212. The letter from a German farmer is found on p. 201.

South Carolina: For elections see *FFE*, vol. 1. Charles Pinckney's letter is on p. 209. William Smith to the voters is on pp. 176–81. David Ramsay's comments are on p. 195. John F. Grimké's letter is on p. 295. Charles Pinckney's letter to Rufus King is on p. 209.

New Hampshire: For elections see *FFE*, vol. 1. William Plumer's account of the elections is on p. 789. "A Friend to the People" is on p. 776. "Friend to Amendments" is on p. 789. Nicholas Gilman to Tench Coxe, May 10, 1789, is in the Coxe Papers at the Historical Society of Pennsylvania. The description of Abiel Foster is in Burnett, *Letters of the Continental Congress*, vol. 7, p. 402n.

Virginia: For elections and other references to *FFE* see vol. 2. Richard Bland Lee to James Madison is on p. 269. "The secret is out," William T. Hutchinson *et al.*, eds., *Madison Papers*, vol. 11, p. 339. "Mr. Henry on the floor," Hutchinson, *Madison Papers*, vol. 11, p. 356. "Exert my faculties," *FFE*, p. 259. "That nothing but the reverence," James Curtis Ballagh, ed., *The Letters of Richard Henry Lee*, vol. 2, p. 479. "Is indeed the devoted Servant," *Madison Papers*, vol. 11, p. 337. "Mr. Henry," *FFE*, p. 398. Federalist James Duncanson's summary is in *FFE*, p. 405. Alexander White's election is in *FFE*, p. 310. "I pointedly gave it," *Madison Papers*, vol. 11, p. 90. James Wilkinson is quoted in *FFE*, p. 313. The quotes from the Alexandria and the Falmouth merchants are in *FFE*, p. 316. "And the most active unceasing endeavours," *FFE*, p. 328. "To come forward in this govt.," *FFE*, p. 347. "Amendments, if pursued," *FFE*, p. 330. "It is my sincere opinion," *FFE*, pp. 330–31. "The Freeholders," *FFE*, p. 336. "It was my misfortune," *FFE*, p. 408. "A Kinsman of Mr. Henry," *FFE*, p. 349. Arthur Lee's broadside, *FFE*, p. 352. "But my duty in the Assembly," *FFE*, pp. 353–54. "Whether Mr. Page's interest," *FFE*, p. 350. "If I am elected," *FFE*, p. 356. "A discharge of 11 heavy cannon," *FFE*, p. 358. Writer to the *Portsmouth Journal*, *FFE*, p. 358. "Col. Parker appears to be very temperate," *Madison Papers*, vol. 12, p. 37. "The district being wholly poisoned," *FFE*, p. 404. "Knowing that it would be impossible," *FFE*, p. 381. "Was a truly honest good man," in George C. Rogers, Jr., ed., "Letters of William Loughton Smith," *South Carolina Historical Magazine* (hereafter *S.C. Hist. Mag.*) 69, p. 120. "Probable, tho' great expectations are entertained," *FFE*, p. 360. "I was pressed," *FFE*, p. 362. "It is thought the Elections," *FFE*, p. 382. "The sense of the People," *Madison Papers*, vol. 11, p. 40.

New York: For elections see *FFE*, vol. 3. "Our Legislature are sitting," p. 327. "Totally forgetting their own dignity," p. 387. "The Genl: Assembly," p. 344. "Beware of Lawyers," p. 482. "The preservation of the government itself," p. 477. "I think I have been the means," p. 497. "A party from Orange," p. 498. "But at the same Time declared," p. 502. "The Legislature assemble," p. 518. "Judged it most prudent," p. 533. "Nothing but delicacy," p. 534. "The probability was," p. 547. Rufus King's memorandum of his conversation with Governor Clinton, p. 515. "In one of my last letters," p. 555.

North Carolina: "I have been very earnestly solicited," in Griffith J. McRee's *Life and Correspondence of James Iredell*, p. 272. "The appointment of the other Senator," *Gazette of the United States*, January 9, 1790. "Was a great politician," Elkanah Watson, *Men and Times of the Revolution*, p. 251. "The time, place, and manner," in Jonathan Elliot, *Debates in the Convention of the State of North Carolina*, p. 71. The characterization of Timothy Bloodworth comes from McRee, *Iredell*, p. 149.

Rhode Island: "That shameless Prostitute," Jonathan Trumbull to George Washington, *FFE*, vol. 2, p. 10. "That little trollop of a sister," Benjamin Lincoln to Theodore Sedgwick, *FFE*, vol. 1, p. 459. "About two thirds of the Freemen," Nicholas and John Brown to Richard Henry Lee, May 1, 1789, John Brown Papers, Rhode Island Historical Society. "The Candidates for Senators were at first numerous" in John P. Kaminski, "Political Sacrifice and Demise — John Collins and Jonathan J. Hazard, 1786–1790," *Rhode Island History* 35, p. 95. "Finding that Constitution," William Ellery to Benjamin Huntington, June 12, 1790, Rhode Island State Archives. "Our Senators will be on their Way," Henry Sherburne to Henry Knox, June 17, 1790, Knox Papers, Massachusetts Historical Society.

"A Collective Body of Men": "The elections have been hitherto," John Clement Fitzpatrick, ed., *Writings of Washington*, vol. 30, p. 185. "There are few shining geniuses," Seth Ames, ed., *Works of Fisher Ames*, vol. 1, p. 33. "I thought him a little out of his head," George Nicholas to John Brown, November 12, 1789, Kentucky Historical Society. "Our debates are conducted with moderation," in "South Carolina Federalist Correspondence," *American Historical Review* 14, pp. 776–77. "You will remember that Congress is but a collective body of men," Paine Wingate to Jeremy Belknap, May 12, 1789, in Paine Wingate's *Life and Letters*, vol. 2, p. 313. "On my alluding to the fact" is also in Wingate, *Life and Letters*, vol. 2, pp. 525–26.

Part Two: The Business of the Congress

The First Session: "Last night they fired 13 cannon," quoted in Charles Henry Hart's "Mary White — Mrs. Robert Morris," *Pennsylvania Magazine of History and Biography* (hereafter *PMHB*) 2, p. 172. "This is a very mortifying situation," Ames, *Works*, vol. 1, pp. 31–32. "This extraordinary delay," *FFE*, vol. 3, p. 431. "The southerners give this delay," *Massachusetts Centinel*, March 25, 1789. "This Town is not half so large," in "Letters from Old Trunks," *Virginia Magazine of History and Biography* 43, p. 290. "So that the common terms," *Virginia Gazette*, February 12, 1789. "No pains have been spared," Oliver Ellsworth to Abigail Ellsworth, March 8, 1789, Ellsworth Papers, Connecticut Historical Society. "Assuredly surpasses the Accommodations," Pierce Butler to Reverend Weeden Butler, June 21, 1789, Butler-Weeden Correspondence, British Museum. "The City of N. York have made wonderful exertions," *FFE*, vol. 3, p. 428. "Really elegant & well designed," Frederick Muhlenberg to Benjamin Rush, March 5, 1789, Gratz Collection, Historical Society of Pennsylvania. "We have Work enough," James Jackson to Anthony Wayne, May 1789, Wayne Papers, Clements Library, University of Michigan, Ann Arbor. Samuel Davis's journal has been published as "Journal of a Tour to Connecticut" in volume 2 of the *Proceedings of the Massachusetts Historical Society*. "At the Inns on the Road," *Madison Papers*, vol. 12, p. 343. "The pleasure which our open doors," *Madison Papers*, vol. 12, p. 357. "There are certain foibles," *Madison Papers*, vol. 12, p. 302. "How would all the little domestic," Wingate, *Life and Letters*, vol. 2, p. 302. "My Mind revolts," in Kenneth R. Bowling and Helen E. Veit, eds., *The Diary of William Maclay and Other Notes on Senate Debates* (hereafter *Maclay Diary*), p. 78. "He does not always vote right," *Maclay Diary*, p. 146. "It is certainly a defect," *Maclay Diary*, p. 330. "Foolerries fopperies," *Maclay Diary*, p. 29. "All the World," *Maclay Diary*, p. 27. "J. Adams espoused," *Madison Papers*, vol. 12, p. 182. "Not a soul," Ames, *Works*, vol. 1, p. 36. "Experience has clearly proved," Fisher Ames to to Judge Sargeant, May 5, 1789, Autograph Collection, Essex Institute. "The House of Delegates is a wise Body," Michael Jenifer Stone to his brother, July 3, 1789, Library of Congress. For Thomas Fitzsimons and Thomas Hartley on the tariff see Hampton L. Carson, "The First Congress of the United States," *PMHB* 13, p. 142. "Laboured with Spite," *Maclay Diary*, p. 58. "Taxing this article as high," *Annals of Congress*, vol. 1, pp. 103–4. "If any man supposes," quoted in George Adams Boyd, *Elias Boudinot, Patriot and Statesman*, p. 160. "We are not to deliberate," *Annals of Congress*, vol. 1, p. 127. "I have just heard," I. Tucker to George Thatcher, April 26, 1789, Thatcher Papers, Chamberlain Collection, Boston Public Library. "Molasses is a necessary of life," T. B. Wait to George Thatcher, May 7, 1789, George Thatcher Papers, Massachusetts Historical Society. "Attachment of the old," Lambert Cadwalader to John Armstrong, May 8, 1789, Gratz Collection, Historical Society of Pennsylvania. "There could not have been selected," *Maclay Diary*, p. 51. "But the members," *Maclay Diary*, pp. 72–73. "Had we not cried out," in Rogers, "Letters of Smith," *S.C. Hist. Mag.* 69 p. 4. "I wish to teach those nations," *Madison Papers*, vol. 12, p. 109. "This discrimination was showing," *Maclay Diary*, p. 54. "The Senate, God bless them," Ames, *Works*, vol. 1, p. 45. "I am happy to find," Levi Hollingsworth to Benjamin Contee, June 30, 1789, Historical Society of Pennsylvania. "With vast perseverance," Ames, *Works*, vol. 1, p. 64. "Rose and read over," *Maclay Diary*, p. 86. "I think it will be a very expensive machine," Wingate, *Life and Letters*, vol. 2, p. 318. "The Grand procession," *Maclay Diary*, p. 88. "It certainly is a Vile law," *Maclay Diary*, p. 116. "The Government will begin," Oliver Ellsworth to Noah Webster, June 8, 1789, The Pierpont Morgan Library. "When I told Morris," Benjamin Goodhue to Samuel Phillips, September 13, 1789, Phillips Family Papers, Massachusetts Historical Society. "Somebody had said Judges," *Maclay Diary*, p. 155. "He cared not for the Arts people Used," *Maclay Diary*, pp. 133–34. "Men of interprize and genius," *Madison Papers*, vol. 12, p. 293. "In spite of Doctor Logan," Robert Morris to Richard Peters, September 13, 1789, Peters Papers, Historical Society of Pennsylvania. "This proves fully," quoted in *Madison Papers*, vol. 11, p. 293. "It must appear extremely impolitic," *Annals of Congress*, vol. 1, p. 424. "The wheels of the national machine," quoted in Rutland, *James Madison*, p. 61. "To break the spirit," Rutland, *James Madison*, p. 65. "Seven out of thirteen," in Lloyd's *Congressional Register*, vol. 2, p. 107. "It consisted of most satisfactory amendments," *Fayetteville Gazette*, September 14, 1789. "Little better than whip-syllabub," *Madison Papers*, vol. 12, p. 341. "Gerry is not content," George Clymer to Richard Peters, June 1789, Historical Society of Pennsylvania. "There was a curious medley of them," Frederick Muhlenberg to Benjamin Rush, August 18, 1789, Historical Society of Pennsylvania. "That the business of Amendments," Robert Morris to Richard Peters, August 24, 1789, Peters Papers, Historical Society of Pennsylvania.

The Great Departments of Government: "Everybody here is occupied to dispose of the offices," Frederick von Steuben to William North, December 21, 1788, Washington University, St. Louis, Missouri. "This has been the most important question," Rogers, "Letters of Smith," *S.C. Hist. Mag.* 69, pp. 7–8. "Upon more mature reflection," Rogers, "Letters of Smith," *S.C. Hist. Mag.* 69, pp. 7–8. "In Order to pay his Court," *Maclay Diary*, p. 97. "But for the House of Representatives," *Maclay Diary*, p. 105. "I have seen more caballing," *Maclay Diary*, p. 113. "Mr. Izard was so provoked," *Maclay Diary*, p. 114. "His Rule through Life" is in Stewart Mitchell, ed., *New Letters of Abigail Adams*, p. 21. "Experience has wrought," Abraham Baldwin to Edward Telfair, June 17, 1789, Edward Telfair Papers, Duke University. "The first Error," *Maclay Diary*, p. 231. "The first thing done," *Maclay Diary*, p. 243.

George Washington: "When I saw Washington," "Memoir of the Hon. William Tudor," *Collections of the Massachusetts Historical Society*, 2d ser. 8, p. 318. "I cannot refrain from observing," Margaret M. O. O'Dwyer, "A French Diplomat's View of Congress, 1790," *WMQ*, 3d ser. 21, p. 413. "Our August President," Abigail Adams to Mary Cranch, in Mitchell, *New Letters*, p. 15. "He never rides out," Mitchell, *New Letters*, p. 20. "Republicans are borne down," *Maclay Diary*, p. 342.

Thomas Jefferson: "Jefferson is a slender Man," *Maclay Diary*, p. 275. "Many of them indeed are trifling," in Julian Boyd *et al.*, eds., *Jefferson Papers*, vol. 16, p. 579.

Alexander Hamilton: "A national debt," Alexander Hamilton to Robert Morris, April 30, 1781, *Hamilton Papers*, vol. 2, p. 635. "The tendency of a national bank," *Hamilton Papers*, vol. 7, p. 256. "He looks thirty-eight or forty years old," in Jacques Pierre Brissot de Warville, *New Travels in the United States of America*, pp. 147–48. "Placed in one of our public buildings," *Hamilton Papers*, vol. 10, p. 482. "Chearfully obey their wish," *Hamilton Papers*, vol. 10, p. 515.

Henry Knox: "To prevent the usurpation," Report of the Secretary of War, January 12, 1790, in Linda Grant DePauw *et al.*, eds., *Documentary History of the First Federal Congress*, vol. 6, p. 281. "It is essential to show all lawless adventurers," Report of the Secretary of War on the Frontiers, January 24, 1791, in DePauw, *Documentary History of the First Federal Congress*, vol. 5, p. 1369. "Knox is the easiest Man," *Maclay Diary*, p. 306.

Abigail Smith Adams: "Indeed I have been fully employd," Mitchell, *New Letters*, p. 19. "It is next to impossible to get a servant," Mitchell, *New Letters*, p. 47. "I feel low spirited and Heartless," Mitchell, *New Letters*, p. 59. "I have a journey before me," Mitchell, *New Letters*, p. 63. "Gentlemen and Ladies solicitous," in Charles Francis Adams, *Letters of Mrs. Adams*, p. 405. "There is much more society," Adams, *Letters of Mrs. Adams*, p. 420. "On tuesday from 3 to 4," Abigail Adams to Cotton Tufts, February 6, 1791, Reel 373, Adams Papers, Massachusetts Historical Society.

The People Petition: "Because it was the duty of the legislature," *Virginia Independent Chronicle*, August 11, 1790.

"Address of the People Called Quakers": "No more than to request Congress," Ebenezer Hazard to Jeremy Belknap, June 5, 1790, Belknap Papers, Massachusetts Historical Society. "Signed by a man," Lloyd, *Congressional Register*, February 12, 1790, p. 330. "That the Quakers have no right," Lloyd, *Congressional Register*, p. 317. "Language low, indecent and profane," Ames, *Works*, vol. 1, p. 75. "The galleries were thronged," Rogers, "Letters of Smith," *S.C. Hist. Mag.* 69, p. 108. "We took each other," quoted in George C. Rogers, Jr., *Evolution of a Federalist*, p. 197. For debate in the House on the Quaker petition, see *Annals of Congress*, vol. 2, pp. 1453–64. "The house have certainly greatly debased their dignity," *Maclay Diary*, p. 226. "For ten days past," George Thatcher to Hezh. Rogers and A. Haven, March 21, 1790, Thatcher Collection, Massachusetts Historical Society.

Baron von Steuben: "All appeared to be of opinion," Roger Sherman to Governor Samuel Huntington, May 12, 1790, Dearborn Collection, Houghton Library, Harvard University. "Bonny Johnney Adams," *Maclay Diary*, p. 278. "I shall not be disappointed," Wingate, *Life and Letters*, vol. 2, p. 363. "Begs to interest the same feelings," *Federal Gazette*, April 26, 1790. "Not one third are individually possessed," *Freeman's Journal*, July 21, 1790.

Catharine Littlefield Greene Miller: "Loose no time in bringing my affair," *Hamilton Papers*, vol. 7, p. 458. "But my dear friend," *Hamilton Papers*, vol. 8, p. 165. "Gen. Greene's Case," William L. Smith to Edward Rutledge, March 24, 1792, in Rogers, "Letters of Smith," *S.C. Hist. Mag.* 69, p. 240.

The Second Session: "Dreadful," Ames, *Works*, vol. 1, p. 96. "The business before them," Abigail Adams to Cotton Tufts, April 18, 1790, Misc. Ms. Boxes, New-York Historical Society. "I feel so struck of an heap," *Maclay Diary*, p. 183. "With all our Western Lands for Sale," *Maclay Diary*, p. 205. "Congress is daily engaged," Aedanus Burke to Samuel Bryan, March 3, 1790, Miscellaneous Letters, R.G. 59, M-179, Roll 3, National Archives. "The Secretarys People," *Maclay Diary*, p. 240. "The speculation in certificates," *Maclay Diary*, p. 184. "Since this report," *Annals of Congress*, vol. 1, pp. 1131–32. "As he came up he passed two expresses," *Maclay Diary*, p. 185. "Packets are sent everywhere," Abraham Baldwin to Joel Barlow, January 16, 1790, Misc. Ms. Collection, Manuscripts and Archives, Yale University Library. "Mr. Madison made a strange Motion," Thomas Hartley to Jasper Yeates, February 14, 1790, Yeates Papers, Historical Society of Pennsylvania. "To adopt his ideas," Theodore Sedgwick to Peter Van Schaack, February 13, 1790, Sedgwick Papers, Massachusetts Historical Society. "A fanciful idea," Abraham Baldwin to Joel Barlow, April 7, 1790, Misc. Ms. Collection, Yale University Library. "Mr. M–d — n pleading the cause," 1790, John Trumbull Papers, Yale University Library. "Until indeed the subject," Rutland, *James Madison*, p. 81. "Told him plainly," *Maclay Diary*, p. 51. "Where is the injustice," Abiel Foster to William Plumer, May 10, 1790, Plumer Collection, New Hampshire State Library. "But if their only crime," quoted in George Athan Billias, *Elbridge Gerry: Founding Father and Republican Statesman*, p. 239. "Mr. Smith of S C," Mitchell, *New Letters*, p. 37. "Seemed to aim," *Maclay Diary*, p. 203. "The Proposition of Mr Madison," Jonathan Trumbull to Theodore Woodbridge, March 20, 1790, Woodbridge Papers, Connectiuct Historical Society. "Must be a little mortified," William Thompson Read, *Life and Correspondence of George Read*, p. 516. "Belonging to states whose debts," Theodore Sedgwick to Henry Van Schaack, January 31, 1790, Sedgwick Papers, Massachusetts Historical Society. "He speaks of the assumption," Fisher Ames to John Lowell, May 2, 1790, Boston Public Library. "Whether he is really a convert," Theodore Sedgwick to Pamela Sedgwick, March 4, 1790, Sedgwick Papers, Massachusetts Historical Society. "As our Debt is the largest," Caleb Strong to Nathan Dane, February 6, 1790, Yale University Library. "Looking on to avail herself," Pierce Butler to Alexander Gillon, April 23, 1790, Pierce Butler Letterbook, University of South Carolina, Columbia. "By G — it must be done," *Maclay Diary*, p. 207. "Is too giddy and unsettled," *Maclay Diary*, p. 234. "Had a proposal," *Maclay Diary*, p. 235. "Have demanded justice," *Annals of Congress*, vol. 2, pp. 1525–26. "Sedgwick from Boston," *Maclay Diary*, pp. 241–42. "The debate on the assumption," Abraham Baldwin to Joel Barlow, May 8, 1790, Misc. Ms. Collection, Yale University Library. "We hear that Colo Bland," *Madison Papers*, vol. 13, p. 239. "A demonstration to the World," *Maclay Diary*, p. 220. "His cholor fairly choacked him," *Maclay Diary*, p. 295. "*It was seriously apprehended*," William L. Smith to Edward Rutledge, July 14, 1790, Pinckney Family

Papers, Library of Congress. "The assumption being carried," William L. Smith to Edward Rutledge, postscript of July 17 to July 14, 1790, letter, Pinckney Family Papers, Library of Congress. "The Act for making provision," William Few to Edward Telfair, August 17, 1790, Georgia Archives, Atlanta. "The place of the seat of government," *Annals of Congress*, vol. 2, p. 789. "The Assumption could never have been carried," Rogers, "Letters of Smith," *S.C. Hist. Mag.* 69, p. 125. "The place of the seat of government," *Annals of Congress*, vol. 1, p. 789. "The seat of government is of great importance," *Madison Papers*, vol. 12, p. 375. "Laboured long to show," *Maclay Diary*, p. 186. "The News papers," George Thatcher to James Sullivan, July 27, 1790, Thatcher Papers, Massachusetts Historical Society. "Rose laughing heartily," *Maclay Diary*, p. 277. "The Universal Consent," *Maclay Diary*, p. 277. "Now it was That Izard," *Maclay Diary*, p. 286. "Congress are much embarrassed," Thomas Jefferson to Thomas Mann Randolph, June 20, 1790, *Jefferson Papers*, vol. 16, p. 540. "The two houses are much divided," Elbridge Gerry to James Monroe, June 25, 1790, Worthington Chauncey Ford, ed., "Letters of Elbridge Gerry," *New England Historical and Genealogical Register* 49, p. 436. "Agreed to place the permanent Residence on the Potowmack," *Maclay Diary*, p. 302. "Serious intention of moving," Charles Carroll to Mary Caton, July 11, 1790, MS. 220, Carroll-McTavish Papers, Maryland Historical Society. "Now King took up his Lamentation," *Maclay Diary*, p. 309. "For every art that can be devised," Ballagh, *Letters of Lee*, vol. 2, p. 532. "This measure has been carryed," Philip Schuyler, July 4, 1790, L. W. Smith Collection, Morristown National Historical Park, Morristown, New Jersey. Jefferson's account of the Compromise of 1790, *Jefferson Papers*, vol. 17, p. 207. "Lee & White from Virginia," in Rogers, "Letters of Smith," *S.C. Hist. Mag.* 69, p. 132. "The Patomacke scheme is so absurd," Benjamin Goodhue to Stephen Goodhue, July 1790, Essex Institute. "These Yorkers are the vilest of people," *Maclay Diary*, p. 312. "The Citizens of Philada.," *Maclay Diary*, p. 331.

The Congress Leaves New York: "Thus we have a prospect at length," Joseph M. Beatty, Jr., "The Letters of Judge Henry Wynkoop," *PMHB* 38, pp. 200–201. "Lay all the blame," Robert Morris to Mary White Morris, July 2, 1790, Henry E. Huntington Library. "Some of the caricatures sold about the streets," Beatty, "Letters of Wynkoop," *PMHB* 38, p. 204. "The prints contain some angry pieces," DeWitt Clinton to George Clinton, July 20, 1790, New-York Historical Society.

The Third Session: "Have encountered difficulty," Joshua Seney to Frances Seney, December 9, 1790, Gratz Collection, Historical Society of Pennsylvania. "The scarcity of good Houses," William L. Smith to Edward Rutledge, January 14?, 1791, South Carolina Historical Society, Charleston. "To tell the Truth, I know no so unsocial a city," *Maclay Diary*, p. 331. "Every day almost I have an invitation to dine," Theodore Sedgwick to Pamela Sedgwick, January 28, 1791, Sedgwick Papers, Massachusetts Historical Society. "Mrs. Bingham has certainly," Abigail Adams to Abigail Adams Smith, December 26, 1790, quoted in Robert C. Alberts's *The Golden Voyage*, p. 212. "In a Stile beyond every thing," *Maclay Diary*, p. 357. "The building in which we set is neat," Theodore Sedgwick to Pamela Sedgwick, January 9, 1791, Sedgwick Papers, Massachusetts Historical Society. "The most evident necessity," Ames, *Works*, vol. 1, p. 37. "Their Indian affairs," Wingate, *Life and Letters*, vol. 2, p. 385. "A more exceptional mode of taxation," quoted in William K. Boyd, *History of North Carolina*, p. 48. "Considering the aversion," James Madison to Ambrose Madison, January 2, 1791, *Madison Papers*, vol. 13, p. 341. "That You may refrain," *Maclay Diary*, p. 375. "He wanted the United States," *Maclay Diary*, p. 379. "There exists some difference in bearing a burden," Philadelphia *General Advertiser*, January 27, 1791. "This will probably be the case," Philadelphia *Federal Gazette*, January 28, 1791. "In the course of his Phillipic," Philadelphia *General Advertiser*, January 18, 1791. "We Should have liked it Better," Theodore Foster to Welcome Arnold, February 22, 1791, Gratz Collection, Historical Society of Pennsylvania. "Was perhaps never more vexed," *Maclay Diary*, p. 377. "After a most strenuous opposition," John Steele, circular letter to his constitutents, January 27, 1791, William Blount Collection, Library of Congress. "Being a new Mode of Taxation," Alexander White to Gentlemen, April 26, 1791, Shephard Papers, Draper Manuscripts, State Historical Society of Wisconsin. "Considered As an Aristrocratic engine," *Maclay Diary*, p. 347. "It is totally in Vain to oppose this bill," *Maclay Diary*, p. 355. "I am now more fully convinced," *Maclay Diary*, p. 362. "On the Subject with every," *Maclay Diary*, p. 365. "A National Bank is establishing," Pierce Butler to G. P. Reade, February 5, 1791,

Butler-Weeden Correspondence, British Museum. "I consider it in its present form," William Few to Edward Telfair, January 15, 1791, Telfair Papers, Hargrett Rare Book and Manuscript Library, University of Georgia Libraries. "The great object of the Bank Bill," James Gunn to Edward Telfair, January 26, 1791, Telfair Papers, University of Georgia Libraries. "You will learn by the publick papers," Abigail Adams to Cotton Tufts, February 6, 1791, Reel 373, Adams Papers, Massachusetts Historical Society. "A great part of our two years," quoted in Winfred E. A. Bernhard, *Fisher Ames*, pp. 170–71. "Will become the great centre of the revenue," Ames, *Works*, vol. 1, p. 96. "The Ostensible Objections," Benjamin Huntington to Samuel Huntington, February 3, 1791, Jenkins Collection, Historical Society of Pennsylvania. "Mr. Maddison spoke yesterday," Benjamin Bourn to Zepaniah Andrews, February 3, 1791, Rhode Island Historical Society. "It will be a very unfortunate event," Theodore Sedgwick to Henry Van Schaack, February 18, 1791, Sedgwick Papers, Massachusetts Historical Society. "Elsworth said they amounted," *Maclay Diary*, p. 388. "We leave unfinished the Post Office," Alexander White, February 27, 1791, Charles Frances Jenkins Collection, Historical Society of Pennsylvania. "This session has been marked," Abigail Adams to Cotton Tufts, March 11, 1791, Misc. Ms. Boxes, New-York Historical Society.

Part Three: Portraits of the Members

John Adams: For address to the Senate see DePauw, *Documentary History of the First Federal Congress*, vol. 1, Senate Legislative Journal, pp. 22–23. "My office requires," John Adams to John Quincy Adams, May 17, 1789, quoted in Page Smith, *John Adams*, vol. 2, p. 769. "Up now got," *Maclay Diary*, p. 30. "Dignities distinctions," *Maclay Diary*, p. 139. "A Man must take," quoted in Smith, *John Adams*, vol. 2, p. 754.

Frederick Muhlenberg: "Never did I dread a Business more," to Benjamin Rush, March 5, 1789, Gratz Collection, Historical Society of Pennsylvania. "I sincerely confess," to Benjamin Rush, August 18, 1789, Historical Society of Pennsylvania. "By his portly person," January 1790, quoted in Harold Donaldson Eberlein and Cortlandt Van Dyke Hubbard, *Diary of Independence Hall*, p. 320. "To hold two I suppose," *Maclay Diary*, p. 6.

Fisher Ames: "A representative is a kind of wife," March 17, 1789, Fisher Ames to William Eustis, William Eustis Papers, Massachusetts Historical Society. "Ames, delivered, a long String of studied Sentences," *Maclay Diary*, p. 203. "I care little where Congress may sit," Ames, *Works*, vol. 1, p. 80.

Abraham Baldwin: "Boards are little better than shingles," to Joel Barlow, June 14, 1789, Misc. Ms. Collection, Yale University Library. "In my opinion," to Edward Telfair, June 17, 1789, Edward Telfair Papers, Duke University.

Richard Bassett: "Being bred Up in low life," *FFE*, vol. 2, p. 77. "A Mere Mushroom," *FFE*, vol. 2, p. 78. "A religious enthusiast," in Max Farrand, ed., *Records of the Federal Convention*, vol. 3, p. 93. "Poor little Delaware," Read, *Life and Correspondence*, pp. 516–17. "Bassett got up and recanted," *Maclay Diary*, p. 163.

Egbert Benson: Benson's reminiscences in the hand of Henry C. Van Schaack are in the special manuscript collection of the Van Schaack family, Columbia University Libraries.

Elias Boudinot: "There are occasions," *FFE*, vol. 3, p. 45. "I feel myself very happy," quoted in Boyd, *Elias Boudinot*, p. 156. "So hardy as to deny," *Maclay Diary*, p. 151. "He was noted for his jocular," Benjamin Rush to John Adams, April, 5, 1808, L. H. Butterfield, ed., *Letters of Benjamin Rush*, vol. 2, p. 964. "I am up at 7 o'Clock," Boyd, *Elias Boudinot*, p. 160.

Benjamin Bourn: "A Gentleman whose Principles and Conduct," Jeremiah Olney to Philip Schuyler, Alexander Hamilton, and Henry Knox, December 7, 1790, Rhode Island Historical Society. "You may be assured," to Moses Brown, January 12, 1791, Rhode Island Historical Society.

John Brown: "Of respectable talents," to Esteban Miro, February 14, 1789, *FFE*, vol. 2, p. 313. "I am now fully convinced," John Brown to Harry Innes, September 28, 1789, *Jefferson Papers*, vol. 16, p. 170. "The opposition to Mr. Brown," George Nichols to James Madison, December 31, 1790, *Madison Papers*, vol. 13, p. 340.

Aedanus Burke: "Who so forcefully demonstrated," Brissot de Warville, *New Travels*, p. 244. "Is become very pleasant," William L. Smith to John Faucheraud Grimké, March 3, 1790, Emmet Collection, New York Public Library. "Has behaved exceedingly well," William L. Smith to Edward Rutledge, February 28, 1790, in Rogers, "Letters of Smith," *S.C. Hist. Mag.* 69, p. 109. "Took occasion to Shew," William Smith to Otho Holland Williams, April 4, 1790, MS. 387.1, Gilmor Papers, Maryland Historical Society. "Was like a Dagger," William L. Smith to Edward Rutledge, April 2, 1790, in Rogers, "Letters of Smith," *S.C. Hist. Mag.* 69, p. 112. "After sometime he again rose," William Smith to Otho Holland Williams, April 4, 1790, MS. 387.1, Gilmor Papers, Maryland Historical Society. "Railed so tremendously," *Maclay Diary*, p. 348.

Lambert Cadwalader: "There have been much Altercation," to John Armstrong, May 8, 1789, Gratz Collection, Historical Society of Pennsylvania. "To the good breeding," in William Henry Rawle, "Col Lambert Cadwalader," *PMHB* 10, p. 14.

Charles Carroll of Carrollton: "We have one Roman Catholic Senator," Paine Wingate to Jeremy Belknap, May 12, 1789, in Wingate, *Life and Letters*, vol. 2, p. 314. "He thought it of no consequence," *Maclay Diary*, p. 11. "Tho' he had been the first to speak," *Maclay Diary*, p. 8. "I am confident," Charles Carroll to Mary Caton, July 11, 1790, MS. 220, Carroll-McTavish Papers, Maryland Historical Society.

Daniel Carroll: "A time would come," *Annals of Congress*, vol. 1, p. 576. "Which he could observe," *Annals of Congress*, vol. 1, p. 880. "It is absolutely necessary," *Maryland Gazette*, July 30, 1790. The Baltimore vote was published in the *New York Daily Advertiser*, October 10, 1790.

George Clymer: "Peevish and fretting," *Maclay Diary*, p. 7. "Disgust and disappointment," George Clymer to Richard Peters, June 8, 1789, Peters Papers, Historical Society of Pennsylvania. "I could have wished that a more decided preference," George Clymer to Dr. Thomas Ruston, May 14, 1789, Historical Society of Pennsylvania. "For confirming the Government," *Maclay Diary*, p. 241. "Clymer is supposed deep," John Armstrong to Robert McPherson, November 26, 1788, *FFE*, vol. 1, p. 368.

Tristram Dalton: "Having for near forty years," Tristram Dalton to Caleb Strong, January 1, 1789, Strong Papers, Forbes Library, Northampton, Massachusetts. "The impost bill will come up tomorrow," quoted in Josiah H. Welch, "Tristram Dalton," *Historical Society of Old Newbury Bulletin* 7, p. 29. "Must be greatly chagrined," Theodore Sedgwick to Pamela Sedgwick, July 13, 1790, Sedgwick Papers, Massachusetts Historical Society. "Would be as agreeable to my disposition," Tristram Dalton to Rufus King, September 25, 1790, New-York Historical Society.

Oliver Ellsworth: "Mr. Elsworth who was principally concerned," in Rogers, "Letters of Smith," *S.C. Hist. Mag.* 69, p. 22. "This Vile Bill," *Maclay Diary*, p. 91. "Elsworth had a String of Amendments," *Maclay Diary*, p. 135. "Respecting Consuls & Vice Consuls," *Maclay Diary*, p. 359. "A most elaborate Speech," *Maclay Diary*, pp. 111–12. "Rhode Island is at length," Oliver Ellsworth to Abigail Ellsworth, June 7, 1790, Oliver Ellsworth Papers, Connecticut Historical Society.

William Few: "Although I had never spent one hour," in William Few, "Autobiography," *Magazine of American History* 7, p. 352. "The State has been long insulted," William Few to Joseph Clay, Few Papers, Duke University. "Already we begin to perceive," William Few to Edward Telfair, January 15, 1791, Telfair Papers, University of Georgia Libraries. "The scorching climate of Georgia," Few, "Autobiography," *Magazine of American History* 7, p. 355.

Catharine Nicholson Few: "I request my fair correspondent," Thomas Paine to Catharine Few, January 5, 1789, printed in Moncure Daniel Conway, *Writings of Thomas Paine*, vol. 3, p. 433.

Elbridge Gerry: "Grave, garrulous, crotchety," William Duer, *Reminiscences of an Old Yorker*, p. 72. "As an awful Tribunal," quoted in Billias, *Elbridge Gerry*, p. 228. "There is not a member," Abigail Adams to Mary Cranch, July 12, 1789, Mitchell, *New Letters*, p. 15. "Gerry has as high notions," Benjamin Goodhue to Samuel Phillips, August 11, 1789, Phillips Family Papers, Massachusetts Historical Society. "Mr. G what can I say," Abigail Adams to Cotton Tufts, September 1, 1789, Misc. Mss. A, New-York Historical Society.

Nicholas Gilman: "Which subjected some of the southern members," Nicholas Gilman to Tench Coxe, May 10, 1789, Coxe Papers, Historical Society of Pennsylvania. "To the general Idea of assumption," Nicholas Gilman to John Sullivan, July 25, 1790, New Hampshire Miscellany, Library of Congress. "He changed his mind very suddenly," *Concord Herald*, November 23, 1790. "Also in favour," *Concord Herald*, November 23, 1790. "Was closely attach'd," *Concord Herald*, August 20, 1790. "It is a vulgar error," *New Hampshire Gazette*, August 20, 1790.

Benjamin Goodhue: "Not the holder of one farthing," Benjamin Goodhue to Michael Hodge, February 15, 1790, "Letters of Benjamin Goodhue of Salem to Michael Hodge," *Essex Institute Historical Collections* 84, p. 150. "Has engrossed all my thoughts," "Letters of Goodhue to Hodge," *Essex Institute Historical Collections* 84, p. 162. "You Know I am apt to be gloomy," Benjamin Goodhue to S. Phillips, April 17, 1790, Phillips Family Papers, Massahusetts Historical Society. "Mr. Goodhue," Fisher Ames to Thomas Dwight, June 11, 1790, Ames, *Works*, vol. 1, p. 80. "He was not of splendid talents," William Bentley, *Diary*, vol. 4, p. 270.

Samuel Griffin: "Mr. Griffin is the Representative," Miles King to James Madison, March 3, 1789, *Madison Papers*, vol. 12, p. 2.

Thomas Hartley: "As I have been punctual," Thomas Hartley to Jasper Yeates, March 22, 1789, Yeates Papers, Historical Society of Pennsylvania. For William Maclay on Hartley see *Maclay Diary*, pp. 250 and 263. "So many local Interests," Thomas Hartley to Jasper Yeates, June 19, 1789, Yeates Papers, Historical Society of Pennsylvania. "My Mind has been made up," Thomas Hartley to Jasper Yeates, June 19, 1789, Yeates Papers, Historical Society of Pennsylvania.

Ralph Izard: "A contemptible affectation," Ralph Izard to Edward Rutledge, May 16, 1789, The South Caroliniana Library, University of South Carolina. "Up now rose Izard," *Maclay Diary*, p. 134. "Large enough to hold my Coach," Ralph Izard to Tench Coxe, October 26, 1790, Coxe Papers, Historical Society of Pennsylvania. "Had a Warmth of Temper," in L. H. Butterfield, *Autobiography of John Adams*, pp. 70–71.

James Jackson: "And to keep out the din," Fisher Ames to Thomas Dwight, July 25, 1790, Ames, *Works*, vol. 1, p. 87. "Is the whole morality," quoted in Sanderson, *Biography of the Signers*, vol. 2, p. 49.

William Samuel Johnson: "Is so engross'd," John Randolph to St. George Tucker, August 19, 1789, Tucker Papers, Library of Congress. "Deny'd there was any such thing," *Maclay Diary*, p. 288. "Doctor Johnson spoke," *Maclay Diary*, p. 380.

Rufus King: "This State think," George Thatcher to Sarah Thatcher, May 14, 1789, Thatcher Papers, Massachusetts Historical Society. William Pierce's characterization of King is printed in Farrand, *Records*, vol. 3, p. 87. "Although from the character," George Lux to George Read, *FFE*, vol. 3, p. 554. "Is reputed to be the most eloquent man," Brissot de Warville, *New Travels*, p. 148. "Like an Indian," *Maclay Diary*, p. 379.

Mary Alsop King: "I am pleased with these intermarriages," John Jay to John Adams, May 4, 1786, printed in Henry P. Johnston, ed., *The Correspondence and Public Papers of John Jay*. "The best looking woman," quoted in Robert Ernst, *Rufus King, American Federalist*, p. 137.

John Langdon: "Tho' fully Sensible," John Langdon to Benjamin Rush, March 21, 1789, Benjamin Rush Papers, Library Company of Philadelphia. "It is a *great national* measure," quoted in Lawrence Shaw Mayo, *John Langdon of New Hampshire*, p. 238. "Langdon who lodges nearly opposite," *Maclay Diary*, p. 254.

John Laurance: "It was supposed that a man of information," *New York Daily Advertiser*, March 3, 1789. "The most alarming apprehensions," *Pennsylvania Gazette*, May 13, 1789.

Richard Bland Lee: "I went up to the Election," Donald Jackson and Dorothy Twohig, *The Diaries of George Washington*, vol. 5, p. 445. "Mr. Richard Bland Lee gained," Robert Carter to Sarah Carter, January 30, 1789, *FFE*, vol. 2, p. 316. "Mr. Lee voted against," *New York Daily Advertiser*, November 26, 1790. "I conceive [it] impracticable," Richard Bland Lee to Charles Lee, January 10, 1790, New York Public Library. "The success of this measure," quoted in Robert S. Gamble, *Sully: The Biography of a House*, p. 26. "Is so calculated to conciliate," Richard Bland Lee to Theodorick Lee, June 26, 1790, printed in Gamble, *Sully*, p. 25. Broadside of August 21, 1790, Broadside no. 3041, Manuscripts Division, University of Virginia Library.

Richard Henry Lee: "The man who gave independence," *Maclay Diary*, p. 290. "How they will terminate," Richard Henry Lee to Samuel Adams, August 8, 1789, in Ballagh, *Letters of Lee*, vol. 2, p. 496. "It is too much the fashion," Richard Henry Lee to Francis Lightfoot Lee, September 13, 1789, Ballagh, *Letters of Lee*, vol. 2, p. 500. "You may be assured," to Patrick Henry, Ballagh, *Letters of Lee*, vol. 2, pp. 501–2. "It is impossible," June 10, 1789, Ballagh, *Letters of Lee*, vol. 2, pp. 523–24.

Samuel Livermore: Letter to the *New Hampshire Gazette*, December 9, 1790. William Plumer is quoted in James McLachlan's *Princetonians, 1748–1768*, p. 52.

James Madison: "I confess," John Page to James Madison, August 6, 1788, *Madison Papers*, vol. 11, p. 235. Fisher Ames's comments on James Madison are in letters of May 3, May 18, and May 24, 1789, to George Minot, Ames, *Works*, vol. 1, pp. 35, 42, and 49. "Is certainly an extraordinary Man," Thomas Hartley to Jasper Yeates, March 14, 1790, Yeates Papers, Historical Society of Pennsylvania. "Was that of a person conscious of his talents," Brissot de Warville, *New Travels*, p. 147.

James Monroe: "As I had no private object to gratify," quoted in William Penn Cresson, *James Monroe*, p. 103. "Will contribute greatly," Cresson, *James Monroe*, p. 108.

Robert Morris: "Miss Fortune," quoted in Clarence L. Ver Steeg, *Robert Morris, Revolutionary Financier*, p. 36. William Pierce's assessment is in Farrand, *Records*, vol. 3, p. 91. "To obtain the Money," Robert Morris to Benjamin Franklin, July 13, 1781, Ferguson and Catanzariti, *Morris Papers*, vol. 1, p. 283.

Mary White Morris: "I am indeed very sensible," Mary Morris to Robert Morris, January 9, 1788, Henry E. Huntington Library. "My station is always at the right hand," Abigail Adams to Mary Cranch, January 5, 1790, in Mitchell, *New Letters*, p. 35. "Mrs. Morris talked a good deal," *Maclay Diary*, p. 74. "A beautiful grove behind the house," Abigail Adams to Elizabeth Shaw, March 20, 1791, in Adams, *Letters of Mrs. Adams*, p. 420.

John Page: Correspondence concerning rhyme-making is addressed to St. George Tucker, February 25 and 26 and March 18, 1790, Tucker-Coleman Papers, Department of Manuscripts and

Rare Books, Earl Gregg Swem Library, College of William and Mary. "I never was less disposed to marry," John Page to St. George Tucker, May 3, 1789, Tucker-Coleman Papers, Department of Manuscripts and Rare Books, Earl Gregg Swem Library, College of William and Mary. "Uncommon exertions," John Dawson to James Madison, August 1, 1790, *Madison Papers*, vol. 13, p. 291. "Very often looking at the portrait," Charles Coleman Sellers, *Portraits and Miniatures of Charles Willson Peale*, p. 155.

Josiah Parker: "Represents every thing," Edmund Randolph to James Madison, July 23, 1789, *Madison Papers*, vol. 12, p. 306. "The first gentleman," letter from Providence, October 21, 1790, printed in Philadelphia *General Advertiser*, November 1, 1790. "A quondam Parson," John Dawson to James Madison, August 1, 1790, *Madison Papers*, vol. 13, p. 291.

George Partridge: Samuel Davis's "Journal of a Tour to Connecticut" is printed in *Proceedings of the Massachusetts Historical Society* 2, p. 21. "I perceive that the pay," George Partridge to Sylvanus Bourne, August 23, 1789, Houghton Library, Harvard University. "Firmness, sobriety," Joshua Thomas to Theodore Sedgwick, January 19, 1791, Massachusetts Historical Society.

William Paterson: "Gay life has never been my Wish," William Paterson to Euphemia White Paterson, May 1, 1789, William Paterson Papers, Rutgers University, quoted in Gertrude Wood, *William Paterson of New Jersey*, p. 105. "Of All the Members of our House," *Maclay Diary*, p. 104. "The next Session," William Paterson to Euphemia White Paterson, August 1, 1790, William Paterson Papers, Rutgers University. "He talks of resigning," *Maclay Diary*, p. 217.

George Read: "I came to this place," George Read to John Dickinson, June 16, 1789, in Read, *Life and Correspondence*, p. 481. "Up now rose Mr. Read," *Maclay Diary*, p. 17. "Was swinging on his legs," *Maclay Diary*, p. 114. "A Man of Obstructed Elocution," *Maclay Diary*, p. 104. "Legal abilities are said," Farrand, *Records*, vol. 3, p. 93. "Was esteemed a plodding," James Tilton, *Biographical History of Dionysius*, p. 8.

Philip Schuyler: "Mr. Hamilton had employed," Louis-Guillaume Otto, January 15, 1790, O'Dwyer, "French Diplomat's View of Congress," *WMQ*, 3d ser. 21, p. 416. "He was a profound mathematician," Watson, *Men and Times*, pp. 332–33. "This wretch," *Maclay Diary*, p. 326. "Schuyler is the supple Jack," *Maclay Diary*, p. 390. "On end," *Maclay Diary*, p. 129.

Theodore Sedgwick: "You know some people think," Samuel Henshaw to Theodore Sedgwick, June 2, 1789, Sedgwick Papers, Massachusetts Historical Society. "Is there [to be] no way," quoted in Richard E. Welch, Jr., *Theodore Sedgwick, Federalist*, p. 71. "Any funding system at all," Theodore Sedgwick to Pamela Sedgwick, April 3, 1790, Sedgwick Papers, Massachusetts Historical Society. "Most agreeable to my inclination," Theodore Sedgwick to Pamela Sedgwick, July 5, 1789, *FFE*, vol. 1, p. 5. "I declare," Sara Cabot Sedgwick and Christina Sedgwick, *Stockbridge 1739–1939*, p. 172.

Pamela Dwight Sedgwick: "I am grieved," Pamela Sedgwick to Theodore Sedgick, July 8, 1790, Sedgwick Papers, Massachusetts Historical Society. "Whose Character as a good Painter," Pamela Sedgwick to Theodore Sedgwick, 1794, Sedgwick Papers, Massachusetts Historical Society.

Roger Sherman: "In spite of his gaunt," Duer, *Reminiscences*, p. 72. "When gentlemen have recourse," Sanderson, *Biography of the Signers*, vol. 2, p. 52. "We ought not to interweave," Sanderson, *Biography of the Signers*, vol. 2, p. 53. "Our old Republican friend," Richard Henry Lee to Samuel Adams, August 8, 1789, Ballagh, *Letters of Lee*, vol. 2, p. 496.

William Smith: "A Man of great commercial," January 13, 1789, *FFE*, vol. 2, p. 199. "Some Warm gentlemen," William Smith to Otho Holland Williams, March 18, 1790, MS. 908, Otho Holland Williams Papers, Maryland Historical Society. "Unfortunately for poor Baltimore," quoted in Sister Mary Virginia Geiger, *Daniel Carroll: A Framer of the Constitution*, p. 162.

William Loughton Smith: "While we remain in this state," quoted in Rogers, *Evolution of a Federalist*, p. 175. "The intemperate & bigoted zeal," William L. Smith to Tench Coxe, April 14, 1789, Coxe Papers, Historical Society of Pennsylvania. "I do not see how the Government," William L. Smith to Tench Coxe, March 18, 1790, Coxe Papers, Historical Society of Pennsylvania. "My being unopposed manifests," William L. Smith to Edward Rutledge, January 14?, 1791, South Carolina Historical Society, Charleston.

John Steele: "Proved what can be effected," *North Carolina Chronicle*, December 27, 1790. "That I have not directly," *North Carolina Chronicle*, December 27, 1790. "I am now writing you a letter," John Steele to Joseph Winnston, May 22, 1790, John Steele Papers, Southern History Collection, University of North Carolina, Chapel Hill.

Caleb Strong: "I assure you that my patience," Caleb Strong to Samuel Phillips, April 15, 1789, Phillips Papers, Massachusetts Historical Society. "Strong, you can do more," quoted in John Langley Sibley, *Sibley's Harvard Graduates*, vol. 16, p. 97. "Mr. Strong, Mr. Ellsworth," Fisher Ames to George Minot, July 8, 1789, Ames, *Works*, vol. 1, p. 64.

Thomas Sumter: "The people of America," *Annals of Congress*, vol. 1, pp. 832–33. "Our conduct in adjourning," *Annals of Congress*, vol. 1, p. 780. "Is really more a Delegate," William L. Smith to Edward Rutledge, April 2, 1790, in Rogers, "Letters of Smith," *S.C. Hist. Mag.* 69, p. 113. "I employed all my rhetoric," Smith to Rutledge, July 25, 1790, in Rogers, "Letters of Smith," *S.C. Hist. Mag.* 69, p. 123. "Just as the Session terminated," Smith to Rutledge, March 1791, in Rogers, "Letters of Smith," *S.C. Hist. Mag.* 69, pp. 225–26.

Jonathan Trumbull: "Not a little pleased," George Washington to Jonathan Trumbull, December 4, 1788, in Fitzpatrick, *Writings of Washington*, vol. 30, p. 149. "The competitor," Henry Wynkoop to Dr. Reading Beatty, April 2, 1789, in Beatty, "Letters of Wynkoop," *PMHB* 38, p. 50.

Thomas Tudor Tucker: "May not be inclined," *Annals of Congress*, vol. 1, pp. 949–50. "He says he will vote," William L. Smith to Edward Rutledge, February 28, 1790, in Rogers, "Letters of Smith," *S.C. Hist. Mag.* 69, p. 109. "Tucker seemed sunk," in Rogers, "Letters of Smith," *S.C. Hist. Mag.* 69, p. 131.

Jeremiah Wadsworth: "Indefatigable in his exertions," George Washington to the president of the Congress, in Fitzpatrick, *Writings of Washington*, vol. 12, p. 277. "It is the home," Brissot de Warville, *New Travels*, p. 116. "Wadsworth has sent off," *Maclay Diary*, p. 185. "Wadsworth . . . has thought," Theodore Sedgwick to Pamela Sedgwick, March 22, 1790, Sedgwick Papers, Massachusetts Historical Society. "I have receiv'd from Wadsworth," John Trumbull to Jonathan Trumbull, July 18, 1784, John Trumbull Papers, Yale University Library.

Hugh Williamson: "A beautiful girl," John Dawson to James Madison, January 29, 1789, in Burnett, *Letters of the Continental Congress*, vol. 8, p. 820. "Success in politics," Alfred Moore to Samuel Johnston, February 23, 1791, Hayes Collection, South Carolina Department of Archives. "That posterity will not be solicitous," quoted in William Dunlap, *History of the Rise and Progress of the Arts of Design*, vol. 1, p. 409.

Henry Wynkoop: "It would not be easy," *Maclay Diary*, p. 169. "He has not firmness," *Maclay Diary*, p. 233. "But if I had talked to a mute Camel," *Maclay Diary*, p. 257. "I must confess for my part," Henry Wynkoop to Dr. Reading Beatty, April 22, 1790, in Beatty, "Letters of Wynkoop," *PMHB* 38, p. 194. "The way in Which," *Maclay Diary*, p. 232.

SELECTED BIBLIOGRAPHY

Adams, Charles Francis, ed. *Letters of Mrs. Adams, the Wife of John Adams*. Boston, 1915.

Alberts, Robert C. *The Golden Voyage: The Life and Times of William Bingham*. Boston, 1969.

Ames, Seth, ed. *Works of Fisher Ames*. 2 vols. Boston, 1854.

Ammon, Harry. *James Monroe: The Quest for National Identity*. New York, 1971.

Anderson, William G. *The Price of Liberty: The Public Debt of the American Revolution*. Charlottesville, Va., 1983.

Annals of the Congress of the United States, 1789–1824. 42 vols. Washington, D.C., 1834–1856.

Austin, James T. *The Life of Elbridge Gerry*. Boston, 1829.

Ballagh, James Curtis. *The Letters of Richard Henry Lee*. 2 vols. New York, 1911.

Beatty, Joseph M., Jr. "The Letters of Judge Henry Wynkoop." *Pennsylvania Magazine of History and Biography* 38 (January, April 1914): 39–64, 183–205.

Bentley, William. *Diary*. 4 vols. 1911. Reprint. Gloucester, Mass., 1962.

Bernhard, Winfred E. A. *Fisher Ames, Federalist and Statesman*. Chapel Hill, N.C., 1965.

Billias, George Athan. *Elbridge Gerry: Founding Father and Republican Statesman*. New York, 1976.

Boardman, Roger Sherman. *Roger Sherman, Signer and Statesman*. 1938. Reprint. New York, 1971.

Bowling, Kenneth R. "Politics in the First Congress." Ph.D. diss., University of Wisconsin, 1968.

———. "Dinner at Jefferson's: A Note on Jacob E. Cooke's 'The Compromise of 1790.'" *William and Mary Quarterly*, 3d ser. 28 (October 1971): 630–40.

———. "The Bank Bill, the Capital City and President Washington." *Capitol Studies* 1 (Spring 1972): 59–71.

———. "New Light on the Philadelphia Mutiny of 1783." *Pennsylvania Magazine of History and Biography* 101 (October 1977): 419–50.

———. "'A Tub to the Whale': The Founding Fathers and Adoption of the Federal Bill of Rights." *Journal of the Early Republic* 8 (Fall 1988): 222–52.

Bowling, Kenneth R., and Helen E. Veit, eds. *The Diary of William Maclay and Other Notes on Senate Debates*. Baltimore, 1988.

Boyd, George Adams. *Elias Boudinot, Patriot and Statesman*. Princeton, N.J., 1952.

Boyd, Julian *et al.*, eds. *The Papers of Thomas Jefferson*. 22 vols. to date. Princeton, N.J., 1950– .

Boyd, William K. *History of North Carolina*. Vol. 2. Chicago and New York, 1919.

Brissot de Warville, Jacques Pierre. *New Travels in the United States of America, 1788*. Edited by Durand Echeverria. Cambridge, Mass., 1964.

Burnett, Edmund Cody. *Letters of Members of the Continental Congress*. 8 vols. Reprint. Gloucester, Mass., 1963.

Butterfield, L. H., ed. *Letters of Benjamin Rush*. 2 vols. Princeton, N.J., 1951.

———. *The Diary and Autobiography of John Adams*. Vol. 4. Cambridge, Mass., 1962.

Carson, Hampton L. "The First Congress of the United States." *Pennsylvania Magazine of History and Biography* 13 (July 1889): 129–52.

Coghlan, Francis. "Pierce Butler, 1744–1822: First Senator from South Carolina." *South Carolina Historical Magazine* 78 (April 1977): 104–19.

Collier, Christopher. *Roger Sherman's Connecticut: Yankee Politics and the American Revolution*. Middletown, Conn., 1971.

Conley, Patrick T. "Rhode Island in Disunion, 1787–1790." *Rhode Island History* 31 (November 1972): 99–115.

Conway, Moncure Daniel. *The Writings of Thomas Paine*. Vol. 3. Reprint. New York, 1969.

Cooke, Jacob E. "The Compromise of 1790." *William and Mary Quarterly*, 3d ser. 27 (October 1970): 523–45.

——. Rebuttal of "Dinner at Jefferson's: A Note on Jacob E. Cooke's 'The Compromise of 1790,'" by Kenneth R. Bowling. *William and Mary Quarterly*, 3d ser. 28 (October 1971): 640–48.

Cresson, William Penn. *James Monroe*. 1946. Reprint. Hamden, Conn., 1971.

Davis, Samuel. "Journal of a Tour to Connecticut." *Proceedings of the Massachusetts Historical Society* 2 (April 1869): 9–32.

DePauw, Linda Grant *et al.*, eds. *Documentary History of the First Federal Congress*. 7 vols. to date. Baltimore, 1972– .

Dictionary of American Biography. 10 vols. New York, 1936.

Dowdy, Dru. "A School for Stoicism: The Life and Letters of Thomas Tudor Tucker." M.A. thesis, College of William and Mary, 1984.

Driver, Carl, S. *John Sevier, Pioneer of the Old Southwest*. Chapel Hill, N.C., 1932.

Duer, William Alexander. *Reminiscences of an Old Yorker*. New York, 1867.

Dunlap, William. *History of the Rise and Progress of the Arts of Design in the United States*. 1834. Reprint. New York, 1969.

Dupriest, James E., Jr. *William Grayson: A Political Biography of Virginia's First United States Senator*. Mansassas, Va., 1977.

"Eben F. Stone Papers." *Essex Institute Historical Collections* 83 (April 1947): 201–19.

Eberlein, Harold Donaldson, and Cortlandt Van Dyke Hubbard. *Diary of Independence Hall*. Philadelphia, 1948.

Elliot, Jonathan. *The Debates in the Several State Conventions on the Adoption of the Federal Constitution*. 5 vols. Philadelphia, 1907.

Ernst, Robert. *Rufus King, American Federalist*. Chapel Hill, N.C., 1968.

Fabian, Monroe H. "Joseph Wright's Portrait of Frederick Muhlenberg." *Antiques* 97 (February 1970): 256–57.

Farrand, Max, ed. *The Records of the Federal Convention of 1787*. 4 vols. Revised edition. New Haven, Conn., 1937.

Ferguson, E. James, and John Catanzariti, eds. *The Papers of Robert Morris*. 6 vols. to date. Pittsburg, Pa., 1973– .

Few, William. "Autobiography of Colonel William Few of Georgia." *The Magazine of American History* 7 (1881): 340–58.

Fitzpatrick, John Clement, ed. *The Writings of George Washington, from the Original Manuscript Sources, 1745–1799*. 39 vols. 1931–1944. Reprint. Westport, Conn., 1970.

Flanders, Henry. "Thomas Fitzsimmons." *Pennsylvania Magazine of History and Biography* 2 (October 1878): 306–14.

Ford, Worthington Chauncey, ed. "Letters of Elbridge Gerry." *New England Historical & Genealogical Register* 49 (October 1895): 435–36.

Gamble, Robert S. *Sully: The Biography of a House*. Chantilly, Va., 1973.

Geiger, Sister Mary Virginia. *Daniel Carroll: A Framer of the Constitution*. Washington, D.C., 1943.

Gerlach, Don R. *Philip Schuyler and the Growth of New York, 1733–1804*. Albany, N.Y., 1968.

Gilpatrick, Delbert Harold. *Jeffersonian Democracy in North Carolina*. New York, 1931.

———. "Contemporary Opinion of Hugh Williamson." *North Carolina Historical Review* 17 (January 1940): 26–36.

Gregorie, Anne King. *Thomas Sumter*. Columbia, S.C., 1931.

Grigsby, Hugh Blair. *The History of the Virginia Federal Convention of 1788*. Reprint. Two volumes in one. New York, 1969.

Groce, George C., Jr. *William Samuel Johnson: A Maker of the Constitution*. New York, 1937.

Harrison, Richard A. *Princetonians, 1769–1775: A Biographical Dictionary*. Princeton, N.J., 1980.

Hart, Charles Henry. "Mary White—Mrs. Robert Morris." *Pennsylvania Magazine of History and Biography* 2 (July 1878): 157–84.

Hatch, Alden. *The Wadsworths of the Genesee*. New York, 1959.

Hutchinson, William T. *et al.*, eds. *The Papers of James Madison*. 15 vols. to date. Chicago and Charlottesville, Va., 1962– .

Jackson, Donald, and Dorothy Twohig. *The Diaries of George Washington*. 6 vols. Charlottesville, Va., 1979.

Jaffe, Irma B. *John Trumbull: Patriot-Artist of the American Revolution*. Boston, 1975.

Jensen, Merrill *et al.*, eds. *The Documentary History of the First Federal Elections*. 3 vols. to date. Madison, Wis., 1976– .

Johnston, Henry P., ed. *The Correspondence and Public Papers of John Jay*. Reprint. New York, 1971.

Kaminski, John P. "Political Sacrifice and Demise—John Collins and Jonathan J. Hazard, 1786–1790." *Rhode Island History* 35 (August 1976): 91–98.

Kaminski, John P., and Gaspare J. Saladino, eds. *The Documentary History of the Ratification of the Constitution*. Volume 13: *Commentaries on the Constitution, Public and Private*. Madison, Wis., 1981.

Kenyon, Cecilia M. "Men of Little Faith: The Anti-Federalists on the Nature of Representative Government." *William and Mary Quarterly*, 3d ser. 12 (January 1955): 1–43.

King, Charles R., ed. *The Life and Correspondence of Rufus King*. 6 vols. New York, 1894–1900.

"Letters from Old Trunks." *Virginia Magazine of History and Biography* 43 (October 1935): 290–93.

"Letters of Benjamin Goodhue of Salem to Michael Hodge." *Essex Institute Historical Collections* 84 (April 1948): 144–63.

Lodge, Henry Cabot. "Memoir of Hon. Caleb Strong." *Proceedings of the Massachusetts Historical Society* 1 (April 1879): 290–316.

Longacre, James B., and James Herring. *The National Portrait Gallery of Distinguished Americans*. 4 vols. Philadelphia, 1839.

Lloyd, Thomas. *Congressional Register of the Proceedings and Debates of the First House of Representatives Taken in Shorthand by Thomas Lloyd*. 2 vols. New York, 1789–1790.

McCaughey, Elizabeth P. *From Loyalist to Founding Father: The Political Odyssey of William Samuel Johnson*. New York, 1980.

McDonald, Forrest. *Alexander Hamilton*. New York, 1979.

McLachlan, James. *Princetonians, 1748–1768: A Biographical Dictionary*. Princeton, N.J., 1976.

McRee, Griffith J. *Life and Correspondence of James Iredell*. 2 vols. New York, 1857.

Mayo, Lawrence Shaw. *John Langdon of New Hampshire*. Reprint. Port Washington, N.Y., 1970.

"Memoir of the Hon. William Tudor." *Collections of the Massachusetts Historical Society*, 2d ser. 8 (1819): 285–325.

Mitchell, Stewart, ed. *New Letters of Abigail Adams*. Boston, 1947.

Morris, Richard B., ed. *Alexander Hamilton and the Founding of the Nation*. New York, 1957.

Oberholtzer, Ellis Paxson. *Robert Morris: Patriot and Financier*. New York, 1903.

O'Dwyer, Margaret M. O. "A French Diplomat's View of Congress, 1790." *William and Mary Quarterly*, 3d ser. 21 (July 1964): 408–44.

Pattison, Robert E. "The Life and Character of Richard Bassett." *Papers of the Historical Society of Delaware* 29 (November 1900): 3–19.

Polishook, Irwin H. *Rhode Island and the Union*. Evanston, Ill., 1969.

Rawle, William Henry. "Colonel Lambert Cadwalader of Trenton, New Jersey." *Pennsylvania Magazine of History and Biography* 10 (April 1886): 1–14.

Read, William Thompson. *Life and Correspondence of George Read*. Philadelphia, 1870.

Rogers, George C., Jr. *Evolution of a Federalist: William Loughton Smith of Charleston (1758–1812)*. Columbia, S.C., 1962.

————, ed. "The Letters of William Loughton Smith to Edward Rutledge." *South Carolina Historical Magazine* 69 (January, April, October 1968): 1–25, 101–38, 225–42.

Rutland, Robert A. *James Madison, the Founding Father*. New York, 1987.

Sanderson, John. *Biography of the Signers to the Declaration of Independence*. 9 vols. Philadelphia, 1828.

Sedgwick, Sara Cabot, and Christina Sedgwick. *Stockbridge, 1739–1939*. Great Barrington, Mass., 1939.

Sellers, Charles Coleman. *Portraits and Miniatures by Charles Willson Peale*. 1952. Reprint. Philadelphia, 1968.

————. *Charles Willson Peale*. New York, 1969.

Sibley, John Langley, and Clifford K. Shipton. *Sibley's Harvard Graduates: Biographical Sketches of Those Who Attended Harvard College*. Boston and New York, 1873– .

Sizer, Theodore, ed. *The Autobiography of Colonel John Trumbull*. New Haven, Conn., 1953.

Smith, Page. *John Adams*. 2 vols. New York, 1962.

"South Carolina Federalist Correspondence." *American Historical Review* 14 (1908–1909): 776–77.

Syrett, Harold C., and Jacob E. Cooke, eds. *The Papers of Alexander Hamilton*. 26 vols. New York, 1961–1979.

Thacher, James. *American Medical Biography*. 2 vols. Reprint. New York, 1967.

Tilton, James. *The Biographical History of Dionysius, Tyrant of Delaware, Addressed to the People of the United States of America*. Philadelphia, 1788.

Torres, Louis. "Federal Hall Revisited." *Journal of the Society of Architectural Historians* 29 (December 1970): 327–38.

Trenholme, Louise Irby. *The Ratification of the Federal Constitution in North Carolina*. New York, 1932.

U.S. Congress. House. Committee on Energy and Commerce. *Petitions, Memorials and Other Documents Submitted for the Consideration of Congress, March 4, 1789, to December 14, 1795*. 99th Cong., 2d sess., 1986.

Ver Steeg, Clarence L. *Robert Morris, Revolutionary Financier*. Philadelphia, 1954.

Wallace, Paul A. W. *The Muhlenbergs of Pennsylvania*. Philadelphia, 1950.

Watson, Elkanah. *Men and Times of the Revolution, or, Memoirs of Elkanah Watson*. New York, 1856.

Welch, Josiah H. "Tristram Dalton." *Bulletin of the Historical Society of Old Newbury* 7 (March 1974): 22–32.

Welch, Richard E., Jr. *Theodore Sedgwick, Federalist*. Middletown, Conn., 1965.

White, Henry Clay. *Abraham Baldwin, One of the Founders of the Republic and Father of the University of Georgia, the First of American State Universities*. Athens, Ga., 1926.

William and Mary Quarterly. "James Madison 1751–1836: Bicentennial Number." 3d ser. 8 (January 1951).

Wingate, Paine. *Life and Letters of Paine Wingate*. 2 vols. Medford, Mass., 1930.

Wood, Gertrude Sceery. *William Paterson of New Jersey*. Fair Lawn, N.J., 1933.

Young, Eleanor. *Forgotten Patriot: Robert Morris*. New York, 1950.

INDEX

Italicized page numbers refer to illustrations.

The First Federal Congress has been designed by Meadows & Wiser of Washington, D.C. It was typeset by General Typographers of Washington, D.C., in the 1968 version of Mergenthaler VIP New Baskerville with Fry's Baskerville display type. It was printed on eighty-pound Warren Lustro Dull Cream by Wolk Press of Woodlawn, Maryland.

Photography Credits

J. Edward Baer: p. 202 (Read armchair); *Stephen Barth*: p. 350; *Ken Burris*: p. 235; *J. Elberson*: p. 213; *Andrew Harkins*: p. 204; *Frank Kelly*: p. 292; *Jennifer Mange*: p. 336 (snuff box); *Steven E. Nelson, Fay Foto, Boston*: p. 335; *Colin L. Price*: p. 116; *Terry Richardson*: p. 239; *Joseph Szaszfai*: pp. 253, 341, 344; *Rolland White*: cover and pp. 26, 29, 32, 35, 36, 43, 44, 49, 50, 63, 67, 71, 72, 74, 79, 80, 86, 87, 88, 91, 93, 98, 101, 109, 124, 138, 147, 185, 220, 223, 224, 249, 274, 279, 281, 289, 296, 315, 343; *Graydon Wood*: p. 240